DISCARDED

All Politics Is Global

All Politics Is Global

EXPLAINING INTERNATIONAL
REGULATORY REGIMES

Daniel W. Drezner

PRINCETON UNIVERSITY PRESS

PRINCETON AND OXFORD

Copyright © 2007 by Princeton University Press
Published by Princeton University Press, 41 William Street,
Princeton, New Jersey 08540
In the United Kingdom: Princeton University Press, 3 Market Place,
Woodstock, Oxfordshire OX20 1SY

All Rights Reserved

Library of Congress Cataloging-in-Publication Data

Drezner, Daniel W.
All politics is global : explaining international regulatory regimes / Daniel W. Drezner.
p.   cm.
Includes bibliographical references and index.
ISBN-13: 978-0-691-09641-4 (hardcover : alk. paper)
ISBN-10: 0-691-09641-4 (hardcover : alk. paper)
1. Globalization—Government policy. 2. Globalization—Political aspects.
3. Globalization—Social aspects. 4. Globalization—Economic aspects. I. Title.
JZ1318.D74   2007
341.2—dc22
2006017741

British Library of Cataloging-in-Publication Data is available

This book has been composed in Minion Typeface with Helvetica Neue display

Printed on acid-free paper. ∞

press.princeton.edu

Printed in the United States of America

10   9   8   7   6   5   4   3   2   1

This book is dedicated to my lovely and loving wife,

ERIKA DREZNER

for settling with finality the question of who regulates our home.

Contents

Tables

Preface

AT THE START OF this project, I participated in two events that offered contrasting narratives about the regulation of the global economy. This book has been, in part, an attempt to reconcile these opposing parables.

In April 2002, I attended a Salzburg Seminar on global economic institutions. Most of the participants spoke bitterly about economic globalization and its supporting global governance structures. The resentment was genuinely multicultural; heated rhetoric came from a Filipino activist, a Brazilian academic, a Burundian minister, a Russian economist, an American journalist, an Ecuadorian expatriate, and a South African union organizer.[1] The common denominator to their complaints was that they saw global governance as a battle between capitalists and democrats—with the capitalists winning. On one side were the transnational corporations capable of buying and selling governments and international economic institutions. On the other side were nongovernmental organizations and local social movements that represented the suffering classes, the people most likely to lose out in a world of untrammeled economic globalization.

These activists' vision of change was an arena for global civil society to engage their corporate antagonists. From their perspective, acting through home governments was pointless, since these governments were bought and paid for by global capital. Walden Bello, director of Focus on the Global South, argued that the protestors' agenda "can only succeed if it takes place within an alternative system of global economic governance."[2] For these activists the sources of political power were clear; multinational corporations make the rules now, and with a lot of discipline and a little luck, global civil society would be the rule-makers of the future. Governments are either obsolete or a creature of business, and therefore left out of the equation. The UN Global Compact is the epitome of this sort of global governance.[3]

Thirteen months earlier, I witnessed an entirely different answer to the question of who writes the rules of the global economy. I was sitting in a conference

[1] Support for the globalization phenomenon was equally multicultural, coming from a Vietnamese trade official, a Romanian academic, a Taiwanese economist, Italian and Spanish bureaucrats, a Ugandan lecturer, American policy analysts, and a Latvian nonprofit director.

[2] Walden Bello, "The Global Conjuncture: Characteristics and Challenges." Keynote speech at the National Convention against Globalization, New Delhi, India, March 21, 2001. Accessed at http://www.focusweb.org/publications/2001/The%20Global%20Conjuncture.htm, July 1, 2002.

[3] Information about the Global Compact can be accessed at its Web site, http://www.unglobalcompact.org.

room in the U.S. Treasury Department, a hundred yards from the White House. An interagency team of United States government officials was engaged in rather active consultations with a hemispheric ally. Six months earlier, the United States, European Union, and their allies in the Financial Action Task Force on Money Laundering had threatened multilateral sanctions against this country unless it enacted and enforced laws to stop money laundering in its financial sector. This step was taken because the United States and other great powers were concerned that criminals were exploiting the integration of capital markets to hide their illicit wealth. These governments wanted to reduce the negative externalities of globalization by ratcheting up global regulatory standards designed to combat money laundering.

The targeted country responded by passing six pieces of legislation. At the extraordinary session I attended, the Americans and their counterparts were examining the new laws line by line. When a U.S. official pointed out a loophole or a vague passage in the text, the other country's representatives noted it and promised a legislative amendment to fix the problem. Within six months of the meeting, the ally had complied with all U.S. requests, and the threat of sanctions was removed.

In this setting, the answer to the question of who regulates the global economy was equally clear and yet completely different from the first story. States make the rules. In particular, the great powers cajole and coerce those who disagree with them into accepting the same rulebook. Corporations and transnational activist networks do not appear in this story. Indeed, as chapter 5 will demonstrate, they were marginal actors throughout this policy initiative. International governmental organizations played an important but not independent role; they were the agents of states.

The disconnect between these two narratives raises some important questions. Does globalization require a transfer of authority from the national to the global level of governance? When will global governance structures effectively regulate the world economy? Which actors shape those governance structures? What factors determine the content of global regulatory standards? What is the role of nonstate actors—corporate and civic—in influencing and redirecting these regimes?

This book argues that what I saw at the Treasury Department is the more accurate picture of the regulation of globalization. The elements of global civil society that oppose globalization assume that transnational capital drives the preferences and actions of other actors in the global political economy. The argument developed in the following pages suggests otherwise. Great power governments remain the most important actors in establishing and enforcing the rules of the global economy. Great power preferences over regulatory questions are obviously influenced to some extent by the behavior of private actors, including multinational corporations. However, it is the groups that face the greatest barriers to market exit or internal adjustment—in other words, the *least* globalized elements of domestic polities—who exert a stronger influence on government preferences. These actors, by exercising their political voice, raise the adjustment costs to governments of regulatory coordination.

More generally, the perception by nonstate actors that globalization weakens the power of the regulatory state is inaccurate. As long as the study of international political economy has been around, one of the basic measures of aggregate power has been relative market size.[4] The current era of globalization merely reinforces the importance of that metric of power. Governments that regulate large markets have always mattered in the global political economy. Globalization does not negate this fact, nor does it empower other actors to the point where they can consistently alter national preferences.

To be fair, my fellow participants at Salzburg were not completely wrong in their judgments. They were correct to point out that international regulatory regimes are not models of democracy—but they erred in identifying the source. Globalization does not alter what have been the facts of life in international relations for the past three centuries—great power governments, and not multinational corporations, make the rules for the global economy. The actors that they identify as important—nongovernmental organizations, international governmental organizations, and multinational corporations—do affect the process of global economic governance. In the end, however, these actors function as intervening variables, not as underlying causal factors.

This book is also intended to address the ongoing debate between mainstream IR theorists and their critics about what globalization means for the study of international relations. What is taking place today in the debates about globalization and global governance echoes similar debates from three decades ago. During the early 1970s the global economy seemed to be buffeted by one shock after another. This triggered a surge of research into the ways in which complex transnational interdependence could alter the behavior of states. This research emphasized the ways in which nonstate actors and the global economy constrained states.[5] A few years later, another wave of scholarship arose asking how the political externalities of interdependence would be regulated in an anarchic world. The result was the literature on international regimes, which pointed out the ways in which states remained the primary actors in establishing the rules of the game, while other actors and factors were "intervening variables."[6]

---

[4] Albert Hirschman, *National Power and the Structure of Foreign Trade* (Berkeley: University of California Press, 1945).

[5] See, for example, Robert Keohane and Joseph Nye, *Transnational Relations and World Politics* (Cambridge, MA: Harvard University Press, 1973); Keohane and Nye, *Power and Interdependence* (Boston: Scott Foresman, 1978).

[6] Oran Young, "International Regimes: Problems of Concept Formation," *World Politics* 32 (April 1980): 331–56; Stephen D. Krasner, ed., *International Regimes* (Ithaca, NY: Cornell University Press, 1983).

A similar yin and yang is taking place in the current theoretical debates about economic globalization. The first wave of this literature arrived more than a decade ago, and highlighted the ways in which the globalization phenomenon placed added constraints on the state. This book belongs to a growing field of scholarship that looks at globalization and global governance from a state-centric perspective.[7] By giving states pride of place, it is easier to discern the effects of new actors and factors. Much like the prior wave of scholarship, this book concludes that they matter as an intervening variable. The argument presented here differs in many ways from other state-centric arguments, but there is agreement on one fundamental point: globalization is not irrelevant to global governance, but it is not transformative either.

Graduate students firmly believe that once they become professors, oodles of time will open up for them to pursue their research. As one who had accepted this maxim as an article of faith in graduate school, I can say now that this is utter rubbish. The number of professional and personal obligations inexorably increases as one moves from student to professor, leaving less time for writing and research. The fact that I was able to complete this book during my years as an assistant professor means only one thing—I have a lot more people to thank now than when I wrote *The Sanctions Paradox.*

My biggest debt is to my former colleagues at the University of Chicago, who provided the perfect intellectual climate to start this project. The international relations group for most of my years there—Charlie Glaser, Jack Goldsmith, Lloyd Gruber, Charles Lipson, John Mearsheimer, Jennifer Mitzen, Duncan Snidal, and Alexander Wendt—were honest enough to ask all of the tough questions, and kind enough to suggest some possible answers. Beyond the IR group, I benefited enormously from the advice and friendship of Carles Boix, Shelley Clark, Luis Fernando Medina, Melissa Harris-Lacewell, Jacob Levy, and Patchen Markell.

Beyond the faculty, bits and pieces of the arguments presented here appeared in my undergraduate lectures and graduate seminars at Chicago, as well as the PIPES and Comparative Politics workshops on that campus. I re-

---

[7] David Vogel and Robert Kagan, eds., *The Dynamics of Regulatory Change: How Globalization Affects National Regulatory Policies* (Berkeley: University of California Press, 2004); Miles Kahler and David Lake, eds., *Governance in a Global Economy: Political Authority in Transition* (Princeton, NJ: Princeton University Press, 2003); Dale Murphy, *The Structure of Regulatory Competition* (New York: Oxford University Press, 2004); Walter Mattli, ed., "The Politics and Economics of International Institutional Standards Setting," *Journal of European Public Policy* 8 (June 2001); Beth Simmons, "The International Politics of Harmonization: The Case of Capital Market Integration," *International Organization* (Summer 2001): 589–620. The precursor for all of this work is David Vogel, *Trading Up: Consumer and Environmental Regulation in a Global Economy* (Cambridge, MA: Harvard University Press, 1995).

main most grateful to those students who attended my workshop presentations and took my courses in Global Governance, Global Political Economy, American Foreign Economic Policy, and Globalization and Its Discontents. They listened to my thoughts on the topic—and most of them were kind enough to stay awake the whole time. I am particularly grateful to Bethany Albertson, Jonathan Caverley, Persis Elavia, Zack Kertcher, Jenna Jordan, Jennifer London, Emily Meierding, Michelle Murray, Adam Nelson, Bilgehan Ozturk, Brian Portnoy, Susie Pratt, Sebastian Rosato, John Schuessler, Alexander Thompson, Sarah Wetmore, and Lora Viola. The feedback and/or inspiration I received from these students at various stages of this project proved invaluable in the revising stages. At different junctures, two research assistants at the University of Chicago made my life much, much, much easier—Bonnie Weir and Amanda Butler. I hope that as they progress in their own careers, they find RAs who are just as diligent.

I put the finishing touches on this book at The Fletcher School at Tufts University. Many thanks to Stephen Bosworth, Laurent Jacque, Michael Glennon, and Joel Trachtman for easing the transition eastward.

Portions of this book have been presented at a plethora of different venues on two continents. In North America, multiple drafts of these arguments were presented at various annual meetings of the American Political Science Association, International Studies Association, and Midwestern Political Science Association. Chapters were also presented at seminars at Brown University, the College of DuPage, the University of California at Berkeley, the University of Pennsylvania, the University of Toronto, Duke, Dartmouth, Georgetown, Notre Dame, Penn State, Princeton, Stanford, Tufts, the University of Wisconsin, the University of Southern California, and the "North-South" seminar on International Relations created by the University of Chicago and Northwestern. I am grateful to the participants and discussants at all of these venues for their thoughts and criticisms—particularly Ken Abbott, Karen Alter, David Bach, Samuel Barkin, Mia Bloom, Risa Brooks, Tom Callaghy, Lars-Erik Cederman, Steve Chan, Ruth Collier, Tyler Cowen, Christina Davis, Raj Desai, Beth DeSombre, Henry Farrell, Benjamin Frankel, Erik Gartzke, Gary Goertz, James Goldgeier, Joshua Goldstein, Judith Goldstein, Emilie Hafner-Burton, Brian Hanson, Virginia Haufler, Ian Hurd, John Ikenberry, Miles Kahler, Bob Keohane, Judith Kelley, Sarah Cleeland Knight, Jeffrey Kopstein, Steve Krasner, Jennifer Lind, Tamar London, George Lopez, Ian Lustick, Ed Mansfield, Kate McNamara, Sophie Meunier, Linda B. Miller, Helen Milner, Andrew Moravcsik, Cliff Morgan, Layna Mosley, Dale Murphy, Chuck Myers, Abe Newman, Daniel Nexon, Glenn Palmer, Jon Pevehouse, Marsha Pripstein Posusney, Aseem Prakash, Daryl Press, Simone Pulver, Peter Rosendorff, Kenneth Schultz, Beth Simmons, Rogers Smith, Harvey Starr, Mike Tomz, David Vogel, Jana Von Stein, and Bill Wohlforth.

Policy-relevant portions of this manuscript have been presented at the Council on Foreign Relations, the Cordell Hull Institute, and the American Enterprise Institute. The advice and support of William Antholis, Alyssa Ayres, Jagdish Bhagwati, Henry Bienen, Marshall Bouton, Scott Cooper, Hugh Corbet, Daniel Esty, Irina Faskianos, Alton Frye, Jack Goldsmith, Richard Haass, Fred Iklé, Jim Lindsay, Sebastian Mallaby, Kenneth Roth, Leigh Sloane, and David Victor were particularly useful. I have on occasion trotted snippets of this project into the blogosphere as well. Tyler Cowen, Kevin Drum, Loren Wilson, and Matthew Yglesias were kind enough to craft thoughtful responses.

In Europe, my early thoughts on the subject were voiced at the April 2002 Salzburg Seminar on Global Economic Institutions, my intermediate thoughts were presented at the June 2003 meeting of the International Eastern European Political Science Association meeting in Budapest, and my later thoughts were presented at a special *Journal of European Public Policy* forum on "Policy Convergence in Europe" at the University of Hamburg. Richard Gardner, Saadia Pekkanen, Olin Robison, Jeffrey Schott, Kari Tapiola, and John Williamson made Salzburg an even more enjoyable environment than usual (a high threshold to meet). In Budapest, Anna Leander was an excellent discussant. At Hamburg, Christoph Knill, Katharina Holzinger, Claudio Radaelli, Andy Jordan, Duncan Liefferink, and Martin Marcussen proffered a steady drumbeat of good ideas.

For the empirical chapters, many scholars who know a lot more about these topics than I were generous in receiving my ideas, treating them seriously but critically, and steering me in the right direction. On the Internet chapter, I thank Tim Büthe, Henry Farrell, Walter Mattli, and Steve Weber for their input. On the financial regulation chapter, my biggest debt is to the ultra-competent staff at the U.S. Department of the Treasury who tolerated my presence for close to a year while they went about their business—particularly Sherman Boone, Paulette Durham, Anna Gelpern, Mark Giancola, Nilmini Gunaratne, Danny Glaser, Juhan Jaakson, Keith Krulak, Wilbur Monroe, Jody Myers, Bill Murden, Brad Setser, and Mark Sobel. For the genetically modified organisms case, Mark Aspinwall, Yves Tiberghien, and Alasdair Young provided valuable references and pointers. For the chapter on intellectual property and public health, I learned a great deal from Tina Choi, Emilie Hafner-Burton, Cynthia Horne, Abe Newman, Elliot Posner, Kal Raustiala, and Eric Shimp.

Several funding sources made the research and writing of this book possible and even enjoyable. At the outset of this project, I received a Council on Foreign Relations International Affairs Fellowship to work at the Treasury Department. Many thanks to Eva Fearn, Elise Carlson Lewis, and Alton Frye for their advice and aid throughout that year; thanks in particular to the incomparable Irina Faskianos for keeping me engaged in CFR activities after becoming a term member. During the drafting of the book, I received two research grants from the University of Chicago's Social Science Division—which would not have happened without the assistance of Fione Dukes, Mark Hansen, and Richard Saller. At the conclusion of this project I received a nonresident Transatlantic fellowship from the German Marshall Fund of the United States. I owe a considerable debt to Craig Kennedy for making that possible.

At Princeton University Press, Chuck Myers was interested in this book from the outset. His invaluable support, advice, and patience during the drafting process have made this a much better manuscript. Scott Gray and Lauren Lepow were excellent sherpas to guide *All Politics is Global* from manuscript to book form. Dawn Hall's copyediting saved me from several embarrassing mistakes. The inestimable Kathy Anderson provided another pair of proof-reading eyes for me at Chicago. At the page proof stage, Luisa Melo, Anu Piilola, and Carol Roberts saved me from as many typos and misspellings as humanly possible.

Some parts of this book have appeared in different venues. A previous draft of chapter 4 appeared in *Political Science Quarterly,* and parts of chapters 3, 5, and 6 appeared in the *Journal of European Public Policy.*[8] I thank the editors of those publications for releasing their copyright.

My healthy skepticism about the power of global civil society does not diminish my healthy respect for local civil society—particularly the network of friendships my family and I built up during our years at Chicago. After a peripatetic existence during the 1990s, Erika and I were fortunate enough to settle down in Hyde Park without needing to move every year. Our friends both in and out of the university community made those years comfortable for us—a rare and precious commodity that we shall not soon forget.

The only thing more important than friends is family. My son Sam was born just as I was starting this project, and my daughter Lauren was born just as I was wrapping up the penultimate draft. When I started graduate school, I thought that nothing was more important than studying world politics. Looking in on my sleeping children as I type this, I will always be grateful to them for expanding my horizons about what's really important.

Daniel W. Drenzer
Medford, MA
September 2006

[8] Daniel W. Drezner, "Globalization, Coercion, and Competition: The Different Pathways to Policy Convergence," *Journal of European Public Policy* 12 (October 2005): 841–59; Drezner, "The Global Governance of the Internet: Bringing the State Back In," *Political Science Quarterly* 119 (Fall 2004): 477–98.

Glossary of Acronyms

ARV	Anti-retroviral drugs
ASEAN	Association of Southeast Asian Nations
BIS	Bank of International Settlements
Bt	bacillus thuringiensis
CAFTA	Central American Free Trade Agreement
CAP	Common Agricultural Policy
CCITT	Consultative Committee on International Telegraphy and Telephony
ccTLD	country code Top Level Domains
DNS	Domain Name System
FATF	Financial Action Task Force on Money Laundering
FDI	foreign direct investment
FSF	Financial Stability Forum
FTA	Free trade agreement
G-7	Group of Seven countries
G-20	Group of Twenty countries
GAC	Government Advisory Committee
GATT	General Agreements on Tariffs and Trade
GBDe	Global Business Dialogue on E-Commerce
GCS	Global civil society
GMO	genetically modified organism
gTLD	global Top Level Domain
gTLD-MOU	Generic Top Level Domain Memorandum Of Understanding
IAHC	International Ad Hoc Committee
IASC	International Accounting Standards Committee
ICA	International commercial arbitration
ICANN	Internet Corporation for Assigned Names and Numbers
ICRA	Internet Content Rating Association
IETF	Internet Engineering Task Force
IFI	International Financial Institution
IFWP	International Forum on the White Paper
IGO	International governmental organization
ILO	International Labor Organization
IMF	International Monetary Fund
IOSCO	International Organization of Securities Commissions
IPR	Intellectual property rights
ISO	International Organization for Standardization

ISOC	Internet Society
ISP	Internet service provider
ITU	International Telecommunications Union
IWC	International Whaling Commission
LDC	less developed country
MAI	Multilateral Agreement on Investment
MSF	Médecins Sans Frontières (Doctors Without Borders)
NAFTA	North American Free Trade Agreement
NAS	National Academy of Sciences
NCCT	Non-Cooperative Countries and Territories
NGO	Nongovernmental organization
NSI	Network Solutions Incorporated
NSS	National security strategy
OECD	Organization for Economic Cooperation and Development
OFC	Offshore financial center
OSI	Open Systems Interconnection
PEPFAR	President's Emergency Plan for AIDS Relief
PhRMA	Pharmaceutical Research and Manufacturers of America
ROSC	Reports on the Observance of Standards and Codes
SALW	Small arms and light weapons
SPS	Sanitary and Phytosanitary Agreement
TCP/IP	Transmission Control Protocol/Internet Protocol
TRIPS	Trade-Related Intellectual Property Rights
UNAIDS	Joint United Nations Programme on HIV/AIDS
USTR	United States Trade Representative
WIPO	World Intellectual Property Organization
WSIS	World Summit on the Information Society
WTO	World Trade Organization

PART I • THEORY

CHAPTER ONE

Bringing the Great Powers Back In

GLOBALIZATION IS RESPONSIBLE for a lot of bad international relations theory. The poor state of theorizing is *not* because economic globalization is irrelevant. The reduction of traditional barriers to exchange, such as tariffs and capital controls, has introduced a bevy of new conflicts over the residual impediments to global economic integration—the differences among domestic rules and regulatory standards. The affected issue areas include but are not limited to labor standards, environmental protection, financial supervision, consumer health and safety, competition policy, intellectual property rights, and Internet protocols. These differences matter: the Organization for Economic Cooperation and Development (OECD) estimates that these standards and regulations affect approximately $4 trillion in traded goods. At the start of the new millennium, these issues have been important enough to trigger an increase in the foreign affairs budgets for U.S. regulatory agencies even as the State Department's budget declined.[1]

Regulatory issues are important in and of themselves. They matter in world politics because of the way they affect the distribution of resources as well. Fundamentally, however, international regulatory regimes strike a political chord because they symbolize a shift in the locus of politics. The title of this book is a play on Tip O'Neill's well-known aphorism that "all politics is local."[2] In the current era, this statement is at least open to question. For many issues that comprise the daily substance of our lives—how to treat workers, how much to pollute, what can go into our food, what can be accessed on the Internet, how much medicine will cost—the politics have gone global.

The proliferation of new global issue areas has increased scholarly attention on how the global economy is regulated in an era of globalization. However, the theoretical debates on this topic leave much to be desired; Miles Kahler and David Lake recently concluded, "Contemporary scholarship . . . has

---

[1] OECD data from Walter Mattli, "The Politics and Economics of International Institutional Standard Setting: An Introduction," *Journal of European Public Policy* special issue 8 (2001): 329; Budget data from Anne-Marie Slaughter, *A New World Order* (Princeton, NJ: Princeton University Press, 2004), 36–37.

[2] Tip O'Neill with Gary Hymel, *All Politics Is Local and Other Rules of the Game* (New York: Times Books, 1994).

yielded only a partial, unsystematic, and ultimately inconclusive body of theorizing on the relationship between globalization and governance."[3]

Most strands of research on this topic share a common assumption—the decline of state autonomy relative to other factors and actors. Globalization undercuts state sovereignty, weakening a government's ability to effectively regulate its domestic affairs. Global market forces are powerful enough to deprive governments of their autonomy and agency. As Thomas Friedman phrases it, globalization binds states into the "Golden Straitjacket," forcing them to choose between "free market vanilla and North Korea."[4] Prominent pundits, policymakers, and scholars echo the assertion that globalization drastically reduces the state's ability to govern.[5] At the same time that state autonomy is in decline, other theorists argue that globalization empowers a web of nonstate actors, including multinational corporations, nongovernmental organizations (NGOs), and transnational activist networks.[6] Some theorists go so far as to assert that globalization requires a wholesale rejection of existing theoretical paradigms.[7]

The trouble with this belief is the lack of variation in the independent variable and the presence of variation in the dependent variable. According to these narratives, globalization increases the number and power of factors and actors that inexorably promote policy convergence, forcing states into agreement on regulatory matters. The problem with this scenario is that there are a number of regulatory issue areas—data privacy, stem cell research, global warming, genetically modified foods—where regulatory convergence has been

[3] Miles Kahler and David Lake, "Globalization and Governance," in *Governance in a Global Economy: Political Authority in Transition,* ed. Kahler and Lake, 15–16 (Princeton, NJ: Princeton University Press, 2003).

[4] Thomas Friedman, *The Lexus and the Olive Tree* (New York: Farrar, Strauss, and Giroux, 1999), 86.

[5] Richard Falk, "State of Seige: Will Globalization Win Out?" *International Affairs* 73 (January 1997): 123–36; Arthur Schlesinger Jr., "Has Democracy a Future?" *Foreign Affairs* (September/October 1997): 7–8; Susan Strange, *The Retreat of the State: The Diffusion of Power in the World Economy* (Cambridge: Cambridge University Press, 1996); Dani Rodrik, *Has Globalization Gone Too Far?* (Washington, DC: Institute for International Economics, 1997); Richard Rosecrance, *The Rise of the Virtual State* (New York: Basic Books, 1999).

[6] Ronnie Lipschutz, "Reconstructing World Politics: The Emergence of a Global Civil Society," *Millennium* 21 (Spring 1992): 389–420; Jessica Matthews, "Power Shift," *Foreign Affairs* 76 (January–February 1997): 50–66; Margaret Keck and Kathryn Sikkink, *Activists Beyond Borders* (Ithaca, NY: Cornell University Press, 1998).

[7] Philip Cerny, "Globalization and the Changing Logic of Collective Action," *International Organization* 49 (Autumn 1995): 595–625; Cerny, "Globalization and Other Stories: the Search for a New Paradigm in International Relations," *International Journal* 51 (December 1996): 617–37; Ian Clark, *Globalization and International Relations Theory* (Oxford: Oxford University Press, 1999); James H. Mittelman, "Globalization: An Ascendant Paradigm?" *International Studies Perspectives* 3 (February 2002): 1–14; Mittelman, "What Is Critical Globalization Studies?" *International Studies Perspectives* 5 (August 2004): 219–30.

limited at best. Structural theories lack the capacity to explain variation in coordination outcomes.

This book argues that the great powers—defined here as governments that oversee large internal markets—remain the primary actors writing the rules that regulate the global economy. The key variable affecting global regulatory outcomes is the distribution of interests among the great powers. A great power concert is a necessary and sufficient condition for effective global governance over any transnational issue. Without such a concert, government attempts at regulatory coordination will be incomplete, and nonstate attempts will prove to be a poor substitute.

A few complexities are contained within this simple argument. For example, when will the great powers agree to coordinate their regulatory standards? I argue that globalization increases the rewards for policy coordination, but has a negligible impact on the adjustment costs of coordination. Whether regulatory coordination takes place is a function of the adjustment costs actors face in altering their preexisting rules and regulations. When the adjustment costs are sufficiently high, not even globalization's powerful dynamics can push states into cooperating.

Adjustment costs are a function of the ability of the affected domestic actors to use exit rather than voice in reacting to the impact of regulatory coordination.[8] The more that domestic groups have invested in the status quo, the greater their costs of exit. Private actors with constrained exit options have a strong incentive to invest in assets specific to longstanding domestic legal and regulatory structures; these specific assets increase the economic and political costs of regulatory coordination. The less viable the exit option, the more that political voice is used, and the greater the political and economic adjustment costs. These costs will be high when the regulatory issue in question affects relatively immobile or mature sectors or markets—the regulation of land, labor, or consumer products. Ironically, the least globalized elements of great power polities exert the strongest effect on the likelihood of global regulatory coordination.

Smaller states and nonstate actors in the international system do not affect regulatory outcomes, but they do affect the processes through which coordination is attempted. The reason their effect on the process is irrelevant to the outcome is that global governance processes are substitutable. Powerful states can and will engage in forum-shopping within a complex of international regimes.[9] They can and will use different policy tools to create those structures, depending on the constellation of state interests. Options include delegating regime management to nonstate actors; creating international regimes with

---

[8] Albert Hirschman, *Exit, Voice, and Loyalty: Responses to Firms, Organizations, and States* (Cambridge, MA: Harvard University Press, 1970).

[9] On the concept of regime complexes, see Kal Raustiala and David Victor, "The Regime Complex for Plant Genetic Resources," *International Organization* 58 (Spring 2004): 277–309.

strong enforcement capabilities; generating competing regimes to protect material interests; and unilateral, extraterritorial measures to establish regional spheres of influence. The preferences and actions of other states and nonstate actors will constrain certain great power strategies, however.

While relative power remains the salient fact in determining regulatory outcomes at the systemic level, it is of little importance in determining great power preferences. The result is a "revisionist" theory that resembles Jeff Legro and Andrew Moravcsik's "two-step" approach to international relations theory.[10] The first step is identifying the domestic actors and institutions that explain the origin of state preferences. The second step is to take those preferences as given for international interactions, and to explain the bargaining outcomes as a function of the distribution of interests and capabilities. Domestic factors account for preference formation, but not the outcomes of international bargaining. That is how the theory will be developed here.

WHY THIS MATTERS

The regulation of the global economy is intrinsically important. Markets rely on rules, customs, and institutions to function properly.[11] Global markets need global rules and institutions to work efficiently. The presence or absence of these rules, and their content and enforcement, is the subject of this book. In a globalizing economy, what are the rules? Who makes them? How are they made?

The answers to these questions matter to policymakers and publics alike. Policymakers have to deal with an ever-increasing amount of regulatory questions. The number of national regulatory agencies has exploded during the current era of globalization.[12] The street protests that started at the World Trade Organization (WTO) Ministerial meeting in Seattle in 1999 have spread to almost every significant meeting of a multilateral economic institution. They are a testament to the passions that globalization arouses.[13] This should not be surprising. Some of the most contentious issues in world politics over the past decade—financial contagion, global warming, genetically modified foods, terrorist financing, sweatshop labor—are, at their core, regulatory disputes.

[10] Jeffrey Legro, "Culture and Preferences in the International Cooperation Two-Step," *American Political Science Review* 90 (March 1996): 118–37; Andrew Moravcsik, "Taking Preferences Seriously: A Liberal Theory of International Politics," *International Organization* 51 (Autumn 1997): 513–53; Jeffrey Legro and Andrew Moravcsik, "Is Anyone Still a Realist?" *International Security* 24 (Spring 1999): 55–106.

[11] John McMillan, *Reinventing the Bazaar: A Natural History of Markets* (New York: W. W. Norton, 2002), 14.

[12] David Levi-Faur and Jacint Jordana, "The Global Diffusion of Regulatory Capitalism," *Annals of the American Academy of Political and Social Science* 598 (March 2005): 12–32.

[13] Jeffry Frieden, *Global Capitalism: Its Fall and Rise in the Twentieth Century* (New York: W. W. Norton, 2006), chap. 20.

The September 11, 2001 terrorist attacks and their aftermath only increased the salience of these issues. The United States considers it vital to develop stringent global standards to block terrorist financing and monitor shipping containers. The possibility of bioterror attacks increases the demand for states to coordinate their environmental and food safety regulations. The use of the Internet by terrorist networks to communicate with one another has raised the question of how governments can effectively patrol cyberspace without choking off e-commerce.[14] More generally, the U.S. response has highlighted the philosophical disagreements between Americans and Europeans over the proper modes of global governance.[15] The 9/11 attacks did not reduce the questions raised by the globalization of national economies; they highlighted how the globalization of national security also generates demands for regulatory coordination.

Scholarly work in this area is necessary in part because the popular discourse on the subject has been dreadful. If it is true that public intellectuals earn more attention from being spectacularly wrong than from drawing an accurate, complex picture of the world, then "pop globalization" writers have certainly garnered attention. Consider Thomas Friedman's aforementioned assertion that globalization acts as a Golden Straitjacket.[16] This description is simple, pithy, and wrong. The persistent diversity of capitalist systems around the world contradicts Friedman's claims about the binding constraints of free market capitalism.[17] Surveys of financial traders undercut Friedman's belief that an "Electronic Herd" runs roughshod over every facet of government intervention in the economy.[18] Globalization does not even force firms in the same sector to compete in the same way.[19] Friedman, like most other popular writers on this subject, offers a simple model of economic determinism—in which the interests of transnational capital dominate all other considerations—to explain how globalization works. This approach does not hold up to careful scrutiny.[20] What is truly scary, however, is that Friedman is an oasis of clarity

[14] Paul Davidson, "FBI Uneasy about Plan to Deregulate Fast Net," *USA Today*, July 9, 2002, 3B.

[15] Robert Kagan, *Of Paradise and Power* (New York: Knopf, 2003); Daniel W. Drezner, "Lost in Translation: The Transatlantic Divide over Diplomacy," in *Growing Apart: America in a Globalizing World*, ed. Jeffrey Kopstein and Sven Steinmo (Cambridge: Cambridge University Press, 2007).

[16] Friedman, *The Lexus and the Olive Tree*; see also Friedman, *The World Is Flat* (New York: Farrar, Strauss, and Giroux, 2005).

[17] Suzanne Berger and Ronald Dore, eds., *National Diversity and Global Capitalism* (Ithaca, NY: Cornell University Press, 1996); Peter Hall and David Soskice, eds., *Varieties of Capitalism: The Institutional Foundations of Comparative Advantage* (New York: Oxford University Press, 2001).

[18] Layna Mosley, *Global Capital and National Governments* (Cambridge: Cambridge University Press, 2003).

[19] Suzanne Berger et al., *How We Compete: What Companies around the World Are Doing to Make It in Today's Global Economy* (New York: Doubleday, 2006).

[20] Daniel W. Drezner, "Globalization and Policy Convergence," *International Studies Review* 3 (Spring 2001): 53–78; Drezner, "Bottom Feeders," *Foreign Policy* 121 (November/December 2000): 64–70.

compared with other popular explanations proffered about globalization and global governance.[21]

This popular discourse has helped to fuel public anxieties about the future of globalization and global governance. In the United States, globalization prompts fierce domestic debates. Polling data reveals that U.S. citizens believe the integration of the United States with the rest of the world has greatly constrained U.S. policy autonomy, creating ambivalence about further international integration.[22] In the European Union, globalization has been inexorably linked to Americanization, which has not endeared the concept to a majority of its citizens.[23] The anxiety about globalization and global governance is even greater in the rest of the world, since other countries are far more dependent on the global economy than the United States. Global public opinion surveys demonstrate majority support in the developing world for capitalism—but want it to be accompanied by "strong government regulations."[24]

Just as the questions raised in this book matter greatly to public discourse, they also affect scholarly debates about the international political economy (IPE). Fifteen years ago, the study of IPE was essentially limited to explaining the variations in the global rules governing merchandise trade, exchange rates, and foreign direct investment (FDI).[25] That was then. The latest era of globalization has raised a plethora of new issues to explain. Can existing IPE paradigms explain the variation of outcomes within and across these new issue areas—or are new paradigms needed?

This study also provides clues to the relationship between states and nonstate actors. The debate about the relevance of nonstate actors is not new,[26] but the current era of globalization has intensified the arguments. Some scholars exaggerate the impotence of the state, interpreting a failure to perfectly regulate

---

[21] Geoffrey Hardt and Antonio Negri, *Empire* (Cambridge, MA: Harvard University Press, 2000).

[22] *Perspectives on Trade and Poverty Reduction: A Survey of Public Opinion* (Washington, DC: German Marshall Fund of the United States, 2005); *Global Views 2004: American Public Opinion and Foreign Policy* (Chicago: Chicago Council on Foreign Relations, 2004), chap. 4; Program on International Policy Attitudes, "Americans on Globalization, Trade, and Farm Subsidies," January 22, 2004, available at http://www.pipa.org/archives/us_opinion.php, accessed March 2006. It should be noted that these attitudes were also prevalent during the boom years of the late 1990s as well. See Kenneth Scheve and Matthew Slaughter, *Globalization and the Perception of American Workers* (Washington, DC: Institute for International Economics, 2001); Scheve and Slaughter, "Economic Insecurity and the Globalization of Production," *American Journal of Political Science* 48 (October 2004): 662–74.

[23] See Joel Krieger, "Egalitarian Social Movements in Western Europe: Can They Survive Globalization and the EMU?" *International Studies Review* 1 (Fall 1999): 69–84.

[24] Program on International Policy Attitudes, "20 Nation Poll Finds Strong Global Consensus: Support for Free Market System, but also More Regulation of Large Companies," January 11, 2006, available at http://www.worldpublicopinion.org/pipa/articles/home_page/154.php?nid=&id=&pnt=154&lb=hmpg2, accessed March 2006.

[25] Robert Gilpin, *The Political Economy of International Relations* (Princeton, NJ: Princeton University Press, 1987).

[26] See the discussion in the preface.

a sphere of social life as an example of a general retreat of the Westphalian system. However, statists have fallen into the same trap, gleefully pointing out the vast areas of world politics where nonstate actors have minimal influence. Both sides tend to generalize from their most favorable cases. The model presented here suggests that states, particularly the great powers, remain the primary actors, but that they will rely on nonstate actors for certain functional purposes. At the same time, nonstate actors can, on occasion, jump-start regulatory agendas to advance their issues—even if the final outcome does not accord with their preferences.

Beyond the study of global political economy, the topic of regulatory coordination raises theoretical questions about global governance that affect a wide variety of debates among international relations theorists. The questions asked in this book address arguments by globalization scholars that the changes wrought on world politics in the past twenty years require completely new theories of international relations.[27] They affect debates in international relations and international law over the extent to which global governance structures can alter or constrain state behavior.[28] At the deepest level, resolving how globalization affects governance wrestles with the fundamental question about whether anarchy is a constant or a variable.[29] For some issue areas, effective global governance means the transfer of authority from the national to the supranational. At what point does global regulatory governance become so routine that the global economy ceases to be anarchical?

Defining Terms

In *Leviathan*, Thomas Hobbes argued that the key step in political science was the formulation of precise terms. That statement applies with a vengeance to the study of global economic regulation. A major reason for the contentious nature of debates about globalization and global governance is the disagreements over the precise meaning of terms. For example, the word "globalization" has been used so frequently to describe so many disparate phenomena that the term has been stripped of any concrete meaning.[30] What one scholar finds important

---

[27] See the works cited in footnote 7.

[28] Abram Chayes and Antonia Handler Chayes, "On Compliance," *International Organization* 47 (Spring 1993): 175–206; George Downs, David Rocke, and Peter Barsoom, "Is the Good News about Compliance Good News about Cooperation?" *International Organization* 50 (Summer 1996): 379–406; Judith Goldstein et al., eds., *Legalization and World Politics* (Cambridge, MA: MIT Press, 2001); Slaughter, *A New World Order*; Jack Goldsmith and Eric Posner, *The Limits of International Law* (New York: Oxford University Press, 2005).

[29] Helen V. Milner, "The Assumption of Anarchy in International Relations Theory: A Critique," *Review of International Studies* 17 (January 1991): 67–85.

[30] For a taxonomy of definitions, see David Held and Anthony McGrew, eds., *The Global Transformations Reader* (Oxford: Polity Press, 2000), part I.

about globalization another will dismiss as irrelevant. Susan Strange argued that a chief deficiency of international political economy was the use of imprecise language; "the worst of them all is 'globalisation'—a term which can refer to anything from the Internet to a hamburger."[31] A dictionary of international relations agrees: "the term is imprecise and its use is often heavily laden with ideological baggage."[32] A different criticism is that the current jargon is merely old wine in new bottles. What is the difference, for example, between globalization and interdependence?[33] How does the concept of global governance differ from international regimes? Before proceeding, clear definitions are needed.

I define *globalization* as the cluster of technological, economic, and political processes that drastically reduce the barriers to economic exchange across borders. This definition is narrower than the one used by a bevy of scholars focusing on the social and cultural dimensions of globalization—for good reasons.[34] Broad definitions tend to commingle causes and effects. This book is specifically interested in the ability of actors to regulate economic and social life, and the impact that globalization has on regulatory efforts. At the same time, my definition is more inclusive than those who use deterritorialization as the primary organizational construct to characterize globalization.[35] The latter definition treats the current moment as historically unique, and therefore has a post hoc flavor to it. My definition acknowledges that there have been previous eras of partial globalization.[36] However, the current era of globalization encompasses most of the world's nations and all of the great powers—including the United States.[37]

---

[31] Strange, *Retreat of the State*, xiii. This term has not gotten any clearer in the past decade. Kwame Anthony Appiah wryly characterized "globalization" as "a term that once referred to a marketing strategy, and then came to designate a macroeconomic thesis, and now can seem to encompass everything and nothing." Appiah, *Cosmopolitanism: Ethics in a World of Strangers* (New York: W. W. Norton, 2006), xiii.

[32] Graham Evans and Jeffrey Newnham, *The Penguin Dictionary of World Politics* (New York: Penguin, 1998), 201.

[33] Robert Keohane and Joseph Nye, "Globalization: What's New? What's Not? (And So What?)" *Foreign Policy* 118 (Spring 2000): 104–19; Keohane, *Power and Governance in a Partially Globalized World* (New York: Routledge, 2002).

[34] James H. Mittelman, *The Globalization Syndrome* (Princeton, NJ: Princeton University Press, 2000); Saskia Sassen, *Globalization and Its Discontents* (New York: The New Press, 1998).

[35] David Held et al., *Global Transformations: Politics, Economics, and Culture* (Stanford, CA: Stanford University Press, 1999); Jan Aart Scholte, *Globalization: A Critical Introduction* (New York: St. Martin's Press, 2000).

[36] For an excellent primer on the nineteenth-century version of globalization in the Atlantic region, see Kevin O'Rourke and Jeffrey Williamson, *Globalization and History* (Cambridge, MA: MIT Press, 1999).

[37] How is this definition of globalization distinct from the concept of interdependence? In the argot of international relations theory, the latter term describes a bilateral interstate relationship rather than a systemic effect. The United States and Canada are interdependent. Globalization, on the other hand, affects all of the actors in the system.

Regulatory coordination is defined as the codified adjustment of national standards in order to recognize or accommodate regulatory frameworks from other countries. Although there are many dimensions of economic regulation, this definition presumes that standards are the primary operationalization through which political authorities establish the global rules of the game. The International Organization for Standardization (ISO) defines standards as, "[the] documented agreements containing technical specifications or other precise criteria to be used consistently as rules, guidelines, or definitions of characteristics, to ensure that materials, products, processes, and services are fit for their purpose."[38] Defining policy coordination via standards has the conceptual advantage of creating a single dimension to compare disparate regulatory preferences. Stringent regulatory standards require actors to invest in significant resources to ensure compliance; lax regulatory standards do not.[39] Walter Mattli observes that, "work on standards by political scientists practically does not exist," suggesting the extent to which the existing literature has missed the mark in assessing the regulation of the global economy.[40]

Regulatory coordination does not automatically imply *policy convergence*, which is defined as the narrowing of gaps in national standards over time.[41] For example, the mutual recognition of other national standards does not necessarily lead to greater policy convergence, but does lead to greater coordination. Furthermore, convergence can occur without conscious coordination, if structural factors affect all actors in an identical fashion. Regulatory coordination is also distinct from *harmonization,* which implies policy convergence to a single regulatory standard. That said, theories predicting policy convergence or even harmonization can ostensibly explain regulatory coordination as well.[42]

Global governance is a more expansive term than policy coordination. Global governance refers not only to the codified adjustment of national rules and regulations; it encompasses the collection of authority relationships designated to monitor, enforce, and amend any transnational set of rules and regulations. Note that this definition can include a variety of arrangements, including "hard

---

[38] Quoted in Mattli, "The Politics and Economics of International Institutional Standard Setting," 330.

[39] One could argue that the stringency metric does not apply to purely technical standards to ensure the interoperability of goods and services across borders (such as the width of credit cards). While this is likely true in some cases, the discussion in part II shows that even technical standards require investment in compliance, with some candidate standards requiring more investment than others.

[40] Mattli, "The Politics and Economics of International Institutional Standard Setting," 332.

[41] Christoph Knill, "Cross-National Policy Convergence: Causes, Approaches, and Explanatory Factors," *Journal of European Public Policy* 12 (October 2005): 764–74; George Hoberg, "Globalization and Policy Convergence: Symposium Overview," *Journal of Comparative Policy Analysis* 3 (August 2001): 127–32.

[42] See Colin Bennett, "What Is Policy Convergence and What Causes It?" *British Journal of Political Science* 21 (April 1991): 287–306; Drezner, "Globalization and Policy Convergence."

law" treaties, "soft law" declarations, private orders, and recommended codes of conduct.[43] As defined, global governance has a more precise definition than the myriad definitions for international regime that are given in the literature.[44] The latter term can include tacit norms or informal social practices;[45] the terms used here imply the existence of codified rules. At the same time, the plurality of institutional arrangements contained within this definition contrasts with institutionalist theory, which tends to think of international regimes as single entities that dominate an issue space.

When can global governance be said to be *effective*? The definitions vary by the author.[46] Some look at whether the regulatory regime affects the substantive issue in question. By this metric, for example, the Kyoto Protocol would be considered effective if it halts the current trend of global warming. Another school of thought examines whether the actors comply with the agreed-upon commitment. By this metric, the Kyoto Protocol would be effective if all of the participating actors adhere to their treaty commitments, even if the Kyoto Protocol does not ameliorate the problem of global warming. Yet another measure is whether defections from global agreements are detected and punished—even if the deviations from existing rules persist. By this metric, the Kyoto Protocol would be considered effective if countries that generated greenhouse gas emissions above their agreed-upon limit were severely sanctioned for their transgressions.

A big problem with measuring effectiveness is that governments often make pledges to coordinate without actually doing so. Consider, for example, the panoply of United Nations environmental treaties and ongoing conferences. As Peter Haas points out:

> It is difficult to evaluate the effectiveness of many of these conferences, in part because of weaknesses and gaps in our ability to monitor progress in achieving conference goals. The record is generally mixed, at best, in terms of achieving the targets and aspirations expressed in the action plans and declarations of the conferences. . . .

---

[43] Duncan Snidal and Kenneth Abbott, "Hard and Soft Law in International Governance," *International Organization* 54 (Summer 2000): 421–56; A. Claire Cutler, Virginia Haufler, and Tony Porter, eds., *Private Authority and International Affairs* (Albany: State University of New York Press, 1999).

[44] Oran Young, "International Regimes: Problems of Concept Formation," *World Politics* 32 (April 1980): 331–56; Stephen D. Krasner, ed., *International Regimes* (Ithaca, NY: Cornell University Press, 1983).

[45] On "tacit norms," see Charles Lipson, "Why are Some International Agreements Informal?" *International Organization* 45 (Autumn 1991): 495–538; on social practices, see Young, "International Regimes."

[46] Chayes and Chayes, "On Compliance"; Downs, Rocke, and Barsoom, "Is the Good News about Compliance Good News about Cooperation?"

The goals are often ambiguous. State reporting about compliance is generally weak and incomplete, and few provisions for verification of state compliance are made at the conferences.[47]

Similarly, Kal Raustiala has demonstrated that because international regulatory regimes are nearly always administered through regulatory regimes at the national level, long-standing domestic institutions can act as an impediment to the implementation of new global regulations.[48] Harmonization of forms does not necessarily translate into genuine policy coordination.

For this project, proper measure of effectiveness measures both the extent of actor compliance and the magnitude of the adjustments that actors are required to make to meet the agreed-upon regulatory standard.[49] To use a numerical example, a global governance structure where states are only 50 percent compliant with an agreement to cut carbon dioxide emissions by 20 percent should be considered more effective than a regulatory regime that produces 100 percent compliance with an agreement to cut emissions by only 1 percent.[50] Compliance matters, but so does the degree of difficulty.

THE LITERATURE

There is no shortage of explanations for how the world economy is regulated in an era of globalization. The scholarly literature on this subject can be divided along two conceptual dimensions, as table 1.1 shows. The first dimension is whether the theory posits that the driving force behind regulatory coordination is economic or ideational. The second dimension is whether actors retain agency in the face of a globalizing economy, or are tightly constrained by structural forces.

The first wave of scholarship—and virtually all of the popular literature on the subject—emphasized the primacy of structural forces over the agency of

[47] Peter Haas, "UN Conferences and Constructivist Governance of the Environment," *Global Governance* 8 (January/March 2002): 80.

[48] Kal Raustiala, "Domestic Institutions and International Regulatory Cooperation: Comparative Responses to the Convention on Biological Diversity," *World Politics* 49 (Summer 1997): 482–83.

[49] This definition elides the question of whether the agreed policy coordination substantially addresses the social or economic externality in question.

[50] I use this same logic in measuring the magnitude of concessions in response to economic sanctions. See Daniel W. Drezner, *The Sanctions Paradox: Economic Statecraft and International Relations* (Cambridge: Cambridge University Press, 1999), chap. 4. For regulatory coordination, another dimension of effectiveness covers the scope of the agreement. To use the example of the Kyoto Protocol again, the failure of the United States or Australia to sign on downgrades the efficacy of the agreement, even if it achieves significant changes of behavior among the signatories.

TABLE 1.1
A Taxonomy of Globalization Theories

	Agent-Based Approaches	Structure-Based Approaches
Material pressures dominate	Mainstream IPE- approaches	Race-to-the-bottom
Ideational pressures dominate	Global civil society (GCS)	World polity paradigm

actors. These approaches argue that states are at the mercy of systemic forces, be they material or ideational. With these approaches, coordination occurs because of structural effects that force policy convergence; all countries respond to transnational constraints in the same way. While these approaches are conceptually elegant, they share the twin flaws of dubious theoretical presumptions and meager empirical support.[51]

Structural models focusing on the material effects of trade and capital flows tend to posit a "race-to-the-bottom" outcome. According to this model, capital has become increasingly footloose, to the point where states could not limit its mobility even if they tried.[52] In such a world, capital will seek the location where it can earn the highest rate of return. High rates of corporate taxation, strict labor laws, or rigorous environmental protection lower profit rates by raising the costs of production. Capital will therefore engage in regulatory arbitrage, moving to (or importing from) countries with the lowest regulatory standards. Nation-states eager to attract capital—and fearful of losing their tax base—lower their regulatory standards so as to raise the rate of return for corporate investment. The end result is a world where regulatory standards are at the lowest common denominator.

As David Vogel and Robert Kagan observe, "The political influence of the 'race to the bottom' imagery has been considerable."[53] While some scholarly advocates for this approach exist, its prominence is largely due to its long intellectual history and its recurrent popularity among the commentariat. Scholars in the social sciences have been fretting about races to the bottom

---

[51] Drezner, "Globalization and Policy Convergence."

[52] See John Goodman and Louis Pauly, "The Obsolescence of Capital Controls?" *World Politics* 46 (October 1993): 50–82; Sebastian Edwards, "How Effective Are Capital Controls?" *Journal of Economic Perspectives* 13 (Fall 1999): 65–84.

[53] David Vogel and Robert Kagan, eds., *The Dynamics of Regulatory Change: How Globalization Affects National Regulatory Policies* (Berkeley: University of California Press, 2004), 2.

since Adam Smith's *Wealth of Nations*.[54] Naomi Klein epitomizes the public intellectual cachet of this metaphor when she asserts: "[T]he incentives to lure investors are increasing and the wages and standards are being held hostage to the threat of departure. The upshot is that entire countries are being turned into industrial slums and low-wage ghettos, with no end in sight."[55] Implicitly or explicitly, this theory is at the root of most of the antiglobalization sentiment voiced in Seattle and elsewhere.[56]

There are anecdotal examples that support the idea of a race to the bottom,[57] but the bulk of the evidence strongly suggests that these assertions are flatly wrong. Official international governmental organization reports,[58] statistical

---

[54] "The proprietor of stock is a citizen of the world, and is not necessarily attached to any particular country. He would be apt to abandon the country in which he was ... assessed to a burdensome tax, and would remove his stock to some other country where he could either carry on his business or enjoy his fortune more at his ease. By removing his stock he would put an end to all the industry which it had maintained in the country which he left" (Adam Smith, *The Wealth of Nations*, [New York: Modern Library, 1937], 800). On other eighteenth- and nineteenth-century fears about globalization, see Samir Amin, "The Challenge of Globalization," *Review of International Political Economy* 3 (Fall 1996): 216–59; Emma Rothschild, "Globalization and the Return of History," *Foreign Policy* 115 (Summer 1999): 106–16.

On concerns about race-to-the-bottom effects beyond political science, see Karl Polanyi, *The Great Transformation* (Boston: Beacon Press, 1944), 57; Charles Tiebout, "A Pure Theory of Local Expenditures," *Journal of Political Economy* 64 (October 1956): 416–24; and William L. Cary, "Federalism and Corporate Law: Reflections upon Delaware," *Yale Law Journal* 83 (March 1974): 663–705.

[55] Naomi Klein, *No Logo* (London: Flamingo, 2000), 208, quoted in Martin Wolf, *Why Globalization Works* (New Haven, CT: Yale University Press, 2004), 240.

[56] Frieden, *Global Capitalism*, 466–68. For examples, see Lori Wallach and Michelle Sforza, *Whose Trade Organization? Corporate Globalization and the Erosion of Democracy* (Washington, DC: Public Citizen, 1999); Jerry Mander and Edward Goldsmith, eds., *The Case Against the Global Economy* (San Francisco: Sierra Club Books, 1996); Robin Broad, ed., *Global Backlash: Citizen Initiatives for a Just Economy* (New York: Rowan and Littlefield, 2002).

[57] See, for example, Kathleen Newland, "Workers of the World, Now What?" *Foreign Policy* 114 (Spring 1999): 52–65; Ethan Kapstein, "Workers and the World Economy," *Foreign Affairs* 75 (May/June 1996): 16–24.

[58] On labor issues, see *Organization for Economic Cooperation and Development, Trade, Employment, and Labour Standards: A Study of Core Workers' Rights and International Trade* (Paris, OECD, 1996); *International Trade and Core Labour Standards* (Paris: OECD, 2000); Dorsati Madami, *A Review of the Role and Impact of Export Processing Zones*, Policy Research Working Paper No. 2238 (Washington, DC: World Bank, 1999); and *International Labour Organization, Labour and Social Issues Relating to Export Processing Zones* (Geneva: ILO, 1998). On the environment, see J. M. Dean, "Trade and the Environment: A Survey of Literature," in *International Trade and the Environment*, ed. Patrick Low (Washington, DC: World Bank, 1992); Candice Stevens, "Do Environmental Policies Affect Competitiveness?" *OECD Observer* No. 183 (1993): 22–25; and Gunnar Eskeland and Ann Harrison, "Moving to Greener Pastures? Multinationals and the Pollution-Haven Hypothesis," World Bank Policy Research Working Paper No. 1744, March 1997.

inquiries,[59] comparative analyses,[60] and even studies of deviant cases[61] fail to find any appreciable evidence that countries are systematically lowering their labor or environmental standards in order to attract multinational capital. There is no evidence that economic openness and regulatory laxness are correlated in any way. Reviewing the literature, Martin Wolf comes to the same conclusion: "The great bulk of foreign direct investment continues to go to

[59] Nathan Jensen, *Nation-Sates and the Multinational Corporation: A Political Economy of Foreign Direct Investment* (Princeton, NJ: Princeton University Press, 2006); Dani Rodrik, "Labor Standards in International Trade: Do They Matter and What Do We Do about Them?" in *Emerging Agenda for Global Trade*, ed. Robert Z. Lawrence, Dani Rodrik, and John Whalley (Washington, DC: Overseas Development Council; Baltimore: Distributed by Johns Hopkins University Press, 1996); Rodrik, "Globalization and Labor," in *Market Integration, Regionalism, and the Global Economy*, ed. Richard Baldwin et al. (Cambridge: Cambridge University Press, 1999); Drusilla K. Brown, "International Trade and Core Labor Standards," Discussion Paper 2000–2005, Department of Economics, Tufts University, Medford, MA, January 2000; Robert J. Flanagan, "Labor Standards and International Competitive Advantage," paper presented at the International Labor Standards Conference, Stanford University, Stanford, CA, May 2002; Hye Jee Cho, "Political Risk, Labor Standards and Foreign Direct Investment," paper presented at UCLA's CIBER Doctoral Reseach Seminar, Ventura, CA, June 2002.

On the environment, see James Tobey, "The Impact of Domestic Environmental Policies on Patterns of World Trade," *Kyklos* 43 (May 1990): 191–209; Nancy Birdsall and David Wheeler, "Trade Policy and Industrial Pollution in Latin America: Where Are the Pollution Havens?" *Journal of Environment and Development* 2 (March 1993): 137–49; Adam B. Jaffe, Steven R. Peterson, Paul R. Portney, and Robert N. Stavins, "Environmental Regulation and the Competitiveness of U.S. Manufacturing," *Journal of Economic Literature* 33 (March 1995): 132–63; Ravi Ratnayake, "Do Stringent Environmental Regulations Reduce International Competitiveness?" *International Journal of the Economics of Business* 5 (February 1998): 97–118; Mark N. Harris, László Kónya, and László Mátyás, "Modelling the Impact of Environmental Regulations on Bilateral Trade Flows," *The World Economy* 25 (March 2002): 387–405; Raman Letchumanan and Fumio Kodama, "Reconciling the Conflict between the 'Pollution-Haven' Hypothesis and an Emerging Trajectory of International Technology Transfer," *Research Policy* 29 (2000): 59–79; David Wheeler, "Racing to the Bottom? Foreign Investment and Air Quality in Developing Countries," *Journal of Environment and Development* 10 (September 2001): 225–45; Beata K. Smarzynska and Shang-Jin Wei, "Pollution Havens and Foreign Direct Investment," NBER Working Paper No. 8465, September 2001; and Josh Ederington, Arik Levinson, and Jenny Menier, "Trade Liberalization and Pollution Havens," NBER Working Paper No. 10585, June 2004. For an exception, see Yuqing Xing and Charles Kolstad, "Do Lax Environmental Regulations Attract Foreign Investment?" *Environmental and Resource Economics* 21 (January 2002): 1–22.

[60] Debora Spar, "Attracting High Technology Investment: Intel's Costa Rican Plant," FIAS Occasional Paper No. 11, World Bank, Washington, DC, April 1998; Cees Van Beers, "Labour Standards and Trade Flows of OECD Countries," *The World Economy* 21 (January 1998): 57–73; Paul Q. Hirst and Grahame Thompson, *Globalization in Question*, 2nd ed. (Cambridge: Polity Press, 1999); Ana Teresa Romero, "Labour Standards and Exports Processing Zones: Situation and Pressures for Change," *Development Policy Review* 13 (1995): 247–76; Theodore Moran, *Beyond Sweatshops: Foreign Direct Investment and Globalization in Developing Countries* (Washington, DC: Brookings Institution Press, 2002).

[61] Elizabeth DeSombre, *Flagging Standards: Environmental, Safety, and Labor Regulations at Sea* (Cambridge, MA: MIT Press, 2006); Dale Murphy, *The Structure of Regulatory Competition* (New York: Oxford University Press, 2004), chap. 2; Ronald Mitchell, "Regime Design Matters: Intentional Oil Pollution and Treaty Compliance," *International Organization* 48 (Summer 1994): 425–58.

countries with high labour costs and strong regulatory regimes, not least on the environment."[62] Theoretically, the race to the bottom rests on shaky initial assumptions—and the predicted outcome is not robust to slight alterations in the model.[63] Of the major explanations for global regulatory coordination, this is the easiest one to dismiss.

The world polity approach eschews the material aspects of globalization.[64] According to this paradigm, regulatory coordination is not driven by capital mobility but by the spread of abstract concepts combined with the need for governments to conform to an ideal of the rationalized bureaucratic state.[65] John Meyer—the leading voice of this paradigm—sums up the argument: "globalization means the expanded flow of instrumental culture around the world. Put simply, common models of social order become authoritative in many different social settings."[66] According to this paradigm, the spread of global scientific discourse, establishment of international treaty law, and creation of attendant international governmental organizations (IGOs) leads to institutional isomorphism.[67] These ideational forces of globalization cause the spread of new norms calling for an "expansive structuration" of the state—

[62] Wolf, *Why Globalization Works*, 233.

[63] Daniel W. Drezner, "Globalizers of the World, Unite!" *The Washington Quarterly* 21 (Winter 1998): 209–25; Miles Kahler, "Modeling Races to the Bottom," paper presented at the 1998 annual meeting of the American Political Science Association, Boston, MA, September 1998; Ronald Rogowski, "Globalization without Governance: Implications of Tiebout Models in a World of Mobile Factors," paper presented at the American Political Science Association annual meeting, Washington DC, September 2000; Geoffrey Garrett and Peter Lange, "Internationalization, Institutions, and Political Change," in *Internationalization and Domestic Change*, ed. Robert Keohane and Helen Milner (Cambridge: Cambridge University Press, 1996); Scott Basinger and Mark Hallerberg, "Remodeling the Competition for Capital: How Domestic Politics Erases the Race-to-the-Bottom," *American Political Science Review* 98 (May 2004): 261–76.

[64] The "world polity" school of thought is also referred to as the "world society" paradigm. In the interest of distinguishing this model from later discussions about global civil society, I will stick to the "world polity" terminology.

[65] John W. Meyer, John Boli, George Thomas, and Francisco Ramirez, "World Polity and the Nation-State," *American Journal of Sociology* 103, no. 1 (1997): 144–81; Martha Finnemore, *National Interests and International Society* (Ithaca, NY: Cornell University Press, 1996); David Strang and Sarah Soule, "Diffusion in Organizations and Social Movements," *Annual Review of Sociology* 24 (1998); David Strang and John Meyer, "Institutional Conditions for Diffusion," *Theory and Society* 22, no. 4 (1993): 487–511.

[66] John W. Meyer, "Globalization: Sources and Effects on Nation States and Societies," *International Sociology* 15 (June 2000): 233–34. See also Marie-Laure Djelic and Kerstin Sahlin-Andersson, eds., *Transnational Governance: Institutional Dynamics of Regulation* (Cambridge: Cambridge University Press, 2006).

[67] Ibid. See also Paul Dimaggio and Walter Powell, "The Iron Cage Revisited: Institutional Isomorphism and Collective Rationality in Organizational Fields," *American Sociological Review* 48 (April 1983): 147–60. In this respect, the world polity approach is akin to structural neorealism. Kenneth Waltz, in discussing globalization, asserts great power autonomy but acknowledges that states will adopt the best practices of other states, leading to policy convergence. See Waltz, "Globalization and Governance," *PS: Political Science and Politics* 32 (December 1999): 697.

the development of new rules and bureaucracies to regulate both society and economy. Inexorably, states harmonize their regulations at ever-increasing levels of government intervention.[68]

This school of thought is somewhat vague on the processes through which convergence occurs, making falsification tests difficult.[69] Nevertheless, scholars working within the world polity paradigm have generated statistical evidence for a variety of regulatory functions.[70] There has undoubtedly been a secular increase in government commitment to labor standards, for example, which supports the structuration hypothesis.[71] In particular, empirical studies argue that the growth of the United Nations system, the rationalization of scientific discourse, and the growth of national bureaucracies can explain the explosion of international environmental regulation over the past century.[72]

The evidence for the world polity approach looks compelling but raises troubling methodological issues. It is an open question whether these results demonstrate correlation or causation. Empirically, measures of broad global participation are used to predict narrower forms of policy coordination.[73]

---

[68] As Meyer et al. conclude, "Holding constant the functional pressures of size, resources, and complexity, in recent decades nation-states . . . have clearly expanded inordinately across many different social domains. This is precisely the period during which world polity has been consolidated." Meyer et al., "World Polity and the Nation-State," 156.

[69] Sidney Tarrow observes, "Meyer and his collaborators were more interested in mapping isomorphism than in understanding the mechanisms of diffusion—and in fact, in their work the diffusion process is more frequently inferred from the presence of similar structures than traced through the actions of particular actors." Tarrow, "Transnational Politics: Contention and Institutions in International Politics," *Annual Review of Political Science* 4 (2001): 5–6. Even adherents to this view acknowledge this; see David Strang and Patricia Yei Min Chang, "The International Labor Organization and the Welfare State," *International Organization* 47 (Spring 1993): 237. See also Kate O'Neill, "Agency and Environmental Policy Change," unpublished ms., University of California, Berkeley, CA, June 2000.

[70] Y. S. Kim, Y. S. Jang, and H. Hwang, "Structural Expansion and the Cost of Global Isomorphism: A Cross-National Study of Ministerial Structure," *International Sociology* 17 (December 2002): 481–503; and Xiaowei Luo, "The Rise of the Social Development Model: Institutional Construction of International Technology Organizations, 1856–1993," *International Studies Quarterly* 44 (March 2000): 147–75.

[71] Strang and Chang, "The International Labor Organization and the Welfare State," 235-262; M. Senti, "The impact of international organizations on national social security expenditure: The case of the International Labour Organization (ILO) 1960–1989," *Politische Vierteljahresschrift* 39 (September 1998).

[72] John W. Meyer et al., "The Structuring of a World Environmental Regime, 1870–1990," *International Organization* 51 (October 1997): 623–51; David John Frank, "Science, Nature, and the Globalization of the Environment, 1870–1990," *Social Forces* 76 (December 1997): 409–37; David John Frank, "The Social Bases of Environmental Treaty Ratification, 1900–1990," *Sociological Inquiry* 69 (Fall 1999): 523-50; David John Frank, Ann Hironaka, and Evan Schofer, "The Nation-State and the Natural Environment over the Twentieth Century," *American Sociological Review* 65 (February 2000): 96–116.

[73] For example, it should not be shocking that the growth of scientific unions is used to predict the growth of environmental associations. Frank, "The Social Bases of Environmental Treaty Ratification," 528.

David John Frank admits that the world polity paradigm's testable hypotheses are "almost tautalogous," acknowledging that "it may be the case that one of the competing independent variables (such as economic development) underlies both country linkages to world society and number of environmental treaty ratifications."[74] Including intervening variables on the left-hand side of a regression model artificially reduces the significance levels of the collinear causal variables.[75] This flaw is indicative of the tendency for world polity scholars, in their empirical work, to omit control variables for alternative explanations.[76]

The world polity paradigm suffers from theoretical shortcomings as well. It tends to exaggerate the power of global culture at the expense of domestic rules and institutions. World polity scholars assume that states in the developing world will mimic more advanced economies because their own laws and institutions are amorphous and/or illegitimate enough to permit the constant re-creation of political institutions. This may be an accurate description of some developing countries, but not all. States in Latin America, South Asia, and the Pacific Rim have a sufficient history of self-governance to experience institutional path dependence, making regulatory change considerably more difficult.[77] This argument also assumes global culture is free of contradictory impulses. As will be demonstrated in the chapter on genetically modified organisms, transnational regulatory coordination can generate both material and ideational conflicts among the great powers.[78] If there is disagreement within the core nations of the global economy, it is hard to envision how common standards and practices will naturally diffuse to other countries.

Another category of theorists reject the emphasis on structural factors and emphasize the agency of nonstate actors in the international system. Ann Florini and P. J. Simmons assert that, "Transnational civil society is a piece—an increasingly important piece—of the larger problem of global gover-

---

[74] Ibid, 533.

[75] A related statistical flaw is that in many of these studies, one-tailed t-tests are used to determine significance. If two-tailed tests are used, many of the significant results drop below the 95 percent confidence threshold.

[76] The Frank study only includes world population and carbon dioxide emissions as alternative explanatory variables; the Meyer study only includes population. Many of the variables consistent with alternative explanations of regulatory convergence—growth in global GDP, the rate of urbanization, the growth of international trade, the distribution of power, changes in communication technologies—are not included in either study. Given the admitted collinearity of these alternatives with the associational variables, the likelihood of omitted variable bias cannot be dismissed.

[77] Douglass North, *Institutions, Institutional Change, and Economic Performance* (New York: Cambridge University Press, 1990); Mauro Guillén, *The Limits of Convergence: Globalization and Organizational Change in Argentina, South Korea, and Spain* (Princeton, NJ: Princeton University Press, 2001).

[78] On the ideational side of the equation, see Judith Goldstein, *Ideas, Institutions, and American Trade Policy* (Ithaca, NY: Cornell University Press, 1993); John Kurt Jacobsen, "Much Ado about Ideas: The Cognitive Factor in Economic Policy," *World Politics* 47 (January 1995): 283–310.

nance."[79] Scholars working in this framework posit that the growth of nongovernmental organizations,[80] epistemic communities,[81] public policy networks,[82] transnational social movements,[83] and even private orders[84] amounts to the creation of a global civil society (GCS) that is too ideationally powerful for states to ignore. As the dynamic density of GCS actors increases, so does their effect on outcomes.[85] Some writers go further, arguing that these groups are now powerful enough to bypass the state entirely, leading to a "world civic politics."[86]

Most of the empirical work on global civil society consists of efforts to demonstrate existence rather than pervasiveness. Therefore, most of the case studies take the form of "easy tests."[87] However, even looking at these cases, there is reason to question the explanatory power of the GCS approach. For example, scholars have argued that an epistemic community based in the United Nations Environmental Program and elite research institutes was responsible for persuading governments to agree to cooperate on the Montreal Protocol on stratospheric ozone, the 1992 Rio biodiversity summit, and the

[79] Ann M. Florini and P. J. Simmons, "What the World Needs Now?" in *The Third Force: The Rise of Transnational Civil Society*, ed. Ann Florini (Washington, DC: Carnegie Endowment for International Peace, 2000), 3.

[80] Peter J. Spiro, "New Global Communities: Nongovernmental Organizations in International Decision-Making Institutions," *The Washington Quarterly* 18 (Winter 1994): 45–56; Paul Wapner, "Politics beyond the State: Environmental Activism and World Civic Politics," *World Politics* 47 (April 1995): 311–40.

[81] Peter Haas, "Introduction: Epistemic Communities and International Policy Coordination," *International Organization* 46 (Spring 1992): 1–35.

[82] Wolfgang Reinicke, *Global Public Policy: Governing without Government?* (Washington, DC: Brookings Institution Press, 1998); John Braithwaite and Peter Drahos, *Global Business Regulation* (Cambridge: Cambridge University Press, 1999).

[83] Keck and Sikkink, *Activists beyond Borders*; Robert O'Brien, Anne Marie Goetz, Jan Aart Scholte, and Marc Williams, *Contesting Global Governance* (Cambridge: Cambridge University Press, 2000).

[84] A. Claire Cutler, Virginia Haufler, and Tony Porter, eds., *Private Authority and International Affairs* (Albany: State University of New York Press, 1999); Rodney Bruce Hall and Thomas J. Biersteker, eds., *The Emergence of Private Authority in Global Governance* (Cambridge: Cambridge University Press, 2002).

[85] Margaret Keck and Kathryn Sikkink point out: "Networks operate best when they are dense, with many actors, strong connections among groups in the network, and reliable information flows." Keck and Sikkink, *Activists beyond Borders*, 28.

[86] Ronnie Lipschultz notes: "While the participants in the networks of global civil society interact with states and governments over particular policy issues, the networks themselves extend beyond levels of analysis and state borders, and are not constrained by the state system itself." Lipschutz, "Reconstructing World Politics," 393. See also Wapner, "Politics beyond the State."

[87] One exception is Richard Price, "Reversing the Gun Sights: Transnational Civil Society Targets Land Mines," *International Organization* 52 (Summer 1998): 613–44, but see chapter 9 for a further discussion of the land mine case.

international whaling regime.[88] However, Lawrence Susskind argues that in general, epistemic communities have rarely played a role in environmental governance: "a review of most of the international treaties negotiated since the 1972 Stockholm conference shows that scientific evidence has played a surprisingly small role in issue definition, fact-finding, bargaining, and regime strengthening."[89] Both first-person and analytic accounts of international environmental negotiations also clash with the GCS narrative.[90]

Research into global civil society often blurs public activity with causal effect.[91] For example, GCS activists assert that through mass protests, petitions, and posting treaty drafts on Web sites, they played a crucial role in the failure of the Multilateral Agreement on Investment (MAI), an OECD initiative that stalled out in December 1998.[92] The problem with this interpretation of events is that there is minimal evidence that they were the cause of the MAI's downfall. The member states were far from reaching an agreement—the last draft version of the treaty had contained almost fifty pages of country-specific exemptions.[93] The United States and European Union were deadlocked over the issues of extraterritorial sanctions, application of the most-favored nation principle, and cultural protectionism. Edward M. Graham concludes: "the ne-

---

[88] On the Montreal Protocol, see Peter Haas, "Banning Chlorofluorocarbons: Epistemic Community Efforts to Protect Stratospheric Ozone," *International Organization* 46 (Spring 1992): 187–224; On whaling, see M. J. Peterson, "Whalers, Cetologists, Environmentalists, and the International Management of Whaling," *International Organization* 46 (Spring 1992): 147–86. More generally, see Wapner, "Politics beyond the State," and Ann Marie Clark, Elizabeth Friedman, and Kathryn Hochstetler, "The Sovereign Limits of Global Society," *World Politics* 51 (Fall 1998): 1–35.

[89] Lawrence Susskind, *Environmental Diplomacy: Negotiating More Effective Global Agreements* (Oxford: Oxford University Press, 1994), 64, quoted in Michael Zürn, "The Rise of International Environmental Politics," *World Politics* 50 (Fall 1998): 617–49.

[90] Mostafa Tolba, *Global Environmental Diplomacy* (Cambridge, MA: MIT Press, 1998), 85; Kenneth Oye and James Maxwell, "Self-Interest and Environmental Management," in *Local Commons and Global Interdependence*, ed. Robert Keohane and Elinor Ostrom (London: SAGE, 1995); Murphy, *The Structure of Regulatory Competition*, chap. 4; Young Ho Kim, "The Conditions of Effective NGO Policy Advocacy: An Analysis of Two International Environmental Treaties," paper presented at the International Studies Association annual meeting, New Orleans, LA, March 2002; and Scott Barrett, "The Political Economy of the Kyoto Protocol," *Oxford Reviews of Economic Policy* 14 (Winter 1998): 20–39.

[91] Michele Betsill and Elisabeth Corell, "NGO Influence in International Environmental Negotiations: A Framework for Analysis," *Global Environmental Politics* 1 (November 2001): 65–85.

[92] Stephen Kobrin, "The MAI and the Clash of Globalizations," *Foreign Policy* 112 (Fall 1998): 98; Craig Warkentin and Karen Mingst, "International Institutions, the State, and Global Civil Society in the Age of the World Wide Web," *Global Governance* 6 (April/June 2000): 237–57; Ronald Deibert, "International Plug 'n Play? Citizen Activism, the Internet, and Global Public Policy," *International Studies Perspectives* 1 (July 2000): 235–72; Florini and Simmons, "What the World Needs Now?" 10.

[93] See Edward M. Graham, *Fighting the Wrong Enemy: Antiglobal Activists and Multinational Enterprises* (Washington, DC: Institute for International Economics, 2000), chaps. 1–2.

gotiations were indeed in very deep difficulty before the metaphorical torpedo was fired by the NGOs . . . this torpedo thus was more a coup de grâce than a fatal blow in its own right."[94]

Many of the flaws in the GCS approach echo the problems with the first wave of research on transnational actors three decades ago.[95] Michael Clarke noted that the first wave of transnationalism research, "certainly does not constitute a theory; it is rather a term which recognizes a phenomenon, or perhaps a trend in world politics, a phenomenon from which other concepts flow."[96] Similarly, the GCS scholarship to date has focused more on descriptive inference than causal inference[97]—and even the description often lacks conceptual clarity.[98] The empirical confusion between the visibility of global civil society and their precise role in affecting the aforementioned cases highlights the need for causal inference and careful process tracing.

The final category of theories—mainstream IR paradigms—refers to the paradigms of international relations that have been dominant in the discourse. These approaches accept the primacy of material over ideational factors, and argue that the menu of choice for significant actors is not tightly constrained. They also assume that states are the primary actors in setting regulatory standards. The revisionist approach developed in this book comfortably fits into this family of theories.

There is a burgeoning literature that discusses how states determine the pattern of transnational regulation.[99] While these approaches share many common assumptions, however, significant differences remain. Many liberal institutionalists and virtually all realists begin with the premise that the United

[94] Graham, *Fighting the Wrong Enemy*, 16 and 40.

[95] Robert Keohane and Joseph Nye, *Transnational Relations and World Politics* (Cambridge, MA: Harvard University Press, 1973); Keohane and Nye, *Power and Interdependence* (Boston: Scott Foresman, 1978). On the similarities between the GCS literature and Keohane and Nye's work in the 1970s, see Alejandro Colás, *International Civil Society* (Oxford: Polity Press, 2002), chap. 1.

[96] Michael Clarke, "Transnationalism," in *International Relations: British and American Perspectives*, ed. Steve Smith (Oxford: Basil Blackwell, 1985), 146.

[97] On the distinction, see Gary King, Robert Keohane, and Sidney Verba, *Designing Social Inquiry* (Princeton, NJ: Princeton University Press, 1994), chaps. 2–3.

[98] Sidney Tarrow concurs, concluding, "Analysts in this burgeoning field have been better at describing activities than at conceptualizing them in clear analytical terms." Tarrow, "Transnational Politics," 10. See, more generally, Tarrow, *The New Transnational Activism* (New York: Cambridge University Press, 2005). See also Florini and Simmons, "What the World Needs Now?" 4.

[99] Murphy, *The Structure of Regulatory Competition*; Vogel and Kagan, *The Dynamics of Regulatory Change*; Kahler and Lake, *Governance in a Global Economy*; Mattli, ed., "The Politics and Economics of International Institutional Standards Setting"; Barbara Koremenos, Charles Lipson, and Duncan Snidal, eds., *The Rational Design of International Institutions* (Cambridge: Cambridge University Press, 2003); Aseem Prakash and Jeffrey Hart, eds., *Coping with Globalization* (London: Routledge, 2000); Liliana Botcheva and Lisa L. Martin, "Institutional Effects on State Behavior: Convergence and Divergence," *International Studies Quarterly* 45 (March 2001): 1–26;. Todd Sandler, *Global Collective Action* (New York: Cambridge University Press, 2004).

States remains a hegemonic actor in most facets of the global economy.[100] For these theorists, policy coordination can be explained by a combination of American preferences and the extent of the externalities created by an absence of harmonization. Unless states face a prisoner's dilemma with few cross-border spillovers, policy coordination is likely.[101]

While the assumption of American hegemony works well in the security realm,[102] it is far from clear whether such an assumption is accurate when thinking about the global political economy. As a share of the global economy, the United States had more power and fewer peer competitors in 1945 than at any point during the current era of globalization—yet no scholar would claim that global policy harmonization was stronger back then. This fact highlights another weakness of the hegemony assumption: the belief that military power, or even productive power, is sufficiently fungible to affect outcomes in the global political economy.[103] Even in realms where American power currently appears preeminent, there are coding disputes. For example, Beth Simmons provides an explanation of harmonization in capital market regulation that relies on hegemonic state power. However, other scholars have challenged Simmons's assumption on empirical grounds.[104]

Another body of state-based theories, resting squarely within the institutionalist tradition, focuses on the bargaining problem between states and the relative strength and weakness of state-level and supranational regulatory networks.[105] Regulatory coordination is more likely to take place when preexisting institutions are in place and possess the necessary monitoring and enforcement capabilities.[106] The theoretical work in this area relies on game-theoretic mod-

---

[100] Beth Simmons, "The International Politics of Harmonization: The Case of Capital Market Integration," *International Organization* 55 (Summer 2001): 589–620. G. John Ikenberry, *After Victory* (Princeton, NJ: Princeton University Press, 2000); Joseph Nye, *The Paradox of American Power* (New York: Oxford University Press, 2002); Michael Mandelbaum, *The Case For Goliath: How America Acts as the World's Government in the 21st Century* (New York: PublicAffairs, 2005).

[101] See, in particular, Simmons, "The International Politics of Harmonization."

[102] William Wohlforth, "The Stability of a Unipolar World," *International Security* 24 (Summer 1999): 5–41.

[103] Another flaw rests on how power is operationalized. While many scholars assume economic power rests on a country's share of global production capabilities, the approach developed in the next few chapters demonstrates that the size of a country's aggregate demand matters more than supply. At the macro level, the definition is unimportant, but at the sectoral level, the distinction frequently leads to contrasting predictions.

[104] See the discussion in chapter 5.

[105] Slaughter, *A New World Order*; Mattli, "The Politics and Economics of International Institutional Standards Setting"; Walter Mattli and Tim Büthe, "Setting International Standards: Technological Rationality or Primacy of Power?" *World Politics* 56 (October 2003): 1–42; Koremenos, Lipson, and Snidal, *The Rational Design of International Institutions*; Keohane, *Power and Governance in a Partially Globalized World*.

[106] Robert Axelrod and Robert Keohane, "Achieving Cooperation under Anarchy: Strategies and Institutions," in *Cooperation under Anarchy*, ed. Kenneth Oye (Princeton, NJ: Princeton Uni-

els of interactions between states. The nature of the cooperation problem is more important than state power or preferences—because the question of interest to many international relations scholars is why states choose not to cooperate even if all parties can enhance their utility via cooperation. The empirical work of this research program also tends to focus on individual international governmental organizations and their relative success and failure.

There are theoretical and empirical shortcomings to this approach. Theoretically, an institutionalist approach ignores situations when noncooperation takes place because of preference divergence rather than bargaining failures or credible commitment problems.[107] As Andrew Hurrell points out, "because a great deal of institutionalist writing has been concerned with the creation of institutions within the developed world, there has been a tendency to assume away the existence of fundamental differences in religion, social organization, culture, and moral outlook that may block or, at least, complicate cooperative action."[108]

Empirically, even institutionalists acknowledge flaws within the paradigm.[109] A major problem is that this research suffers from a narrowness of vision. There is a tendency to focus on a single formal organization to the exclusion of other institutions with similar functions. This overlooks an important fact in understanding the processes of regulatory coordination—there is a remarkably thick institutional environment in the global political economy.[110] The number of formal IGOs is sufficiently large that in thinking about global governance, one can talk about "regime complexes" rather than single organizations.[111]

Where does the literature leave us? Most immediate is the need for more refined theories and better empirical work. If the structural approaches have less empirical support it is partially because their predictions are more precise and thus easier to falsify. Agent-based approaches to policy coordination must

---

versity Press, 1986); Lisa Martin, "Interest, Power and Multilateralism," *International Organization* 46 (Autumn 1992): 765–92.

[107] For example, Robert Keohane ascribes the failure of the Kyoto Protocol to "bargaining problems," when in fact the divergence of preferences is so wide that it is far from clear that, until the costs of global warming become more readily apparent, a bargaining core even exists. Keohane, *Power and Governance in a Partially Globalized World*, 32.

[108] Andrew Hurrell, "Power, Institutions, and the Production of Inequality," in *Power in Global Governance*, ed. Michael Barnett and Raymond Duvall (Cambridge: Cambridge University Press, 2005), 35–36.

[109] Jeffry Frieden and Lisa Martin acknowledge that, "theoretical work on international institutions has far outstripped the quantity and quality of empirical work." Frieden and Martin, "International Political Economy: Global and Domestic Interactions," in *Political Science: The State of the Discipline*, ed. Ira Katznelson and Helen Milner (New York: W. W. Norton, 2002), 146.

[110] Cheryl Shanks, Harold Jacobson, and Jeffrey Kaplan, "Inertia and Change in the Constellation of International Governmental Organizations, 1981–1992," *International Organization* 50 (Autumn 1996): 593–627; Judith Goldstein, Douglas Rivers, and Michael Tomz, "Institutions in International Relations," paper presented at the American Political Science annual meeting, Philadelphia, PA, August 2003.

[111] Raustiala and Victor, "The Regime Complex for Plant Genetic Resources."

be able to make falsifiable predictions. Empirically, there is a need to select tests that generate contrasting predictions from different theoretical approaches. To date, a common failure of the approaches reviewed in this chapter is the failure to consider alternative explanations in their empirical work. Single case studies with overdetermined explanations or statistical tests without control variables are insufficient for the accumulation of knowledge.

To be fair, the globalization process imposes formidable roadblocks to theory-building. One obvious challenge is the dizzying plethora of actors, factors, and venues that appear to demand explanation. Some existing paradigms may draw faulty causal inferences about global economic governance, but they are more accurate in their descriptive inferences of how globalization unleashes emergent actors and trends. The literature on global civil society is correct in asserting that globalization has increased the number of nonstate actors in world politics. The world polity approach is correct in pointing to the proliferation of intergovernmental organizations and agreements that dot the global stage. The race-to-the-bottom argument dramatically overpredicts its primary hypothesis, but provides some empirical leverage in highlighting the possibility of regulatory slack.[112] The state-based approaches make more sensible assumptions, but can suffer from a narrowness of theoretical and empirical vision. These critiques, however, offer a useful guide for how to start theorizing about the regulation of globalization.

THE METHODS

This book will use a mixture of formal and expositional argumentation to develop the argument. Game theory can be a valuable tool to clarify the assumptions and the causal logic of a model. It will be used here to show the conditions under which governments will be amenable to policy coordination. The globalization phenomenon has a lot of working parts, however. In addition to states there are other categories of actors, including NGOs, IGOs, and multinational corporations. Throwing all of these actors into the game-theoretic grinder increases the complexity of a formal model to the point where the computational costs outweigh the explanatory benefits. When such circumstances present themselves, I will switch to a less formal method of theory development.

Statistical analysis is of little use in testing this model against competing explanations. Operationalizing a common measure of the dependent variable—effective regulatory coordination—across issue areas is extremely problematic. Examining formal international agreements is one way to measure policy coordination, but there is no observable and verifiable method for mea-

---

[112] Murphy, *The Structure of Regulatory Competition.*

suring effective implementation that travels across disparate issue areas. This matters because for certain distributions of state interests, my model will predict the development of sham standards—nominal policy coordination coupled with ineffective global governance. Furthermore, the model presented here develops a theory of coordination processes as well as outcomes. Given the dynamic nature of the coordination questions under study, the best approach to testing these theories is through the careful selection of case studies, followed by process-tracing and within-case analysis.[113] Case studies can best test the process attributes of the various models of regulatory coordination.

It is commonly argued that the case study methods are inferior to statistical methods in demonstrating empirical validity.[114] However, the proper selection of cases can substantially strengthen the positive empirical claims that can be made. To demonstrate that a great power concert is a necessary and sufficient condition for effective global regulatory governance, I examine the global governance of financial regulation and the Internet. Globalization theorists argue that the nation-state is at its weakest and the plethora of nonstate actors and structural constraints are at their strongest for these two issue areas. All of the ways in which globalization is hypothesized to weaken states occur in a more concentrated form on Internet-related issues. Therefore, in chapter 4, I look at the global governance of the Internet. International finance is commonly assumed to be the synecdoche of all of the ways in which economic globalization empowers markets and constrains states. In chapter 5, I examine the push toward global financial regulation in the wake of the Mexican and Asian financial crises. In chapter 6, I examine the case of genetically modified organisms—an issue area where the United States and European Union have diametrically opposing preferences. This case provides fertile ground to examine the theory of preference formation developed here—and also allows a comparison of the revisionist model against other state-centric models of global regulation. There are also issues for which nonstate actors are given pride of place in explaining shifts in global governance outcomes. In chapter 7, I examine the ongoing battle over intellectual property rights and the patenting of life-saving pharmaceuticals. For these cases, the revisionist model presented here can explain the variation in governance processes, governance outcomes, and the enforcement of rules better than any single competing alternative.

These case studies involve an intensive use of primary and secondary source material. I also rely on interviews with the relevant officials from key governments, IGOs, and NGOs that were involved in these issue areas. In analyzing

---

[113] Alexander George and Timothy McKeown, "Case Studies and Theories of Organizational Decision-Making," in *Advances in Information Processing in Organizations*, ed. R. Coulam and R. Smith (Greenwich, CT: JAI Press, 1985); Alexander George and Andrew Bennett, *Case Studies and Theory Development in the Social Sciences* (Cambridge, MA: MIT Press, 2005).

[114] Arend Lijphart, "Comparative Politics and the Comparative Method," *American Political Science Review* 65 (September 1971): 682–93; King, Keohane, and Verba, *Designing Social Inquiry.*

the global governance structures concerning both financial regulation and money laundering, I rely on an additional data source—my "field work" as an international economist at the U.S. Department of the Treasury's Office of International Banking and Securities Markets.

THE LIMITATIONS

The revisionist model presented here can explain a lot about globalization and global governance, but there is a lot more that lies outside this book's purview. No single book weighing less than ten pounds could explain all of the implications of globalization or the intricacies of global governance, which range from the end of the nation-state to the end of history. It should be stressed what this book does *not* cover: I do not attempt to explain the origins of the recent era of economic globalization or the origins of the international institutions that underlie this era.[115] At this juncture, such a question is primarily of historical interest; this book assumes that regulations matter precisely because high tariffs, quotas, and capital controls are not considered to be viable policy options for most goods and services. The effect of globalization on macroeconomic policies or the size of the welfare state will also not be discussed.[116] The global governance of security-related issues is not covered in the main text. The normative debates about global governance are also not a topic of discussion.[117]

The empirical limitations need to be highlighted as well. The problem with studying global regulatory coordination is the limited number of data points. While there have been previous eras of globalization, states in those times were less concerned with ameliorating the domestic externalities of global capitalism.[118] As a result, the few studies of regulatory coordination prior to 1945 have mainly highlighted the unwillingness in world politics to create effective forms of global governance.[119] The cold war–era largely consisted of efforts

[115] For discussions of this, see Daniel Yergin and Joseph Stanislaw, *The Commanding Heights* (New York: Simon and Schuster, 1998); Frieden, *Global Capitalism*; Jeffrey Winters, "Power and the Control of Capital," *World Politics* 46 (April 1994): 419–52; Benjamin J. Cohen, "Phoenix Risen: The Resurrection of Global Finance," *World Politics* 48 (January 1996): 268–96.

[116] Two excellent reviews of this literature are Geoffrey Garrett, "Global Markets and National Politics: Collision Course or Virtuous Circle?" *International Organization* 52 (October 1998): 787–824, and Günther Schulze and Heinrich Ursprung, "Globalisation of the Economy and the Nation State," *The World Economy* 22 (May 1999): 295–352.

[117] Both security issues and normative implications make cameo appearances in the concluding chapter.

[118] For a discussion of other differences between the pre–World War I era and the more recent era of globalization, see Kahler and Lake, "Globalization and Governance," 11–15.

[119] Most pre-1945 studies of policy coordination focus on monetary policy. See Luca Einaudi, *Money and Politics: European Monetary Unification and the International Gold Standard* (New

to remove the overt barriers to the free flow of goods, services, and capital that were permitted under the Bretton Woods system of embedded liberalism.[120] The cases developed in this book explain the recent past—roughly speaking, from 1980 onward.[121] The small-n nature of the data means that any empirical support found in the cases must be labeled as preliminary; this approach will find or lose empirical support based on the future.

THE REST OF THE BOOK

Part I lays out the theory. It outlines the assumptions behind the revisionist model, works through the theory's causal logic, and examines how it differs from existing work on the subject.

The next chapter develops a theory to explain the relative power and preferences of states. A simple game-theoretic model demonstrates the ways in which market size and adjustment costs influence coordination outcomes. Market size alters the distribution of payoffs by reducing the rewards of regulatory coordination for large market states and increasing the rewards for small market states. This gives the great powers a bargaining advantage and alters the perceptions of other actors so as to reinforce the likelihood of regulatory coordination at a great power's status quo ante. On top of this, market size endows great powers with the option of economic coercion as a way of convincing other actors in the system to change their standards. However, the model also demonstrates that between large markets, power differentials are of minimal importance.

Moving from power to preferences, chapter 2 also develops a theory of national preferences over regulatory standards. Initial regulatory preferences are a function of myriad factors, including a country's stage of economic development and its economic history. What really determines government attitudes toward international regulatory coordination, however, is the adjustment costs

---

York: Oxford University Press, 2001), and Beth Simmons, *Who Adjusts?* (Princeton, NJ: Princeton University Press, 1994). For an exception, see Lawrence Spinelli, *Dry Diplomacy* (Wilmington, DE: Scholarly Resources, 1989) on the Anglo-American disputes over regulating alcohol consumption in the 1920s. The most comprehensive history of global regulatory coordination can be found in Braithwaite and Drahos, *Global Business Regulation*.

[120] John Gerard Ruggie, "International Regimes, Transactions, and Change: Embedded Liberalism in the Postwar Economic Order," *International Organization* 36 (Spring 1982): 379–415; Jonathan Kirshner, "Keynes, Capital Mobility, and the Crisis of Embedded Liberalism," *Review of International Political Economy* 6 (Autumn 1999): 313–37.

[121] Economic analyses of globalization tend to use 1980 as the break point after which the current era of globalization kicked into overdrive. See, for example, Surjit Bhalla, *Imagine There's No Country* (Washington, DC: Institute for International Economics, 2002); Wolf, *Why Globalization Works*; David Dollar and Aart Kraay, "Spreading the Wealth," *Foreign Affairs* 81 (January/February 2002): 120–33.

it faces from altering its national standards. When public or private actors face barriers to exit in response to changes in the regulatory environment, governments will incur higher adjustment costs and are therefore more reluctant to change their regulatory standards. Adjustment costs are expected to be higher for regulatory arenas affecting relatively mature economic sectors or relatively immobile factors of production.

Chapter 3 builds on the insights from chapter 2 and develops a typology of regulatory processes. If there is a large bargaining core among the great powers, then the outcome will be one of coordinated standards. However, the divergence of preferences between the great powers and other actors in the system will strongly shape the process through which global governance structures are fashioned. A split between great powers and other states affects both the bargaining tactics and the bargaining forum. This chapter also considers the influence of various nonstate actors. Working through the outcomes of different constellations of state interests, I develop typologies of both NGOs and IGOs. For NGOs, the distinction between advocacy and service functions is a useful one. For IGOs, I rely on Michael Walzer's typology of membership to categorize IGOs by their criteria for inclusion and exclusion.[122] This leads to a tripartite world of IGOs: clubs, neighborhoods, and universes. The utility and influence of these nonstate actors is a direct function of the distribution of state interests.

Part II shifts from theory to examine international regulation as it is practiced. Chapter 4 examines the spectrum of Internet regulation. This case is a tough test of the revisionist model, because the Internet has been consistently cited as a metaphor for the declining importance of the nation-state. A closer look at this case reveals multiple issue areas within this broad category—copyright protection, content regulation, technical protocols, consumer privacy—that overlap with more traditional regulatory questions. The model generated here can therefore explain the distribution of outcomes. The most interesting case, however, is the evolution of technical protocols. This case best illustrates that states can still determine regulatory outcomes even if they play no formal role in the governance structure. This is demonstrated through a process-tracing of the emergence of the Transmission Control Protocol/Internet Protocol (TCP/IP) and the creation of the Internet Corporation for Assigned Names and Numbers (ICANN).

Chapter 5 traces the creation of the financial codes and standards that were created in the wake of the Asian financial crisis in the late 1990s. The globalization of finance and the concomitant rise in financial instability increased the demand for a new "international financial architecture." Most of the scholarly and policy focus centered on the role of the international financial institutions

---

[122] Michael Walzer, *Spheres of Justice: a Defense of Pluralism and Equality* (New York: Basic Books, 1983), chap. 2.

(IFIs)—the International Monetary Fund (IMF) and World Bank. However, focusing strictly on the IFIs overlooks the ability of the economic great powers to substitute between different governance structures as a means of advancing their common preferences. Because financial regulation produced a cleavage of interests between the developed and developing states, the developed great powers relied on club organizations to create new modes of coordination. The aftermath of the Mexican and Asian financial crises led to the creation of new clubs, such as the Financial Stability Forum (FSF)—and the empowerment of preexisting clubs, such as Bank of International Settlements. While the International Monetary Fund did play a role in the enforcement of these new standards, it was marginalized in the policy coordination process.

Chapter 6 examines the extent of regulatory coordination in the treatment of genetically modified organisms (GMOs). The dynamic density of transnational activist networks is very strong on this environmental question—therefore, models of global civil society would predict stringent regulatory standards for GM products across the globe. In actuality, GMO regulations in most of the world oscillate between the American and European positions. The reason is that the GMO case affects actors with high barriers to regulatory exit—consumers and agricultural producers. These actors are far more likely to mobilize their resources to engage in political voice—raising the domestic costs of adjustment for governments. To date, global civil society has proven unsuccessful in translating its preferences on this issue to governments outside the European Union's sphere of economic influence—but agricultural producers have been equally frustrated in altering European preferences.

This chapter also demonstrates the relative strength of the revisionist model vis-à-vis other state-based theories of regulatory coordination. Some state-based models tend to assume U.S. hegemony on regulatory matters because of its impressive production capabilities. Given its dominance in agricultural output, a hegemonic model would predict an outcome favoring the United States. Other governance models argue that the key variable is the relative strength and coherence of a government's regulatory capacity. By this metric, many scholars would presume that the European Union would have an advantage. A California effect would also predict upwards harmonization to the European Union's level of regulatory stringency. However, the approach developed here predicts what we actually see—a stalemate of rival standards between two great powers. Only the revisionist model generates the correct prediction.

Chapter 7 looks at a deviant case—the push by global civil society to modify the intellectual property rights regime. For the past decade, activists and nongovernmental organizations waged a sustained campaign to force the great powers to allow public health "flexibilities" in the enforcement of Trade-Related Intellectual Property Rights (TRIPS). These groups have claimed some notable successes, culminating in the 2001 Doha Declaration on the TRIPS

Agreement and Public Health. This apparent success challenges the revisionist approach developed here. This chapter critically examines the GCS narrative on TRIPS and public health, and finds two flaws: a neglect of alternative explanations for the policy change, and an overestimation of the magnitude of the policy shift. Over the long run, the ability of the great powers to shift regulatory fora gives them an advantage that global civil society cannot match. Upon further examination, this episode turns out to be a "semi-deviant" case.

Chapter 8 concludes with a discussion of the revisionist model's implications. The model and evidence developed here refutes theoretical assertions that globalization requires the rejection of existing paradigms. Instead, globalization vastly expands the explanatory domain for IR theory, by constantly internationalizing heretofore domestic policy issues. With regard to public policy, the revisionist model provides important clues to nonstate actors about the conditions and strategies that will be successful in influencing global public policy. The normative disapproval of globalization that comes through in much of the literature is due in part to the belief that democratic sovereignty is being trampled by the onslaught of global corporate domination.[123] There is no question that the great powers rule the global political economy, at times without input from other stakeholders in the system. However, globalization is not the guilty party here, and it is far from clear that there is any alternative to the status quo. Relative to the democratic ideal, the governance of today's global political economy is flawed. Compared to the past, however, the current era offers some promise of hope.

---

[123] Manuel Castells, "Global Governance and Global Politics," *PS: Political Science and Politics* 38 (January 2005): 9–16; Peter Singer, *One World: The Ethics of Globalization* (New Haven, CT: Yale University Press, 2002).

CHAPTER TWO

A Theory of Regulatory Outcomes

THIS CHAPTER LAYS OUT the initial assumptions and game-theoretic logic behind the revisionist model of policy coordination. To understand international regulatory regimes, one must understand the preferences and capabilities of great power governments. The approach I develop in this chapter agrees with realists in asserting that state power comes from the size of a government's internal market. My approach diverges from realism in arguing that government preferences on regulatory standards have their origins in the domestic political economy.

To be more specific: I posit that government preferences can be derived from the visible adjustment costs that economies face under the prospect of regulatory cooperation. Economic globalization increases the gross rewards for policy coordination, but does not lessen the domestic adjustment costs that come from regulatory change. These adjustment costs will vary considerably by the affected sectors and factors of production. For regulations affecting relatively immobile factors of production—such as land and labor—or for regulations affecting asset-specific investments—as in mature or nontradable sectors—the affected actors will rely more heavily on the use of political voice than market exit or internal adjustment in their response to any proposed change.[1] The greater the use of political voice, the higher the government's political and economic adjustment costs to regulatory coordination.

In an era of globalization, market size can still be translated into government power. The size of consumer markets affects the coordination of regulatory standards in two ways. First, market size affects the material incentives governments face in choosing whether to coordinate regulatory standards. A sufficiently large internal market drastically reduces a government's incentive to switch its standards, creating a set of expectations that encourages other actors to switch their regulatory standards. In a similar manner, market power facilitates the use of economic coercion. Great powers can use the threat of complete or partial market closure to force recalcitrant states into switching their regulatory standards. Second, market size affects actor perceptions over outcomes. Great powers by dint of their market size can alter the beliefs of other actors

---

[1] Albert Hirschman, *Exit, Voice, and Loyalty: Responses to Decline in Firms, Organizations, and States* (Cambridge, MA: Harvard University Press, 1970).

over the likelihood of possible outcomes. Their standards act as an attractor, causing other actors to converge to their preferences.

From these assumptions regarding power and preferences, this chapter develops three propositions. First, it is possible for issues to exist where the rational outcome for self-interested actors is not to coordinate on regulatory matters. Because the discipline of international political economy tends to be concerned with arenas where cooperation is possible, these situations of mutual beneficial noncooperation are often overlooked. Second, governments with sufficient market size can influence the regulation of globalization through the use of market power and coercive power.[2] Third, while gross power differentials matter, disparities in capabilities *among* the great powers are of minimal importance. Governments that control large markets cannot coerce or cajole other great power governments into regulatory coordination.

The rest of this chapter is divided into seven sections. The next section describes the assumptions about the power of states that underline the approach developed here. The third section operationalizes the concept of state power and concludes that for the time period discussed here, there is a bipolar distribution of power between the United States and the European Union. The fourth section details the assumptions regarding how government preferences work. The fourth section also operationalizes those preferences, based on when the affected domestic actors choose to exercise political voice rather than adjust to new policy proposals. The fifth section formalizes the intuition, presenting a simple, two-actor standards game. The sixth section discusses how asymmetrical market power affects the likelihood of coordination. The final section summarizes and concludes.

THE POWER OF GOVERNMENTS

The revisionist model assumes that governments remain the primary actors in global economic governance. This does *not* mean that governments are insensitive to market forces and market pressures. In a globalized economy, one would expect states to act in a manner that maximizes national income and labor productivity, which requires market-friendly policies and institutions. However, while many authors recognize the structural dependence of the state on capital, the structural dependence of capital on the state should also be acknowledged. Firms rely on governments to establish and enforce the rules of the game for economic interactions. Key business traits ranging from

---

[2] On distinction between the two, see Scott James and David Lake, "The Second Face of Hegemony," *International Organization* 43 (Winter 1989): 1–29. For a more recent typology of power, see Michael Barnett and Raymond Duvall, eds., *Power in Global Governance* (Cambridge: Cambridge University Press, 2005).

corporate governance to innovation strategies to procurement policies are often contingent on preexisting state structures.[3] Legal institutions play a critical role in determining the relative sophistication of national markets.[4] States continue to act as the primary negotiating agents in international fora, and retain the final say in developing the domestic rules that govern economic activity. Governments are far from the only actors in global governance—but they matter the most.

Governments are differentiated by their relative power. Power is defined as the relative size and diversity of an actor's internal market. Markets have a gravitational effect on producers—the larger (and closer) the economy, the stronger the pull for producers to secure and exploit market access.[5] As demand increases, firms will have greater financial incentives to mirror that market's preferences. Similarly, the diversity of a state's economy determines how vulnerable it is to becoming asymmetrically interdependent on other actors. The more diverse the variety of goods produced and consumed in the national market, the less vulnerable the state is to external pressure, be it private or public. A great power has an economy of sufficient size and diversity such that it acts as a natural attractor for profit-seeking actors while being able to rebuff potential coercers. Simply put, great powers are price-makers, not price-takers.

There is plenty of evidence to support the contention that economic power emanates from market size—most directly from the literature on economic sanctions. Economic coercion against states has a mixed record, since most governments have the organizational capability to resist economic pressure and the political incentive to stand firm if they anticipate frequent conflicts with the sanctioning state.[6] In the global political economy, however, firms have different preferences than countries. CEOs do not care nearly as much about relative gains among countries as they care about profits.[7] For example, the success rate of U.S. economic sanctions imposed against foreign firms is

[3] Alfred D. Chandler Jr., *Scale and Scope: The Dynamics of Industrial Capitalism* (Cambridge, MA: Belknap Press, 1990); Paul Doremus et al., *The Myth of the Global Corporation* (Princeton, NJ: Princeton University Press, 1998).

[4] Rafael La Porta, Florencio Lopez-de-Silanes, Andrei Shleifer, and Robert Vishny, "Law and Finance," *Journal of Political Economy* 106 (December 1998): 1113–55; Daron Acemoglu, Simon Johnson, and James A. Robinson, "The Colonial Origins of Economic Development: An Empirical Investigation," *American Economic Review* 91 (December 2001): 1369–1401.

[5] This is one reason why econometric methods to predict international trade flows are called "gravity models"; the presumption is that the larger and closer an economy, the more traded goods that economy will naturally attract. For a review, see Edward Leamer and James Levinsohn, "International Trade Theory: The Evidence," in *Handbook of International Economics, Volume 3*, ed. Gene Grossman and Kenneth Rogoff (Amsterdam: North-Holland, 1997).

[6] Robert Pape, "Why Economic Sanctions Do Not Work," *International Security* 22 (Fall 1997): 90–136; Daniel Drezner, *The Sanctions Paradox: Economic Statecraft and International Relations* (Cambridge: Cambridge University Press, 1999).

[7] Drezner, *The Sanctions Paradox*, 83.

significantly higher than the success rate of U.S. sanctions against foreign governments. Furthermore, the variation in firm compliance with U.S. sanctions is a function of the firm's dependence on the American market.[8] The more important the U.S. market is to a firm's revenue stream, the more likely the corporation will comply with U.S. demands. Multinational corporations may have some measure of leverage vis-à-vis small states, but governments with significant markets can easily coerce them into compliance with their own rules and regulations.[9]

Because of the size and diversity of their internal markets, great powers are also less dependent on international exchange as a source of goods and capital. Robert Keohane and Joseph Nye's concepts of sensitivity and vulnerability are useful in making this distinction.[10] Sensitivity refers to the immediate costs that occur with the disruption of established patterns of economic exchange. Vulnerability refers to the costs that remain *after* a state has tried to adjust to the disruption of trade. In an open global economy, both great powers and less powerful states build up significant levels of sensitivity. However, because of their internal markets and diversified set of endowments, great powers possess significantly lower levels of vulnerability than other states in a globalized world. They have "go-it-alone" power.[11]

Identifying the Great Powers

Power is defined as a combination of internal market size and reduced vulnerability to external disruptions. Who, then, are the great powers? The question is a relative one—the great powers must possess these attributes in comparison to all other actors. Therefore, the most logical way to identify the great powers is to round up the relevant attributes of all the candidates and see which actors distinguish themselves on both dimensions.

Table 2.1 displays relevant economic data for the candidate great powers for 2002, a typical year for the time period under study. For the current era of globalization, the economic great powers are the United States and the Euro-

---

[8] In the post-1945 period, U.S. sanctions against firms had a 50 percent success rate; economic sanctions in support of political goals were estimated to succeed only one-third of the time. Data from George Shambaugh, *States, Firms, and Power* (Albany: State University of New York Press, 1999), chap. 2, and Gary Hufbauer, Jeffrey Schott, and Kimberly Elliott, *Economic Sanctions Reconsidered* (Washington, DC: Institute for International Economics, 1990). See also Kenneth A. Rodman, "Sanctions at Bay?" *International Organization* 49 (Winter 1995): 105–37.

[9] Nick Butler, "Companies in International Relations," *Survival* 42 (Spring 2000): 149–64.

[10] Robert Keohane and Joseph Nye, *Power and Interdependence* (Boston: Scott Foresman, 1978), chap. 1.

[11] Lloyd Gruber, *Ruling the World: Power Politics and the Rise of Supranational Institutions* (Princeton, NJ: Princeton University Press, 2000).

TABLE 2.1
Measures of Great Power Status in 2002

Measure of Economic Power	United States	European Union	Japan	Russia	China	India
Population (in millions)	290	379	127	145	1,286	1,050
GDP (market exchange rates, in billions)	10,434	10,140	3,971	345	1,271	508
GDP (purchasing power parity, in billions)	10,450	9,571	3,651	1,409	5,989	2,664
Per capita GDP	$36,004	$23,063	$31,138	$2,374	$1,001	$482
Share of global merchandise trade	18.6	18.5	7.5	1.7	6.2	1.1
Merchandise trade as a % of GDP (market exchange rates)	18.5	16.6	16.2	53.2	54.3	20.4
Merchandise trade as a % of GDP (purchasing power parity)	17.7	18.0	18.5	11.7	10.5	3.7
Capital market size (in billions)	54,488	51,546	21,628	> 800	> 5,000	> 5,000

Sources: CIA World Factbook; Organization for Economic Cooperation and Development; Eurostat; United Nations Statistical Division; World Trade Organization.

pean Union. These are the only two entities that combine relatively large markets with relatively low vulnerability. As measured by aggregate market size, the United States and European Union both have economies over $10 trillion at the end of 2003.[12] The American and European shares of global merchandise trade are more than twice that of any other "candidate" great power. Using market exchange rates, both the United States and European Union are twice as large as Japan, the next biggest economy. When their market size is combined, the United States and the European Union are responsible for roughly 40 percent of global output, 41 percent of world imports, 59 percent of inward foreign direct investment, 78 percent of outward foreign direct investment, and 88 percent of global mergers and acquisitions.[13]

Other potential candidates for great power status fail one or both of the prerequisites. Japan is less dependent on trade than either the United States

[12] In 2003, America's GDP was estimated at $10.9 trillion; the European Union's GDP was estimated at $10.4 trillion. Japan's GDP came in at approximately $4.2 trillion. *Economist*, February 27, 2004.

[13] Joseph Quinlan, "Drifting Apart or Growing Together? The Primacy of the Transatlantic Economy," Center for Transatlantic Relations, Washington, DC, 2003.

or the European Union, but its domestic market size is only half that of either great power. Furthermore, beyond the aggregate statistics, Japan's overwhelming dependence on its trading partners for critical factors of production renders it more vulnerable to the vicissitudes of the global marketplace.[14] China and India have rapidly growing economies and sizeable populations. In the future, these countries could develop the market power necessary to attain great power status. However, for the time period under study, their economies are neither sizeable nor invulnerable enough in hard currency terms to rival either the United States or the European Union.[15] As these countries develop their markets, they may enter the great power category, but for now these markets remain emerging and not emerged.[16] Russia, at this juncture, fails to impress on either dimension of economic power.

Describing the United States as an economic great power is straightforward—both its market size and economic diversity are unquestioned.[17] The European Union presents a trickier conundrum for international relations theory. It would be highly problematic to describe the European Union as a unitary actor in matters of foreign and security policy. The failure of the EU constitution to be ratified, and the collapse of the Growth and Stability Pact established in the 1991 Maastricht Treaty, also cause one to doubt the "actorness" of the European Union. Does the European Union qualify as a single, coherent bargaining unit? If so, do other regional bodies such as the Association of Southeast Asian Nations (ASEAN) or the North American Free Trade Agreement (NAFTA) qualify as single actors?

For the regulation of the global economy, a strong case can be made for treating the European Union as a single actor. Post-Maastricht, the member governments have delegated significant regulatory and bargaining powers to the European Commission. The Commission has the power to bargain with other states in trade matters, and is charged with monitoring the harmonization of national laws to comply with EU law. The Commission has been granted significant agenda-setting powers in the economic "pillar" of the Union—to the point where it can thwart individual member countries from signing international agreements on regulatory matters.[18] EU members are

---

[14] For an excellent discussion on the effects of Japan's trade dependence on its foreign economic policy, see Christina Davis, *Food Fights over Free Trade* (Princeton, NJ: Princeton University Press, 2003).

[15] When purchasing power parity (PPP) is used to convert gross domestic product, both India and China would appear to have much larger economies. However, from the perspective of multinational corporations, the PPP conversion rate is not as important as the market exchange rate, since that is the relevant factor for a profit-maximizing actor.

[16] See chapter 8 for a discussion of how China and India's rise to great power status would affect the revisionist model.

[17] William Wohlforth, "The Stability of a Unipolar World," *International Security* 24 (Summer 1999): 5–41.

[18] For one example of this with regard to shipping regulation, see Robert Block, "Container-Security Pact Is Reached," *Wall Street Journal Europe*, April 23, 2004, A2.

increasingly adopting common positions in multilateral forums.[19] As Karen Alter has observed, the European Court of Justice's ability to force member governments into compliance with EU rules is unprecedented and distinguishes the European Union from other regional bodies.[20] Mark Pollack notes, "the EU is at or near the end of the continuum in terms of delegation to executive, judicial, and legislative agents. Indeed, no other international executive enjoys both the regulatory and agenda-setting powers of the European Commission."[21] Systematic comparative research of other regional organizations confirms this assessment.[22] Even skeptics of supranational law acknowledge that the European Union is an exception.[23] The United States clearly views the European Union as its primary competitor in promulgating global regulatory standards.[24]

To be sure, it remains the case that Europe's national governments still hold significant sway over social and business regulation. However, even in these areas, the commonalities of policy content are powerful enough to treat Europe as a single actor. After detailed market analyses of the principal European nations, the director of the McKinsey Global Institute observed that, "the common patterns across Europe even in the laws and regulations governing microeconomic behavior are very strong and more important than the individual country differences."[25] The adherence to supranational norms among national bureaucrats in Europe is quite high.[26]

Finally, it should be noted that in issue areas such as trade, competition policy, or regulatory standards, the European Union has already been modeled

[19] John van Oudenaren, "Transatlantic Bipolarity and the End of Multilateralism," *Political Science Quarterly* 120 (Spring 2005): 10.

[20] Karen Alter, *Establishing the Supremacy of European Law: The Making of an International Rule of Law in Europe* (New York: Oxford University Press, 2001).

[21] Mark Pollack, "The Delegation of Powers to the European Commission," paper presented at the International Studies Association annual meeting, Montreal, Canada, March 2004, 41–42; see also Pollack, *The Engines of European Integration* (New York: Oxford University Press, 2003); Giandonenico Majone, "The Rise of the Regulatory State in Europe," *West European Politics* 17 (May 1994): 77–101; and Jonas Tallberg, "Paths to Compliance: Enforcement, Management, and the European Union," *International Organization* 56 (Summer 2002): 609–43.

[22] Yoram Haftel, "Designing for Peace: Regional Integration Arrangements, Institutional Variation, and Militarized Inter-State Disputes," *International Organization* 61 (Spring 2007): forthcoming.

[23] Jack Goldsmith and Eric Posner, *The Limits of International Law* (New York: Oxford University Press, 2005), 126.

[24] George Parker and Tobias Buck, "Washington Bridles at EU Urge to Regulate," *Financial Times*, May 11, 2006.

[25] William W. Lewis, *The Power of Productivity* (Chicago: University of Chicago Press, 2004), 50. Lewis was the director of the McKinsey Global Institute for a decade.

[26] Liesbet Hooghe, "Several Roads Lead to International Norms, but Few Via International Socialization: A Case Study of the European Commission," *International Organization* 59 (October 2005): 861–98.

as a viable single actor.[27] The international political economy literature has increasingly modeled the European Union as having a "collective interest" in its economic negotiations with external actors in world politics.[28] Public policy commentators have increasingly viewed the European Union as a single, powerful entity containing a coherent ideology about business and social regulation.[29] When member preferences converge, they have been increasingly willing to delegate negotiating power to the European Union's supranational institutions.[30] David Vogel and Robert Kagan conclude that, "It is a supranational body, namely the EU, which has harmonized European standards."[31] This does not mean that member governments cannot influence the direction of EU policy—just as regional or sectoral interests constrain the government of the United States with regard to foreign economic policy.[32] Treating the European Union as a single actor in the coordination of global economic regulations is still a significant assumption, but it is hardly a heroic one.

Identifying Government Preferences

I assume that government preferences on regulatory issues have their origins in the domestic political economy. This assumption echoes Jeff Legro's and Andrew Moravcsik's "two-step" approach to international relations theory.[33]

[27] Charlotte Bretherton and John Vogler, *The European Union as a Global Actor* (New York: Routledge, 1999); Michèle Knodt and Sebastian Princen, eds., *Understanding the European Union's External Relations* (New York: Routledge, 2003).

[28] Knodt and Princen, eds., *Understanding the European Union's External Relations*; see also Joseph Grieco, *Cooperation among Nations* (Ithaca, NY: Cornell University Press, 1990); James Caporaso, "The European Union and Forms of State: Westphalian, Regulatory or Post-Modern?" *Journal of Common Market Studies* 34 (March 1996): 29–52; Sophie Meunier, "European Institutions and EU-U.S. Trade Negotiations," *International Organization* 54 (Winter 2000): 103–36; Meunier, *Trading Voices: The European Union in International Commercial Negotiations* (Princeton, NJ: Princeton University Press, 2005); Davis, *Food Fights over Free Trade*; Walter Mattli and Tim Büthe, "Setting International Standards: Technological Rationality or Primacy of Power?" *World Politics* 56 (October 2003): 1–42; Christopher Hill and Michael Smith, eds., *International Relations and the European Union* (New York: Oxford University Press, 2005).

[29] Joseph Nye, *The Paradox of American Power* (New York: Oxford University Press, 2002), 29; Charles Kupchan, *The End of the American Era* (New York: Knopf, 2002); Jeremy Rifkin, *The European Dream* (New York: Tarcher, 2004); Mark Leonard, *Why Europe Will Run the 21st Century* (London: Fourth Estate, 2005).

[30] Andrew Moravcsik, *The Choice For Europe* (Ithaca, NY: Cornell University Press, 1998).

[31] David Vogel and Robert Kagan, eds., *Dynamics of Regulatory Change* (Berkeley: University of California Press, 2004), 8.

[32] Peter Trubowitz, *Defining the National Interest* (Chicago: University of Chicago Press, 1998).

[33] Jeffrey Legro, "Culture and Preferences in the International Cooperation Two-Step," *American Political Science Review* 90 (March 1996): 118–37; Andrew Moravcsik, "Taking Preferences Seriously: A Liberal Theory of International Politics," *International Organization* 51 (Autumn 1997): 513–53; Jeffrey Legro and Andrew Moravcsik, "Is Anyone Still a Realist?" *International*

In their rubric, the first step is identifying the domestic actors and institutions that explain the origin of state preferences. The second step is to take those preferences as an ontological given for international interactions, and to explain the bargaining outcomes as a function of the distribution of interests and capabilities. Domestic factors account for preference formation, but not for outcomes of international bargaining.

Initial Preferences

To say that modeling government preferences from scratch is difficult would be an understatement.[34] I therefore start with a few simplifying assumptions. The first is that a government's ideal point on regulatory issues is its domestic status quo. The logic behind this assumption is simple but important: most regulatory issues start out as domestic problems before globalization makes them international issues. Thus, for each issue area, a government's ideal point is its own preexisting national regulatory framework. The status quo represents the domestic political equilibrium on the relevant issue. Revealed preference suggests that for the government, the political costs of changing that equilibrium exceed the expected benefits—otherwise such change would have already been enacted.[35]

What factors determine the location or content of the regulatory status quo? Initial government preferences on regulatory standards will vary from country to country because of differences in national economic development and economic history. To understand the role that economic development plays, it helps to think of regulation as a luxury good. Economists define luxuries as goods and services that possess high-income elasticities of demand. Consumers desire luxury goods, but are not willing to pay the opportunity costs of acquiring them until they can already afford sufficient amounts of staple goods such that the marginal utility of consuming additional units of these goods has declined. As citizens acquire more income, they will be willing to spend an increasing fraction of their income on luxuries.

Security 24 (Spring 1999): 55–106. In the larger schema of IR theories that rely in part on domestic politics, the approach developed here is a strong version of what Peter Gourevitch labels "preference-driven models." Peter Gourevitch, "Squaring the Circle: The Domestic Sources of International Cooperation," *International Organization* 50 (Spring 1996): 349–73.

[34] On the complexities of divining national preferences, see Jeffry Frieden, "Actors and Preferences in International Relations," in *Strategic Choice and International Relations*, ed. David A. Lake and Robert Powell, 39–76 (Princeton, NJ: Princeton University Press, 1999).

[35] To be clear, it is possible that governments may actually prefer a different regulatory standard to the existing one—but revealed preference shows that the political costs of change exceed the perceived benefits of regulatory change. While international negotiations can conceivably alter this cost-benefit analysis, as we shall see this is less likely for the great powers. For more on this question see Daniel W. Drezner, ed., *Locating the Proper Authorities: The Interaction of Domestic and International Institutions* (Ann Arbor: University of Michigan Press, 2003).

When citizens and governments choose between stringent economic regulation and maximizing economic efficiency, their income level will influence their regulatory preferences. When the broad mass of society is concerned with acquiring the basic necessities of life, strict regulatory standards will be perceived as expensive—and unnecessary—luxury goods. Stringent regulation imposes high opportunity costs, since investments in complying and monitoring such regulations hamper economic growth.[36] As the broad mass of society acquires middle-class levels of income, the marginal rate of substitution between regulatory standards and economic efficiency shifts in the direction of preferring more social regulation. As Ronald Inglehart concludes, "Societies at the early stages of the [development] curve tend to emphasize economic growth at any price. But as they move beyond a given threshold, they begin to emphasize quality of life concerns such as environmental protection and lifestyle issues."[37] As a country's median level of income increases, societal preferences for government regulation will shift in favor of more stringent standards. Empirical correlations exist between rising per capita income and government activity.[38] Citizens in emerging markets will prefer lax regulatory standards. Citizens in developed countries will prefer stringent regulatory standards.

National economic histories—and the embedded institutional structures that determine and are determined by these histories—will also affect the domestic status quo for governments. Scholars studying technological innovation,[39] macroeconomic policy,[40] welfare systems,[41] and corporate governance[42] concur that embedded economic institutions at the national level play a constitutive role in the formation of firm preferences. Peter Hall and David Soskice

---

[36] Alberto Alesina et al., "Regulation and Investment," NBER Working Paper No. 9560, Cambridge, MA, March 2003; Stefano Scarpetti and Giuseppe Nicoletti, "Regulation, Productivity, and Growth," World Bank Policy Research Working Paper No. 2944, Washington, DC, January 2003.

[37] Ronald Inglehart, "Globalization and Postmodern Values," *The Washington Quarterly* 23 (Winter 2000): 219. See also Ronald Inglehart, *Culture Shift in Advanced Industrial Society* (Princeton, NJ: Princeton University Press, 1990).

[38] These studies look specifically at government expenditures and not regulation per se, but it is logical to presume that greater expenditures would be associated with a concomitant increase in regulation. Adolph Wagner, "Three Extracts on Public Finance," in *Classics in the Theory of Public Finance*, ed. R. A. Musgrave and A. T. Peacock (London: Macmillan, 1958); R. M. Bird, "'Wagner's Law' of Expanding State Activity," *Public Finance* 26 (1971): 1–26; Paul Pierson, "The New Politics of the Welfare State," *World Politics* 48 (January 1996): 143–79.

[39] Giovanni Dosi, "Some Notes on National Systems of Innovation and Production," in *Innovation Policy in a Global Economy*, ed. Dariele Archibugi, Jeremy Howells, and Jonathan Michie (Cambridge: Cambridge University Press, 1999); Robert Gilpin, "Economic Evolution of National Systems," *International Studies Quarterly* 40 (September 1996): 411–31.

[40] Geoffrey Garrett, *Partisan Politics in the Global Economy* (Cambridge: Cambridge University Press, 1998).

[41] Gøsta Esping-Anderson, *The Three Worlds of Welfare Capitalism* (Princeton, NJ: Princeton University Press, 1990).

[42] Chandler, *Strategy and Structure*; Doremus et al., *The Myth of the Global Corporation*.

characterize this phenomenon as "varieties of capitalism."[43] They divide advanced industrialized states into liberal and coordinated market economies. In liberal market economies, particularly the United States, there is a strong tradition of minimal government interference in the economy. Regulatory agencies are separated from government ministries to reduce the state's ability to impose significant regulations.[44] Firms coordinate their activities primarily through decentralized market arrangements. In coordinated market economies, firms rely more on nonmarket institutions to allocate scarce resources. Government regulation of the economy—be it through formal rulemaking, as in France, informal consultation, as in Germany, or a mixture of formal rules and informal administrative guidance, as in Japan—is common.[45] Government ministries house their own enforcement agencies, making it easier for the state to regulate. The expectation of government intervention in the economy is greater than in liberal market economies. The European Union, and its prominent role in fashioning environmental and social regulation, can be thought of as a natural extension of coordinated market institutions.[46] Other scholars have independently developed similar versions of the Hall and Soskice typology.[47]

The variation in embedded economic institutions across countries affects firm preferences with regard to government regulation. Firms have an incentive to invest in assets specific to their institutional structure. They will therefore pressure governments to devise and enforce regulatory standards that

---

[43] Peter Hall and David Soskice, eds., *Varieties of Capitalism: The Institutional Foundations of Comparative Advantage* (New York: Oxford University Press, 2001). See also Suzanne Berger and Ronald Dore, eds., *National Diversity and Global Capitalism* (Ithaca, NY: Cornell University Press, 1996); Herbert Kitschelt, Peter Lange, Gary Marks, and John D. Stephens, eds., *Continuity and Change in Contemporary Capitalism* (Cambridge: Cambridge University Press, 1999).

[44] Steve K. Vogel, *Freer Markets, More Rules: Regulatory Reform in Advanced Industrial Countries* (Ithaca, NY: Cornell University Press, 1996).

[45] One explanation for the variation in national levels of comfort with state intervention is the moment at which these states faced a combination of acute geopolitical competition combined with economic backwardness. The later that moment took place, the greater the extent of state intervention. See Alexander Gerschenkron, *Economic Backwardness in Historical Perspective* (Cambridge, MA: Belknap Press, 1962); Thomas Ertman, *Birth of the Leviathan* (New York: Cambridge University Press, 1997).

[46] Charlotte Bretherton and John Vogler, *The European Union as a Global Actor* (New York: Routledge, 1999).

[47] See Robert Gilpin, *Global Political Economy* (Princeton, NJ: Princeton University Press, 2001); Peter A. Gourevitch, "The Macropolitics of Microinstitutional Differences in the Analysis of Comparative Capitalism," in Berger and Dore, *National Diversity and Global Capitalism*, 239–61; Steven K. Vogel, *Freer Markets, More Rules*. Gilpin argues that the Japanese model of a market economy is distinct from the laissez-faire model of the United States and the corporatist model of continental Europe. Gourevitch distinguishes between the "Anglo-American" and "Nippo-Rhenish" forms of capitalism, reinforcing the coordinated/liberal distinction. Vogel makes a similar distinction between countries with preexisting ideologies favoring government disengagement and those favoring a reinforced governmental role in the economy. Obviously, all of these typologies are gross generalizations, a point that Vogel in particular takes great pains to stress.

are consistent with long-lasting embedded institutions. As Hall and Soskice observe, "their [firm's] stance towards new regulatory initiatives will be influenced by judgements about whether those initiatives are likely to sustain or undermine the comparative institutional advantage of their nation's economy. Governments should be inclined to support such initiatives only when they do not threaten the institutions most crucial to the competitive advantage their firms enjoy."[48]

The historical and developmental components can reinforce each other in terms of establishing regulatory preferences—as in the case of continental EU economies. These components can also create contradictory impulses of regulation—as in the case of the United States. What this section makes clear, however, is that there are excellent reasons to explain why there will likely be a heterogeneous grouping of initial preferences on any given regulatory matter when it is first addressed at the global level.

The Benefits of Coordination

I assume that regulatory coordination at the international level brings *gross* benefits—but not always *net* benefits—to participating governments. Uncoordinated, disparate regulatory structures function as implicit barriers to trade. This is particularly true when border measures—such as tariffs or quotas—are at minimal levels, leaving regulations as the remaining barriers to trade. Regulatory coordination reduces the transaction costs of cross-border exchange, leading to an increase in static efficiency, which increases economic benefits for all participating states.

There is reason to believe that regulatory coordination leads to dynamic gains from trade as well.[49] The neoclassical economic model assumes a world of homogeneous firms facing decreasing returns to scale. The mere existence and prominence of multinational corporations suggests that for some economic sectors these assumptions are flawed.[50] If one allows for increasing returns to scale, the economic benefits of uniform standards start to make more sense.

Global regulatory standards provide three distinct benefits to multinational firms, and by extension to home and host countries. First, uniform standards permit companies to maintain single production processes, rather than multiple processes to accommodate for multiple standards regimes. As the CEO of

[48] Hall and Soskice, *Varieties of Capitalism*, 52.

[49] See generally, on this point, Raghuram G. Rajan and Luigi Zingales, *Saving Capitalism from the Capitalists* (Princeton, NJ: Princeton University Press, 2004), and Douglas Irwin, *Free Trade under Fire* (Princeton, NJ: Princeton University Press, 2002).

[50] For a review of theories to explain the existence of multinational firms, see Richard Caves, *Multinational Enterprise and Economic Analysis*, 2nd ed. (Cambridge: Cambridge University Press, 1996).

General Electric argued in June 2005, "For us to remain competitive, we simply cannot navigate a regulatory maze that forces us to tweak and modulate every product and process to suit individual regulatory regimes at their whim."[51] A single global standard permits firms to exploit economies of scale in their day-to-day operations. Conforming to global rules avoids the maintenance of multiple production processes necessary to comply with different regulatory schema.[52] Adherence to global standards also gives multinational firms a cost advantage over domestic firms that must adjust to new standards, providing the opportunity to expand market share and profits.[53] Ronie Garcia-Johnson observed this behavior in her examination of U.S. chemical firms in Brazil and Mexico.[54] Elizabeth DeSombre shows that although multinational firms may oppose increased regulation in their home country, once such regulations are enacted these firms will often switch their position on global regulatory standards. These "bootleggers" want all producers to face the same regulatory constraints internationally as they do domestically, in order to ensure a level playing field in the global market.[55]

Second, the need for multinational firms to develop distinct brands gives them an incentive for a global standard consistent with their corporate culture and brand image. Economists, political scientists, and organizational scholars provide numerous motivations for multinational corporations to develop a strong corporate culture.[56] One reason is that, as firms try to develop globally identifiable brands, they will be sensitive to any regulatory violations anywhere that could tarnish the brand image.[57] Statistical tests show that multinational firms that establish single global standards for their production processes have higher market capitalization than firms with disparate national standards.[58] Anecdotal evidence suggests that this is how the CEO's of multinational corpo-

---

[51] Jeffrey Immelt, "A Consistent Policy on Cleaner Energy," *Financial Times*, June 29, 2005.

[52] David Lazer, "Regulatory Interdependence and International Governance," *Journal of European Public Policy* 8 (May/June 2001): 477.

[53] Michael Porter and Claas van der Linde, "Toward a New Conception of the Environment-Competitiveness Relationship," *Journal of Economic Perspectives* 9 (Autumn 1995): 97–118.

[54] Ronie Garcia-Johnson, *Exporting Environmentalism: U.S. Multinational Chemical Corporations in Brazil and Mexico* (Cambridge, MA: MIT Press, 2000).

[55] Elizabeth DeSombre, *Domestic Sources of International Environmental Policy: Industry, Environmentalists, and U.S. Power* (Cambridge, MA: MIT Press, 2000).

[56] For the economic motivations, see David Kreps, "Corporate Culture and Economic Theory," in *Perspectives on Positive Political Economy*, ed. James Alt and Kenneth Shepsle (New York: Cambridge University Press, 1990). For the political origins, see Doremus et al., *The Myth of the Global Corporation*. For the organizational take, see Herbert Simon, *Administrative Behavior*, 3rd ed. (New York: Free Press, 1976).

[57] *Economist*, "Brands: Who's Wearing the Trousers?" September 8, 2001; Deborah Spar, "The Spotlight and the Bottom Line," *Foreign Affairs* 77 (March/April 1998).

[58] Glen Dowell, Stuart Hart, and Bernard Yeung, "Do Corporate Environmental Standards Create or Destroy Value?" *Management Science* 46 (August 2000): 1059–74.

rations think of their management style.[59] Aseem Prakash has shown how corporate culture explains why some firms exceed mandated regulatory standards in the United States.[60]

It is more difficult for a corporation to present a consistent brand image if its operating environment varies by the national regulatory framework. A single regulatory standard is more consistent with the marketing need for a single corporate culture. Both of these arguments are consistent with empirical findings that firms adhering to single global standards create greater market capitalization than firms attempting to exploit divergent standards.[61]

Third, a single regulatory regime clarifies the political process by which transnational regulatory standards can be changed. Multiple standards require firms to gauge the political environments of all countries with significant markets or production facilities. The greater the number of disparate national standards that exist, the greater the political uncertainty for multinational actors. Coordination helps to generate clear decision-making rules for any future changes in the rules. A single global regime clarifies the process through which standards might change, making it easier for firms to form accurate expectations of their future operating environment. As one corporate official phrased it when discussing the Kyoto Protocol in 2001, "what businesses want is policy certainty."[62] The reduction of uncertainty via global economic governance increases economic efficiency, moving the global economy closer to the Pareto frontier. Coordination thus bestows greater benefits to all countries by increasing the static and dynamic efficiency of economic agents.

[59] Scott Beardsley, Denis Burgov and Luis Enriquez, "The Role of Regulation in Strategy," *The McKinsey Quarterly* 4 (December 2005): 92–102. For a specific example, the chairman of the German insurance firm Allianz wrote in a *Financial Times* op-ed: "At Allianz, the head office sees its role as defining the group's regulatory framework, setting group strategy and financial objectives. How to service local markets, however, is left up to our local subsidiaries. They know their markets much better than the central office in Munich" (Henning Schulte-Noell, "Europe Must Clarify Its Goals," *Financial Times*, June 2, 2002).

[60] Aseem Prakash, *Greening the Firm: The Politics of Corporate Environmentalism* (Cambridge: Cambridge University Press, 2000).

[61] Dowell, Hart, and Yeung, "Do Corporate Global Environmental Standards Create or Destroy Market Value?" 1059–74. Their results also offer another explanation for why races to the bottom rarely occur. According to their findings, the firms that exploit the lowest standards occupy the most precarious positions in terms of profitability. Racing to the bottom is not necessarily the way to maximize any firms' profitability. Instead, it appears to be a last-ditch survival strategy for marginal producers. Therefore, a firm that engages in regulatory arbitrage is trying to maximize its rate of return, but in the process it also signals to financial markets its lack of competitiveness with rivals. This signal is likely to raise a firm's capital costs via increased risk premiums. Even for marginal producers, the expected gain of regulatory arbitrage can be outweighed by the costs of sending a signal of uncompetitiveness to capital markets.

[62] Quoted in Andrew C. Revkin and Neela Benerjee, "Energy Executives Urge Some Gas-Emission Limits on Bush," *New York Times*, August 1, 2001, C1.

The Costs of Coordination

While states may receive gross benefits from the development of international regulatory coordination, any agreement that diverges from the domestic status quo comes with economic and political costs—and these costs can outweigh the expected benefits.

There are direct costs to the governments of any attempted change in the domestic status quo. Governments must invest in the necessary political capital to make any necessary legal and administrative reforms. These costs have the potential to be significant. Bureaucratic agencies and regulators, accustomed to the status quo and reluctant to change training procedures, can devise a number of ways to resist politically directed change from above.[63] Legislative actors have the capacity to either block or reverse administrative changes in regulation. Outside the apparatus of the state, any political opposition that exists to the regulatory change—or any dissatisfaction with the new standards among voters, interest groups, or members of the selectorate—will obviously increase the costs to the government.[64] For governments, mobilizing bureaucratic actors, lobbying legislatures, and mollifying interest groups requires breaching powerful iron triangles.

Governments suffer indirect costs when private actors must expend resources in order to comply with new regulations. Firms, for example, incur economic costs when they are forced to retool their operations to comply with a new regulatory standard. One would expect consumers and local producers to be more comfortable with local rules than any international standard that diverges from those rules. Common regulatory standards can negate the comparative institutional advantage that firms develop in tailoring their production processes to a country's embedded regulatory framework. Neoclassical trade theory suggests that regulatory standards can be thought of as an institutional extension of traditional notions of comparative advantage. Producers maximize their efficiency within a given regulatory environment, and that producer satisfaction translates into increased utility for the government. That environment directly affects the firm's optimal portfolio of outputs. Since cross-border exchange generates increases in utility because of differences in

[63] John Brehm and Scott Gates, *Working, Shirking, and Sabotage: Bureaucratic Response to a Democratic Public* (Ann Arbor: University of Michigan Press, 1997); Martha Derthick, *Agency under Stress: The Social Security Administration in American Government* (Washington, DC: Brookings Institution Press, 1990); Amy B. Zegart, *Flawed by Design: The Complex Evolution of the CIA, JCS, and NSC* (Stanford, CA: Stanford University Press, 1999).

[64] These costs may seem insignificant but they can add up. For developed countries, changes in the status quo can trigger resistance from entrenched bureaucracies. Most developing countries lack the resources to properly train and fund the requisite agencies that would be necessary to properly enforce new regulatory burdens.

comparative advantage, uniform global standards can generate costs in some countries from a loss of competitiveness.

Even multinational corporations are most comfortable operating in the home country environment that conditioned their historical structure and operating processes.[65] Less competitive sectors incur even greater costs from harmonization, since disparate regulatory systems are often the last residual barrier to full integration. For these sectors, coordination implies economic extinction. The short-term costs of such creative destruction can be significant for the national economy on the whole, and devastating to the directly affected actors.

Operationalizing Government Preferences

Now that we have an understanding of the sources of a government's costs and benefits from regulatory coordination, how can these factors be operationalized? Consider the effect of economic globalization on the cost-benefit calculus. The reduction of barriers to exchange across borders increases the benefits derived from coordination. The lower the transaction costs of economic exchange—whether through technological innovation or political accommodation—the greater the rewards that are conferred through policy coordination. Globalization lowers the barriers to entry for all market participants and thereby increases the number of economic actors that stand to benefit from regulatory coordination. Concomitantly, globalization increases the economic benefits to governments for coordination.

While globalization leads to a secular increase to the benefits of coordination, its effect on costs are minimal and contradictory. Costs are a function of the domestic political economy; economic globalization does not alter this, nor does it lessen the gross costs of shifting to new standards. One could argue that globalization, by leading to greater economic growth, increases the allure of leaving a less competitive sector and therefore reduces adjustment costs. However, globalization also increases the speed with which market forces affect these sectors. Thus, the short-term costs for these sectors would also be increased.

With globalization increasing the benefits of coordination while not affecting the costs, we should expect to see greater regulatory coordination over time. However, there may be regulatory arenas for which the adjustment costs still outweigh the benefits. Insurmountable costs can be observed in the extent to which the affected domestic actors exercise political voice rather than market exit in responding to the adverse effects of changing rules and regulations. This is most likely to take place when regulatory coordination affects either economically mature sectors or nontradable portions of the economy.

---

[65] Chandler, *Strategy and Structure: Chapters in the History of the Industrial Enterprise*; Doremus et al., *The Myth of the Global Corporation*.

The definitions of political voice and market exit come directly from Albert Hirschman's *Exit, Voice, and Loyalty.*[66] Actors exercise voice when they respond to adverse circumstances by expressing their dissatisfaction to the authorities responsible for creating the circumstances. The use of voice takes place when the alternative options available to affected parties—internal adjustment or market exit—are deemed costlier options.

It could be argued that the affected actors will employ exit, voice, and other adjustment strategies in tandem. However, as Hirschman observed, it is politically difficult for actors to combine these strategies. For example, "the presence of the exit alternative can . . . tend to *atrophy the development of the art of voice.*"[67] Later on Hirschman notes: "By itself, the high price or the 'unthinkability' of exit may not only fail to repress voice but may stimulate it. It is perhaps for this reason that the traditional groups which repress exit alone have proved to be . . . viable."[68] This is also true when considering internal adjustment strategies. Oona Hathaway, in applying Hirschman's framework to the political behavior of tradable sectors, concurs: "Investment in adjustment . . . necessarily weakens an industry's chance of obtaining administrative or legislative protection because it undermines its claim that it is suffering from severe economic distress."[69] Empirical research has demonstrated that firms and sectors facing barriers to exit are more likely to extract government benefits in the form of subsidies.[70]

Even if voice is the cheapest option, its effective use requires the build-up of significant organizational assets to overcome the collective action problems associated with political action. Actors that are ineffective in the use of voice quietly fade away—because they failed to retain the necessary protections from the government. Actors that successfully employ voice strategies foster expectations of future success.[71] Over time, actors that successfully relied on voice in the past will be likely to ignore the exit strategy as an appropriate policy response—and vice versa.

The argument that voice raises adjustment costs more than exit runs contrary to the conventional wisdom regarding how globalization empowers pri-

---

[66] Hirschman, *Exit, Voice, and Loyalty.*

[67] Ibid., 43 (italics in original).

[68] Ibid., 98.

[69] Oona Hathaway, "Positive Feedback: The Impact of Trade Liberalization on Industry Demands for Protection," *International Organization* 52 (Summer 1998): 579. Similarly, I. M. Destler observes, "Firms with expanding markets tend to concentrate on business. . . . It is the embattled losers who go into politics to seek trade protection" (*American Trade Politics: System under Stress* [Washington, DC: Institute for International Economics, 1986, 3]).

[70] James Alt et al., "Asset Specificity and the Political Behavior of Firms: Lobbying for Subsidies in Norway," *International Organization* 53 (Winter 1999): 99–116; Nikolaos Zahariadis, "Asset Specificity and State Subsidies in Industrialized Countries," *International Studies Quarterly* 45 (December 2001): 603–16.

[71] Hathaway, "Positive Feedback," 608–9.

vate actors. An underlying assumption of globalization theorists is that the reduction of barriers to international exchange increases the number of exit options for mobile factors of production. In theory, this enhances the threat of exit for these actors, forcing states that are structurally dependent on capital to respond to their policy preferences.[72] For example, Dale Murphy concludes: "Firms with nonspecific assets can just 'up and leave' so their threats to relocate are more credible. They need only whisper for governments to hear their voice and respond."[73]

However, there are reasons to believe that the costs of exit to the state are overstated when compared to voice. For governments, the threat of exit is costly for direct economic reasons—the potential loss of revenue from resource reallocation. These costs, however, can be alleviated by the manner in which exit takes place. In a global economy, there are two kinds of market exit. The relevant actors could choose to exit the affected sector and redirect their productive energies toward a different economic activity. This decision imposes minimal economic costs on the government. The other exit option is for the actors to relocate economic activity outside of the country. This has the potential to impose greater economic costs on the government, in the form of lost jobs and tax revenues. Empirically, however, it is far from clear that this cost is especially significant. For example, the offshore outsourcing of production tasks to avoid regulatory burdens does not have immediate or dramatic effects on either unemployment or taxation.[74] The real costs are often indirect in their effect, weakening attempts to politically link regulatory stringency to negative economic effects. While exit can create costs for the government, these costs are often mitigated by the intrinsic nature of responses to market exit.

The exercise of political voice is an indicator of significant economic *and* political costs. Political voice signals that the relevant factors of production face imposing economic adjustment costs. Actors that face high barriers to exit are more likely to resort to voice as their preferred influence mechanism. As Hirschman observes, "The voice option is the only way in which dissatisfied customers or members can react whenever the exit option is unavailable."[75] In and of itself, the use of voice signals the economic costs that would come with

[72] Adam Przeworski and Michael Wallerstein, "Structural Dependence of the State on Capital," *American Political Science Review* 82 (February 1988): 11–29; John Goodman and Louis Pauly, "The Obsolescence of Capital Controls?" *World Politics* 46 (October 1993): 50–82; Wallerstein and Przeworski, "Capital Taxation with Open Borders," *Review of International Political Economy* 2 (August 1995): 425–45.

[73] Murphy, *The Structure of Regulatory Competition*, 18.

[74] See McKinsey Global Institute, "Offshoring: Is It a Win-Win Game?" San Francisco, CA, August 2003; Daniel W. Drezner, "The Outsourcing Bogeyman," *Foreign Affairs* 83 (May/June 2004): 22–34; Erica L. Groshen et al., "U.S. Jobs Gained and Lost through Trade: A Net Measure," *Federal Reserve Bank of New York Current Issues in Economics and Finance* 11 (August 2005): 1–7.

[75] Hirschman, *Exit, Voice, and Loyalty*, 33.

changes in the status quo. Politically, the exercise of voice creates demands for action that must be addressed by the government in power. Actors exercising voice will punish governments that fail to respond to their preferences by switching loyalties to political rivals. Above and beyond the economic costs, the use of voice imposes additional political costs on governments than exit.

Which regulatory issue areas are likely to trigger the exercise of political voice? Regulations that adversely affect actors facing high barriers to exit or actors skilled in the use of voice are likely to generate significant adjustment costs. Changes in regulations that cover nontradable as well as tradable sectors will affect actors meeting the first criteria. Changes in regulations that affect relatively mature, well-established economic sectors will affect actors meeting both criteria.

Mature economic sectors are likely to fulfill both criteria. As Mancur Olson observed, the passage of time without exogenous shocks increases the likelihood that any group of actors can overcome collective action problems and exercise political voice in concert. This logic applies to older economic sectors; over time, national producers within a particular sector should be increasingly able to act in a cartelistic fashion.[76] This behavior is designed to generate rents that cannot be retrieved through market exit. Over time, firms that successfully adapt to complex regulatory environments would be expected to resist actions that lower these entry barriers. Firms within a mature economic sector will have a vested incentive to rely heavily on voice to resist any change in the preexisting regulatory environment. One would expect these actors to specialize over time more in the use of political voice instead of contemplating market exit.

Regulatory changes that affect large sections of society are also likely to trigger political action. Even in an era of globalization, the bulk of economic activity remains geographically rooted; the actors involved in these sectors face prohibitive barriers to using the exit option of leaving the state. This fact applies with even greater force to the government bureaucracies and bureaucrats that need to implement the requisite changes in regulatory oversight of the affected sectors. Regulatory coordination that requires changes in the way that nontradable sectors conduct their business will lead to political mobilization rather than market adjustment. This includes rules that affect either immobile factors of production or immobile markets—that is, land, labor, and product markets.

To sum up: regulatory harmonization generates positive benefits for all participating actors, and those benefits increase with greater globalization. Such coordination also generates adjustment costs for those actors. The costs can be detected by the tendency of affected actors to exercise political voice rather than market exit in response to the prospect of regulatory convergence. This is more likely to take place in regulatory issue areas that affect either mature

---

[76] Mancur Olson, *The Rise and Decline of Nations* (New Haven, CT: Yale University Press, 1982), 40.

economic sectors or broad sections of societal actors. Sectors with long economic histories, or those that emphasize the use of immobile factors of production, are likely to have the greatest adjustment costs. With these assumptions delineated, we can move on to a simple game-theoretic model of regulatory coordination.

A SIMPLE STANDARDS GAME

Consistent with the two-step approach, domestic actors affect preferences, but at the international bargaining stage, the primary actors are governments. This section employs a simple game-theoretic model to capture the bargaining dynamics of interstate regulatory coordination.

The rational choice literature on interstate cooperation has been focused on whether the payoff matrices in a given issue area resemble a Battle-of-the-Sexes game or a Prisoner's Dilemma.[77] For example, environmental protection is often described as a classic tragedy of the commons, while the development of technical standards is often seen as a simple coordination game. However, this obscures the fact that for any issue area, there exists a spectrum of possible agreements and bargains that can be struck, with the distribution of benefits differing from actor to actor. The formal model developed here starts with the premise that James Fearon first highlighted:

> Empirically, there are always many possible ways to encourage an arms, trade, financial, or environmental treaty, and before states can cooperate to enforce an agreement they must bargain to decide which one to implement. Thus, regardless of the substantive domain, problems of international cooperation typically involve first a bargaining problem (akin to various coordination games that have been studied) and next an enforcement problem (akin to a Prisoner's Dilemma game).[78]

Another problem with this literature is that it gives short shrift to how power asymmetries affect both process and outcome.[79] The language of game theory

---

[77] Lisa L. Martin, "Interests, Power, and Multilateralism," *International Organization* 46 (Autumn 1992): 765–92; Beth Simmons, "The International Politics of Harmonization: The Case of Capital Market Integration," *International Organization* (Summer 2001): 589–620; Barbara Koremenos, Charles Lipson, and Duncan Snidal, eds., *The Rational Design of International Institutions* (Cambridge: Cambridge University Press, 2001). For critiques, see James Morrow, "Modeling the Forms of International Cooperation: Distribution Versus Information," *International Organization* 48 (Summer 1994): 387–423, and James Fearon, "Bargaining, Enforcement, and International Cooperation," *International Organization* 52 (Spring 1998): 269–305.

[78] Fearon, "Bargaining, Enforcement, and International Cooperation," 270. Koremenos, Lipson, and Snidal similarly note, "In practice, states have a wide range of choices and many possible cooperative outcomes, often with different distributional consequences" (*The Rational Design of International Institutions*, 2).

[79] Consider, for example, the Rational Design school on international institutions. Koremenos, Lipson, and Snidal state that, "Every state has an interest in the international economy . . . but

can make it difficult to incorporate power considerations into a model of international interactions. In two-player games, for example, symmetrical payoff matrices, or alternating the sequence of moves, often obscure inherent power imbalances.[80] At the same time, some devices to formally incorporate power imbalances—such as giving one actor agenda-setting powers—have the problem of exaggerating power differentials in the other direction.

The approach developed here specifies the sources and effects of asymmetric bargaining power through the payoff functions.[81] Table 2.2 shows the general coordination game that states face. For now, I assume coordination over standards is a two-player game with no coercive option. Two states, A and B, have the choice of coordinating their regulatory standards or not. There exists a unidimensional measure of regulatory stringency, with a higher value implying a more stringent standard. As a convention, it will be assumed that state A's regulatory standards (a) are always more stringent than state B's (b)—in other words, $a > b$. States can choose to stick to their own regulatory framework or agree to switch to the other country's framework.[82]

The payoffs for the status quo—each state retaining their own regulatory standards—are normalized to zero. π_i represents the benefits country i derives from the enhanced economic efficiency achieved through regulatory coordination. π is a function of the intrinsic nature of the regulatory issue in question, the national attributes of country i, and the value of coordinating with country j. Initially, however, I will assume that for all i, $\pi_i = \pi$.

The term d_i equals the economic and political costs of making the necessary adjustments to new regulatory standards for country i. Like π, d is a function of the intrinsic nature of the regulatory issue in question, the national attributes of country i, and the value of coordinating with country j. As with π, to start I will assume that for all i, $d_i = d$, $0 < d < 1$, and that $d = f(a - b)$. This makes the adjustment costs a monotonically increasing function of the gap in the preexisting standards between countries A and B. It is logical to assume that the adjustment costs increase as the gap in initial standards between A and B increases.

Actors must choose whether to adhere to their national standard or be willing to switch to the other player's prior standard. Regulatory coordination increases the size of the public good but can also impose costs on actors that

---

few have the economic power to determine its course." However, this (unelaborated) point is their only mention of the role of power in the Rational Design school (*The Rational Design of International Institutions*, 16).

[80] For a more radical critique, see Andrew Hurrell, "Power, Institutions, and the Production of Inequality," in *Power in Global Governance* ed. Michael Barnett and Raymond Duvall, 34–41 (Cambridge: Cambridge University Press, 2005).

[81] I also employed this technique in *The Sanctions Paradox*.

[82] For convenience, I assume that any mutual recognition agreement is the logical equivalent of agreeing to state B's standards.

Table 2.2
The Standards Game

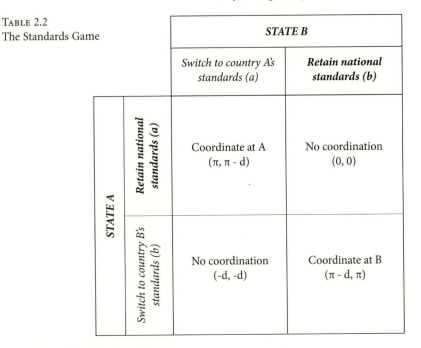

		STATE B	
		Switch to country A's standards (a)	***Retain national standards (b)***
STATE A	*Retain national standards (a)*	Coordinate at A $(\pi, \pi - d)$	No coordination $(0, 0)$
	Switch to country B's standards (b)	No coordination $(-d, -d)$	Coordinate at B $(\pi - d, \pi)$

π = benefits from regulatory coordination
d = adjustment costs of adopting a new regulatory standard
a = initial regulatory standard of state A, a > b
b = initial regulatory standard of state B, a > b

must adjust from the previous status quo. For all states, the most preferred option is coordination at their set of national standards. Because of adjustment costs, a state's worst outcome is to agree to another country's standards but fail to successfully coordinate. This model is consistent with, but not identical to, other international relations models of coordination.[83]

Solving the simplest version of this game reveals two important facts. First, if the costs of adjustment outweigh the perceived benefits of harmonizing regulatory standards, the actor's dominant strategy is to retain its national standards.[84] This leads to a unique equilibrium outcome of no coordination. If d > π, then the *only* equilibrium outcome that exists is no coordination.

This simple result is worth emphasizing because the implicit bias in much of the international relations literature is that cooperation is a socially efficient outcome relative to the status quo. More formally, international relations theo-

[83] Stephen D. Krasner, "Global Communications and National Power: Life on the Pareto Frontier," *World Politics* 43 (April 1991): 336–66. See also Gruber, *Ruling the World.*
[84] The proof is in the appendix to this chapter.

rists assume that virtually all international interactions are variations on simple "games of cooperation," in that cooperation generates a unique and socially efficient outcome that Pareto-dominates noncooperative outcomes.[85] This is true even of models that allow for distributional conflicts among participating actors. In part, this is because the question of interest to many international relations scholars is why states choose not to cooperate even if all parties could enhance their utility via cooperation. Such an approach assumes away plausible scenarios when noncooperation is the optimal strategy—not because of fears of defection or concerns about relative gains, but because of the wide divergence of actor interests. Rather than assume *ex ante* that cooperation is the socially efficient outcome, the model described above allows for the possibility that mutual cooperation does not Pareto-dominate mutual defection.

The second insight from this game presumes that the public benefits from coordination outweigh the economic and political costs of adjustment.[86] This makes coordination a possible equilibrium outcome. As the public good from cooperation increases and the costs from adjusting to new standards decreases, a coordinated outcome becomes more likely. In other words, regulatory coordination is an increasing function of π and b, but a decreasing function of d and a. These results rely on the inclusion of mixed strategies, and are demonstrated in the appendix.[87]

Again, this is a straightforward result that is nevertheless worthy of note. One would expect that as the bargaining "core" between the actors increases, so will the likelihood that a bargain will be struck. Any increase in the benefits from coordination or decrease in the political costs of adjustment increases the size of the core, which increases the likelihood of coordination. Similarly, any increase in the initial gap between national regulatory standards reduces the size of the bargaining core, which reduces the likelihood of coordination. Most game-theoretic approaches are concerned with what happens within a bargaining core. This emphasis elides that coordination is more likely when the size of the bargaining core increases.

The previous section in this chapter demonstrated that globalization increases the gross benefits of regulatory coordination (π) while having little effect on a country's adjustment costs (d). It also argued that the regulation

---

[85] For a formal definition of "games of cooperation," see Jonathan Bendor and Piotr Swistak, "The Evolutionary Stability of Cooperation," *American Political Science Review* 91 (June 1997): 297–98.

[86] That is, $\pi > d$.

[87] On interpreting mixed-strategy equilibria for this kind of symmetrical game, James Johnson and Randall Calvert point out: "In the absence of any reason to focus on one or the other pure-strategy equilibrium, the mixed-strategy equilibrium captures the whole 'problem' of the coordination problem; to solve the problem is to discover a way to achieve one of the pure-strategy payoffs dependably." See Johnson and Calvert, "Interpretation and Coordination in Constitutional Politics," Working Paper No. 15, W. Allen Wallis Institute of Political Economy, Rochester, NY, July 1998, footnote 8.

of mature economic sectors or regulation that covered nontradable as well as tradable sectors would generate high adjustment costs, or high values of d. Combining those insights with the formal game structure leads to two straightforward hypotheses regarding regulatory coordination. First, *ceteris paribus*, economic globalization increases the likelihood of international regulatory coordination. As the benefits increase while the costs remain relatively constant, the size of the bargaining core expands, which increases the likelihood of a coordination outcome. Second, regulatory coordination is less likely when the regulation directly affects mature or nontradable economic sectors— since these sectors are expected to generate the highest level of adjustment costs. Even as globalization increases gross benefits, the costs relative to other sectors or factors of production remain relatively high. Coordination is therefore a less likely outcome.

INTRODUCING ECONOMIC POWER

So far, the model has assumed symmetrical payoffs between the negotiating countries. However, a more reasonable conjecture would be to say that the public good benefits from regulatory coordination depend upon the size of the newly opened market. For example, if the United States and Jordan coordinate their regulatory standards, it reduces the barriers to exchange between the countries. For America, this is a small but positive benefit. Reducing the barriers to exchange with a market that is less than a quarter of one percent of the size of the U.S. economy does not yield substantial rewards.[88] On the other hand, such coordination would generate a significant windfall for Jordan, since the market that opens up to its actors is significantly greater. In this real-world instance, $\pi_{US} < \pi_{Jordan}$. Economists have demonstrated empirically that the benefits of greater openness vary in inverse proportion to size.[89]

This simple example demonstrates why the positive benefits that come from regulatory coordination should vary according to the actor. So, let Y_i equal the market size of country i. And, instead of $\pi_i = \pi$, let π_i be a function of the relative market shares of the two countries, such that country i receives a bigger payoff from coordination as the market size of the partner country increases.[90]

How does this affect the dynamics of the coordination game? The likelihood of a coordination equilibrium at one country's standards is an increasing func-

---

[88] Data on gross domestic product comes from the *CIA World Factbook*.

[89] Elhanan Helpman, *The Mysteries of Economic Growth* (Cambridge, MA: Belknap Press, 2004), 71–72.

[90] Formally, let Y_i equal the size of country i's economy. Then for all i, π_i = a linear transformation of: $Y_j/(Y_i + Y_j)$. Gravity models indicate that geographic proximity would have a similar effect to aggregate market size. In the interest of simplicity, that variable is excluded from the analysis. Its inclusion has no effect on the results presented here.

tion of that country's market size. This probabilistic statement comes from the concept of "stability sets" suggested by John Harsanyi and Reinhardt Selten and developed by Luis Fernando Medina.[91] The intuition stems from how market size affects the perceptions both actors have about the likelihood of their strategic choices. Each country's reaction function is based on the possible distribution of payoffs in the game. Increasing the market size of government A decreases that actor's reward for coordination, while simultaneously increasing B's payoff from coordination at any set of standards. This means that the cost of adjustment carries a larger weight for the more powerful actor's decision-making calculus, while the reverse is true of the smaller actor. Both governments process this information into their reaction functions. The result is that there is a larger zone of beliefs—the stability set—where both players will prefer to select the great power's set of preferred standards.

The logical extension of the effect of market size is that, *ceteris paribus*, once an economy amasses enough relative size, the *only* equilibrium outcome is coordination at that country's standards. Assume that country A is the great power. After a certain point, increasing A's market size vis-à-vis country B reduces A's benefit of coordinating at B's standards to the point that it prefers the status quo to coordination at B's regulatory standards. So, once its market reaches a certain relative size, country A's dominant strategy is to adhere to its preexisting standards. Given A's choice, country B will switch its standards to A's preferred position so long as the benefits from coordination outweigh the adjustment costs. Since B's benefits from coordination increase with A's market size, after a certain point A's economy is big enough to ensure that this will be the case.

The introduction of market power alone increases the likelihood that coordination will take place at the larger country's preferred set of standards. However, great powers have another mechanism through which they can influence the coordination game—the threat of economic coercion. It is easy to point to circumstances in which great powers have threatened or employed economic sanctions over regulatory differences.[92] Furthermore, there is strong empirical evidence that the threat or use of sanctions can yield significant concessions in regulatory disputes.[93]

With this tactic, a state that prefers to retain its own standards will impose economic sanctions if the other state refuses to switch its standards. Table 2.3

[91] See John Harsanyi and Reinhardt Selten, *A General Theory of Equilibrium Selection* (Cambridge, MA: MIT Press, 1988); Luis Fernando Medina, "The Comparative Statics of Collective Action: A Pragmatic Approach to Games with Multiple Equilibria," *Rationality and Society* 17 (Fall 2005): 423–32.

[92] Daniel W. Drezner, "Outside the Box: Explaining Sanctions in Pursuit of Foreign Economic Goals," *International Interactions* 26 (Summer 2001): 379–410.

[93] Daniel W. Drezner, "The Hidden Hand of Economic Coercion," *International Organization* 57 (Summer 2003): 643–59; Drezner, "Outside the Box."

TABLE 2.3
The Modified Standards
Game

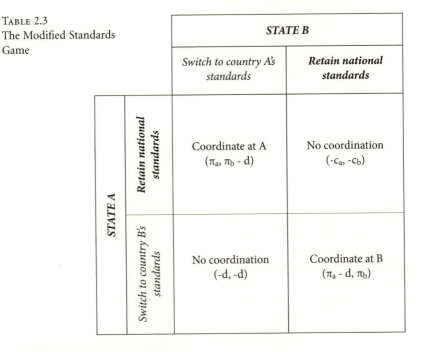

		STATE B	
		Switch to country A's standards	***Retain national standards***
STATE A	*Retain national standards*	Coordinate at A $(\pi_a, \pi_b - d)$	No coordination $(-c_a, -c_b)$
	Switch to country B's standards	No coordination $(-d, -d)$	Coordinate at B $(\pi_a - d, \pi_b)$

π = benefits from regulatory coordination
d_i = adjustment costs of moving a new regulatory standard for country i
c_i = costs of coercion if no coordination

demonstrates how the option to employ pressure tactics changes the payoffs of the coordination game. States with the capability to employ economic coercion can alter the payoff structure of the other player by tactically linking regulatory coordination to the broader benefits derived from economic openness.[94] They can penalize the other actor for choosing to retain their preexisting standards when the great power would prefer the target country to switch its regulations. The introduction of economic coercion alters the dynamics of the coordination game in two ways. First, it widens the size of the bargaining core—the distribution of costs and benefits under which a coordinated outcome is an equilibrium outcome. For the targeted state, the preference to switch standards is no longer a question of whether the benefits exceed the adjustment costs. The question is whether the benefits exceed the costs such that switch is less costly than suffering from economic coercion. Even if the targeted state is worse off from switching, it may represent the least bad alternative when faced with the possibility of sanctions. When necessary, great pow-

---

[94] It is assumed that great powers are able to satisfy the conditions necessary to threaten economic coercion. For more on this condition, see Drezner, *The Sanctions Paradox*, chap. 4.

ers will use economic coercion to force weaker and smaller governments into switching their regulatory standards.

The second way in which coercion alters the dynamic of the game is to reduce the market size necessary to lock in coordination at the great power's standards as the only possible equilibrium outcome. The shadow of potential sanctions lowers the threshold at which the targeted state would prefer switching to the great power's standards rather than accept the status quo. *Ceteris paribus*, the presence of coercion increases the range of situations in which coordination at the great power's most preferred outcome will take place.

The standards game shows that economic power matters, but there is an important caveat to this conclusion: only gross power differences matter. Great powers will be unable to use economic coercion to alter the regulatory standards of another great power. When the two interacting countries are both great powers, neither actor possesses an appreciable bargaining advantage. This is true even if one of the two actors has more relative power. Given the requisite size for both economies to achieve great power status, the likelihood that any dyadic difference in market size sufficiently alters the payoffs enough to generate a single equilibrium outcome is mathematically impossible. Differences in relative power do affect the size of the stability sets for coordination at each actor's preferred set of standards. However, because of the gross economic size of these governments, the effect is marginal at best. As for the coercion option, it is highly unlikely that either actor would be able to satisfy the necessary conditions for extracting significant concessions from another great power—the expectations of future conflict would be too great. Empirically, sanctions among great powers have generated meager results at best.[95] Between great powers, the effects of power largely wash out.

Conclusion

This chapter has laid out the assumptions regarding government power and preferences in a global economy where regulations are the remaining barriers to integration. Great powers are defined by their internal market size and reduced vulnerability to external shocks. This endows them with the necessary market power and coercive power to alter the incentives for weaker states. For the empirical cases that will be evaluated in this book, the only great powers are the United States and the European Union. Their preferences are a function of the domestic adjustment costs they face in changing their domestic regula-

---

[95] Drezner, *The Sanctions Paradox*, chaps. 2, 3, and 4. See also Drezner, "Outside the Box," and Barry Buzan, "Economic Structure and International Security," *International Organization* 38 (Autumn 1984): 597–624.

tory frameworks. When governments are forced to cope with domestic actors who resort to the use of voice rather than exit or market adjustment in response to proposed regulatory change, their adjustment costs increase. For all of the literature arguing that globalization acts as a structure that tears asunder outmoded local institutions, the theory of national preferences articulated here suggests that history still matters. The older the sectors and the regulatory problem in question, the greater the adjustment costs for actors well versed in the use of political voice. For these issues, increasing exposure to globalization will fail to provide a sufficient incentive for regulatory coordination.

A simple game-theoretic model of regulatory coordination reveals several important insights about the global coordination of regulatory standards. There exist some regulatory issue areas for which no coordination is the equilibrium outcome. For those issues where π is sufficiently low and d is sufficiently high, there is no incentive to coordinate regulatory standards in the absence of a colossal hegemon. Those issue areas are likely to be regulatory questions that affect either mature or nontradable economic sectors. Power matters—some of the time. Great powers are more likely to achieve regulatory coordination at their preferred level of standards. Their power affects the location of regulatory coordination in two ways. First, their market size can alter the incentives of actors such that their preferred outcome becomes the only equilibrium. Second, the threat of economic coercion can accelerate the lock-in effect of coordinating at the great power's ideal point. However, between great powers, relative differences in market size do not have an appreciable effect on the outcome.

There are additional implications for the political economy literature on the "second image reversed" question.[96] The arguments about adjustment costs presented here suggest, for example, that in an era of globalization, the salient political cleavages within the domestic political economy will be by sector rather than class. The latter disputes might occur, but the indirect nature of how adjustment costs diffuse through the economy will make these disputes tougher political sells for the disaffected actors. In contrast, sectoral disputes have a more straightforward relationship between openness and adjustment costs, because both labor and capital are similarly affected. These arguments contradict recent assertions that the primary cleavage in the current era of globalization will be based on class.[97]

---

[96] Peter Gourevitch, "The Second Image Reversed: The International Sources of Domestic Politics," *International Organization* 32 (Fall 1978): 881–912; Ronald Rogowski, *Commerce and Coalitions: How Trade Affects Domestic Political Alignments* (Princeton, NJ: Princeton University Press, 1989).

[97] Richard Freeman, "What Really Ails Europe (and America): The Doubling of the Global Workforce," *The Globalist*, June 3, 2005, available at http://www.theglobalist.com/StoryId.aspx?StoryId=4542, accessed March 2006.

APPENDIX
PROOF OF LEMMAS

Lemma 1: If π − d < 0, then the only equilibrium outcome is for both countries to retain their national standards.

Proof: Begin with A's choice of standing firm or switching to B's standards. If B chooses to switch standards, A's utility from retaining its standards is greater than switching (π < d). If B retains its national standard, State A's utility from retaining its standards is still greater than switching standards, given the assumption that the costs of adjustment are greater than the benefits from regulatory coordination (0 > π − d). Therefore, the dominant strategy for A is to retain its own standards. By symmetry, this holds for B as well. QED

Lemma 2: If π > d = (a − b), the likelihood of regulatory coordination is an increasing function of both π and a, but a decreasing function of both d and b.

Proof: If π > d, then the model becomes a symmetrical coordination game with three Nash equilibria: A (switch to B's standards)—B (retain national standards), A (retain national standards)—B (switch to A's standards), and a mixed-strategy equilibrium.

To calculate the mixed strategy equilibrium: Let ρ = probability that A chooses (retain national standards). A chooses a value of ρ such that B is indifferent to its possible strategy set (switching to A's standards and retaining national standards). Therefore, A chooses ρ such that:

$$\rho\,(\pi - d) - (1 - \rho)d = 0 + (1 - \rho)\pi$$
$$\rho\pi - d = \pi - \rho\pi$$
$$\rho = \left(\frac{d + \pi}{2\pi}\right)$$

By symmetry, ρ is also the probability that B chooses to retain its national standards.

The probability of a coordinated equilibrium P (coordinated equilibrium) = P [A (switch to B's standards); B (retain national standards)] + P [A (retain national standards); B (switch to A's standards)], which equals $2\rho(1 - \rho)$. Substituting, we get:

$$P \text{ (coordinated equilibrium)} = 2\rho\,(1 - \rho) = \left(\frac{2\,(d + \pi)\,(\pi - d)}{4\pi^2}\right)$$

Which simplifies to: $\left(\dfrac{\pi^2 - d^2}{2\pi^2}\right)$

Which simplifies to: $1/2 - d^2/2\pi^2$

Changing the values of ρ, d, a, and b within the constraint of $\pi > d = (a - b)$ does not alter the pure strategy Nash equilibria. Changing these values does affect the likelihood of a coordinated equilibrium occurring in the mixed-strategy outcome. Partial differentiation shows that P (coordinated equilibrium):

- Increases with π;
- Decreases with d.

Substitute $(a - b)$ for d. Inspection of partial differentiation reveals that P (coordinated equilibrium):

- Increases with a;
- Decreases with b.

QED

Lemma 3: If $\pi_i > d = (a - b)$ for all i, the likelihood of a coordination equilibrium at A's standards is an increasing function of A's market size (Y_A).

Proof: If $\pi_i > d$ for all i, then the model becomes a symmetrical coordination game with three Nash equilibria: A (switch to B's standards)—B (retain national standards), A (retain national standards)—B (switch to A's standards), and a mixed-strategy equilibrium.

To calculate the mixed strategy equilibrium: Let ρ = probability that A chooses (retain national standards). A chooses a value of ρ such that B is indifferent to its possible strategy set (switching to A's standards and retaining national standards). Therefore, A chooses ρ such that:

$$\rho (\pi_b - d) - (1 - \rho)d = 0 + (1 - \rho)\pi_b$$

$$\rho\pi_b - d = \pi_b - \rho\pi_b$$

$$\rho^* = \left(\frac{d + \pi_b}{2\pi_b}\right)$$

Let q = the probability that B chooses (retain national standards). By symmetry,

$$q^* = \left(\frac{d + \pi_a}{2\pi_a}\right)$$

So, A's optimal reaction function to B's strategy is $R_a(q)$:

$$R_a (q) = \begin{array}{l} q < q^* \mid \text{Retain national standards} \\ q = q^* \mid \text{Retain national standards with probability } \rho = \rho^* \\ q > q^* \mid \text{Switch to B's standards} \end{array}$$

B's optimal reaction function to A's strategy is $R_b(\rho)$:

$$R_b(\rho) = \begin{array}{l} \rho < \rho^* \mid \text{Retain national standards} \\ \rho = \rho^* \mid \text{Retain national standards with probability } q = q^* \\ \rho > \rho^* \mid \text{Switch to A's standards} \end{array}$$

Assume that both actors have a uniform distribution of prior beliefs over ρ and q. The likelihood of an equilibrium of coordination at A's standards $[L (\rho^*, q^*)]$ is therefore:

$$L (\rho^*, q^*) = P [R_b(\rho) > \rho^*] * P [R_a(q) < q^*] = q^* (1 - \rho^*)$$

$$= [(d + \pi_a)/ 2\pi_a] * [1 - (d + \pi_b)/2\pi_b]$$

$$= [\pi_a\pi_b + d (\pi_b - \pi_a) - d^2]/4\pi_a\pi_b$$

$$= 1/4 + d[((\pi_b - \pi_a) - d]/ 4\pi_a\pi_b$$

Partial differentiation demonstrates that L is an increasing function of π_b and a decreasing function of π_a. Remember that for all i, $\pi_i =$ a linear transformation of: $Y_j/(Y_i + Y_j)$. Therefore, as Ya increases, π_b increases and π_b decreases, both of which increase the value of L. Therefore, *ceteris paribus*, as Y_a increases, so does the likelihood of a coordinated equilibrium at A's preferred set of standards. *QED*

Lemma 4: There exists a market size Y* such that, ceteris paribus, *when $Y_A > Y^*$, the only equilibrium outcome is coordination at country A's standards.*

Proof: $\pi_A = Y_B/(Y_A + Y_B)$, and $\pi_B = Y_A/(Y_A + Y_B)$. Since by definition $Y_i > 0$ for all i, π_A and π_B are continuous functions of Y_i that lie between zero and one.

Partial differentiation shows that as Y_A increases, π_B monotonically increases and π_A monotonically decreases.

Since by definition $0 < d < 1$, $\exists\, Y^*$ such that for all $Y_A > Y^*$,

$$\pi_A - d < 0 \tag{1}$$

When this condition holds, A's dominant strategy is to retain its national standards. Given this strategy for A, B will choose to switch standards *iff*:

$$\pi_B - d < 0 \tag{2}$$

π_B is an increasing function of Y_A, so by Brower's fixed point theorem, there must exist a value Y^{**} such that, *ceteris paribus*, for all $Y_A > Y^{**}$, inequalities 1 and 2 both hold. For those values of Y, the only Nash equilibrium outcome is [Retain national standards; switch to A's standards]. *QED*

CHAPTER THREE

A Typology of Global Governance Processes

MODELS SIMPLIFY the world in order to better understand it. The previous chapter used a very simple two-actor model to derive hypotheses about how adjustment costs and market power affect regulatory coordination. However, that model encompassed only governments, and to a lesser extent, domestic and multinational corporations. The actors that many globalization scholars believe to be important in determining the pattern of global governance—international governmental organizations and global civil society—were excluded. What happens when these actors are thrown into the mix?

This chapter argues that the dynamics of the revisionist model are unaffected by the introduction of new actors. Indeed, the main point of this chapter is to demonstrate that governance *processes* need to be separated from governance *outcomes*. Once this analytical separation is made, it becomes clear that the existence of a great power concert remains the necessary and sufficient condition for effective global regulatory coordination to take place. There are myriad processes through which such coordination can take place, however, and other actors can and do affect which process goes forward. Nongovernmental organizations, international governmental organizations, corporate-led private orders, and states outside the great power rank all affect the process of governance. These actors can block the most preferred routes of global governance, forcing great powers to substitute among different global governance structures.

The substitutability principle developed by Benjamin Most and Harvey Starr is essential to understanding the processes of global governance.[1] The substitutability concept is the progenitor of a burgeoning literature on forum-shopping in global governance.[2] States can and will substitute different governance structures, and different policy tools to create those structures, depending on

---

[1] Benjamin Most and Harvey Starr, "International Relations Theory, Foreign Policy Substitutability, and 'Nice' Laws," *World Politics* 36 (April 1984): 383–406. See also Most and Starr, *Inquiry, Logic, and International Politics* (Columbia: University of South Carolina Press, 1989).

[2] Kenneth Abbott and Duncan Snidal, "Pathways to International Cooperation," in *The Impact of International Law on International Cooperation*, ed. E. Benvenisti and M. Hirsch (Cambridge: Cambridge University Press, 2003); Lawrence Helfer, "Regime Shifting: The TRIPS Agreement and New Dynamics of International Intellectual Property Making," *Yale Journal of International Law* 29 (Winter 2004): 1–81; Kal Raustiala and David Victor, "The Regime Complex for Plant Genetic Resources," *International Organization* 58 (Spring 2004): 277–309.

the constellation of state and nonstate interests. While all states will attempt to select fora amenable to their interests, great powers will have the greatest success employing this tactic. Great power options include delegating regime management to nonstate actors, creating international regimes with strong enforcement capabilities, generating competing regimes to protect material interests, and tolerating the absence of effective cooperation because of divergent state preferences. Because most globalization scholars fail to consider the delegation strategy as a conscious state choice, they have misinterpreted the state's role in global governance.

This chapter is divided into six sections. The next section discusses the preferences, capabilities, and strategies that IGOs possess in the model of global governance developed here. The third section discusses the preferences, capabilities, and strategies of NGOs. The fourth section develops a typology of global governance structures, and the attendant roles that IGOs and NGOs play in those structures. The fifth section considers the varying roles that nonstate actors play in the process of regulatory coordination in light of existing debates in the literature. The final section summarizes and concludes.

What about IGOs?

In moving from a two-actor world to a multi-actor world, international governmental organizations matter. At a minimum, they serve as focal points through which multilateral bargaining and contracting takes place.[3] Even the most diehard of offensive realists acknowledge that the presence of IGOs makes it easier for states to act collectively when they choose to do so.[4] IGOs can serve as a clearing-house for relevant information. More generally, they assist in the coordination of enforcement strategies through a combination of the logic of appropriateness and the logic of consequences.[5]

The more established mechanism through which IGOs matter in global governance is through facilitating the logic of consequences in enforcing international rules and regulations. As noted in the previous chapter, the enforcement stage of an agreement is assumed to have a distribution of payoffs akin to a

---

[3] Jack Goldsmith and Eric Posner, *The Limits of International Law* (New York: Oxford University Press, 2005); Lisa L. Martin, "Interests, Power, and Multilateralism," *International Organization* 46 (Autumn 1992): 765–92; Kenneth Abbott and Duncan Snidal, "Why States Act through Formal International Organizations," *Journal of Conflict Resolution* 42 (February 1998): 3–32.

[4] John J. Mearsheimer, "The False Promise of International Institutions," *International Security* 19 (Winter 1994/95): 13–14.

[5] James March and Johan Olsen, "The Institutional Dynamics of International Political Orders," *International Organization* 52 (Autumn 1998): 943–69. It should be noted that despite theoretical debates about the relative importance of each logic, they should be expected to complement rather than substitute for each other.

Prisoner's Dilemma. For cooperation to be a stable outcome in such a game, it must be the case that the punishment of defection by other actors in the system is an incentive-compatible move. So, if one actor defects, other actors must have an incentive to carry out the threatened punishment.

In a bilateral context, this incentive compatibility condition always holds, because the punishing actor is also the one directly affected by any defection. However, when the game moves to a multilateral format, the temptation to act opportunistically arises. If the number of coordinating actors is sufficiently high, then the act of punishing defections takes on a public good quality of its own. Without arenas to provide for coordination, reassurance, and selective incentives, the multilateral enforcement of defections can fall apart.[6] Most IGOs do not directly control the material capabilities to punish defections. Through a combination of professional expertise, information provision and collection, and technical assistance, they can facilitate the ability of national governments to mobilize the necessary resources to punish defectors. For this reason, international organizations reduce the costs and increase the effectiveness of global governance.

There are other grounds for states to rely on IGOs that rest on the logic of appropriateness rather than the logic of consequences. IGOs can enhance the legitimacy of regulatory coordination through three mechanisms. First, international institutions can create a legal obligation for states to comply with the promulgated set of rules.[7] For small and medium-sized countries, the obligation of complying with international treaties and laws can mitigate and reduce domestic opposition to such a move.[8] Although such legal obligations may lack any supranational enforcing power, the desire for a good reputation alone can be sufficient to create incentives to honor agreements. Even non-binding, soft law arrangements codify the concern for reputation among states, and endow a source of legitimating power to IGOs with weak enforcement capabilities.

Second—and related—IGOs can enhance the normative desire to comply with the promulgated rules and regulations through the size of its membership group. Norms derive their power in part from the number of actors that formally accept them.[9] The greater the number of actors that accept a rule or

---

[6] Lisa L. Martin, *Coercive Cooperation: Explaining Multilateral Economic Sanctions* (Princeton, NJ: Princeton University Press, 1992); Martin, "Interests, Power, and Multilateralism."

[7] Abbott and Snidal, "Why States Act through Formal International Organizations"; Kenneth Abbott et al., "The Concept of Legalization," *International Organization* 54 (Summer 2000): 401–20; Kenneth Abbott and Duncan Snidal, "Hard and Soft Law in International Governance," *International Organization* 54 (Summer 2000): 421–56.

[8] Daniel Drezner, ed., *Locating the Proper Authorities: The Interaction of Domestic and International Institutions* (Ann Arbor: University of Michigan Press, 2003).

[9] Martha Finnemore and Kathryn Sikkink, "International Norm Dynamics and Political Change," *International Organization* 52 (Autumn 1998): 887–917. As will be seen, this is not to imply that membership size is the *only* source of legitimacy in world politics.

regulation, the greater the social pressure on recalcitrant actors to change their position.[10] As an IGO's membership increases, its perceived "democratic" mandate concomitantly increases—thereby enhancing its legitimating power. On this dimension, the more powerful compliance-inducing IGOs are those with the widest membership—such as the United Nations organizations.[11]

Third, as previously stated, the secretariats of international organizations can provide valuable technical expertise in the crafting of global rules and regulations. The functional bureaucracies of powerful governments possess reservoirs of expertise that often overshadow that of IGOs. Nevertheless, in some issue areas the power that comes from specialized knowledge and command over discourse also resides in IGO secretariats and staffs. Beyond the intrinsic value of their expertise is the prestige that their policy imprimatur carries with other actors. The most obvious example of such power is in the international financial institutions of the International Monetary Fund and the World Bank. The economists based at these entities have an independent legitimacy generated through their reputation for expertise.[12] Given the arcane nature of most regulatory arenas, IGOs with reservoirs of expertise enhance their influence.

While IGOs can facilitate the fashioning and enforcement of regulatory coordination, this facilitation comes with attendant costs. All else equal, a great power would prefer any regulatory standard to be backed with a powerful logic of appropriateness (i.e., enhanced legitimacy), a powerful logic of consequences (i.e., rigorous enforcement mechanisms), and a mechanism to alter policies in a manner consistent with great power preferences (i.e., decision-making rules that favor powerful actors). The ideal-type IGO for these governance tasks would be an organization with a large membership, a competent but obedient staff assisting in coordination activities, and decision-making rules that privilege the great powers.

The problem is that such IGOs exist only in theory; even institutions that appear to embody these attributes in theory often fail to do so in practice. Great powers are few in number by definition. The decision-making structures of most IGOs, however, rely on consensus decision-making procedures that to some degree factor in the preferences of all members, including smaller but

---

[10] A. Iain Johnston, "The Social Effects of International Institutions on Domestic (Foreign Policy) Actors," in Drezner, ed., *Locating the Proper Authorities.*

[11] Jens Steffek, "The Legitimation of International Governance: A Discourse Approach," *European Journal of International Relations* 9 (June 2003): 249–75. It is certainly debatable whether the one-country, one-vote principle used in most IGOs is truly democratic; however, the question here is whether the *perception* of democracy is present.

[12] Michael Barnett and Martha Finnemore, *Rules for the World: International Organizations in World Politics* (Ithaca: Cornell University Press, 2004), chapter 3; James Keeley, "Toward a Foucauldian Analysis of International Regimes," *International Organization* 44 (Winter 1990): 83–105.

more numerous governments. Even when power differences are formally in-corporated into decision rules—as in the case of the international financial institutions, for example—informal consensus norms still constrain the great powers' ability to push global economic governance through universal membership IGOs.[13] As for a powerful but pliant staff, empirical studies demonstrate the extent to which IGO secretariats will network with nongovernmental organizations as a way of developing policy autonomy.[14] As a result, even if a nation-state commands a significantly smaller market vis-à-vis the great powers *outside* an IGO, it can choose to ally with many other small states to stymie the efforts of more powerful actors *inside* an IGO. The great powers may desire to employ a powerful IGO to provide global governance over a particular issue area, but the preferences of other, weaker actors act as a constraint on this option.

Different distribution of state interests will cause great powers to prefer different types of IGOs as a way of protecting their interests. Great powers will substitute among these different governance structures depending on the distribution of preferences among states. To understand the outcomes that emerge from these possible distributions of interests, it is necessary to construct a typology of international governmental organizations. Borrowing from Michael Walzer,[15] I categorize IGOs by membership: clubs, neighborhoods, and universes. Universal IGOs, such as the United Nations and its emanations, purposefully try to maximize membership and staff size. As a result, these organizations have enhanced legitimacy through large memberships. However, the large number of actors implies an increasing diversity of member preferences. Such organizations also tend to have larger bureaucracies, which in turn leads to more autonomous staffs and secretariats. Both of these factors increase the transaction costs of decision-making.[16]

Club IGOs, such as the Group of Seven countries (G-7) or the OECD, use membership criteria to exclude states with different preference orderings and

---

[13] See chapter 5 for more on this example.

[14] Peter Haas, *Knowledge, Power, and International Policy Coordination* (Columbia: University of South Carolina Press, 1997); Kal Raustiala, "States, NGOs, and International Environmental Institutions," *International Studies Quarterly* 41 (December 1997): 719–40; Barnett and Finnemore, *Rules for the World*.

[15] Michael Walzer, *Spheres of Justice: A Defense of Pluralism and Equality* (New York: Basic Books, 1983), chap. 2. Walzer's typology included a fourth category of membership—families. There are IGOs in world politics that parallel this concept, such as the Commonwealth countries or the Organization of the Islamic Conference. However, these actors play a minimal role in global economic governance, and therefore this category is excluded from the analysis.

[16] On the tradeoff between legitimacy and efficiency, see Alexander Thompson, "Channeling Power: International Organizations and the Politics of Coercion" (PhD diss., University of Chicago, 2001).

bestow benefits for in-group members as a way to ensure collective action.[17] Compared to universal IGOs, clubs have reduced legitimacy because of their limited membership, though this can be partially compensated through other sources of legitimacy such as a reputation for effectiveness. Clubs also have the advantage of a membership with a more homogenous set of preferences. The smaller number of actors also increases a club's ability to coordinate and enforce policy.

Neighborhood IGOs, such as the Association of Southeast Asian Nations (ASEAN) or the Organization of American States (OAS), use geography to place a natural and fixed limitation on membership. That limitation means that these organizations have considerable legitimating power within the region but much less power outside it. States can use these institutions to bolster their bargaining position in global fora, as well as creating regional orders that affect significant trading partners. Regional hegemons will use them to coerce or induce economically dependent allies to adopt their positions.

What about NGOs?

International governmental organizations are part and parcel of mainstream international relations theory. International nongovernmental organizations pose a greater challenge, because by definition these entities are not the creatures of states.[18] However, in presenting NGOs and other nonstate organizations as distinct actors, it helps to compare them to IGOs as a way of isolating their distinct capabilities, strategies, and constraints.

One crucial difference is that NGOs are theorized as having an independent set of preferences. Whereas IGOs remain the creation of states, NGOs are the creation of like-minded private individuals who share a founding idea. These kinds of organizations are distinct in several ways from other kinds of political actors on the global stage. NGOs are more likely to embrace a single "missionary" idea that leads to a coherent set of preferences over means and ends.[19] Principled beliefs determine an institution's preferences over outcomes; causal beliefs determine an institution's preferences over possible strategies. Within NGOs, there is little disagreement over the goals. Indeed, NGOs will try to prevent the introduction of additional goals in order to avoid value conflicts

---

[17] James Buchanan, "An Economic Theory of Clubs," *Economica* 32 (February 1965): 1–14.

[18] There is some contention on this matter. If NGOs receive a disproportionate amount of their funding from official government assistance, then their relationship takes on a different cast.

[19] Stephen Hopgood, *Keepers of the Flame: Understanding Amnesty International* (Ithaca, NY: Cornell University Press, 2006); Daniel W. Drezner, "Ideas, Bureaucratic Politics, and the Crafting of Foreign Policy," *American Journal of Political Science* 44 (October 2000): 733–49.

or tradeoffs.[20] This allows members of a nongovernmental organization to maintain their intensity of preferences over means and ends; it also prevents the NGO from engaging in tradeoffs over competing goals.

What makes NGOs distinctive in world politics is that the principled beliefs they advance tend to emphasize humanitarian, altruistic, or ethical norms. These ends are usually divorced from material rewards that could benefit the NGO itself. To be sure, nongovernmental organizations will want to expand their budgets and staffs, but this is not the primary motivation for their behavior. NGOs are also less likely to compromise their positions when negotiating with other actors.[21] Because of the importance of the founding idea in fostering group cohesion, compromises can be seen as undercutting an organizational mission—and, concomitantly, an NGO's political strength.

Like IGOs, NGOs traffic in the logic of appropriateness to advance their interests. NGOs pursue a litany of public strategies designed to appeal to legitimating norms. These activities can be broadly categorized into advocacy and service functions. Advocacy activities are defined as efforts to alter existing governance structures and standards in directions consistent with NGO preferences. Actors enmeshed in global civil society will use a variety of tactics to campaign for their preferred regulatory outcomes—including the promulgation of ideal-type governance norms, transnational lobbying, "naming and shaming" exercises, and attracting media coverage and interest through mass protests.[22] The connections between NGOs and transnational social movements give these organizations a measure of popular legitimacy akin to IGOs enhancing the legitimacy of global governance structures through increasing membership.

NGOs can also provide service functions—defined as activities that aid in the monitoring and enforcement of existing sets of global standards.[23] Because NGOs have separate and independent networks of information gathering, their ability to observe defection from agreements adds a "fire-alarm" element

---

[20] Hopgood, *Keepers of the Flame*; Chaim Kaufmann and Robert Pape, "Explaining Costly International Moral Action," *International Organization* 53 (Autumn 1999): 631–68.

[21] In their survey of antiglobalization NGOs, Elliott, Kar, and Richardson divided the groups into "confronters" and "engagers." The former outnumbered the latter 59 percent to 41 percent. Kimberly Ann Elliott, Debayani Kar, and J. David Richardson, "Assessing Globalization's Critics: 'Talkers Are No Good Doers?'" in *Challenges to Globalization*, ed. Robert E. Baldwin and L. Alan Winters, 17–62 (Chicago: University of Chicago Press, 2004), appendix A.

[22] On the utility of protests, see Kate O'Neill, "Transnational Protest: States, Circuses, and Conflict at the Frontline of Global Politics," *International Studies Review* 6 (June 2004): 233–51.

[23] Ronald Mitchell, "Sources of Transparency: Information Systems in International Regimes," *International Studies Quarterly* 42 (March 1998): 109–30; Xinyuan Dai, "Information Systems of Treaty Regimes," *World Politics* 54 (July 2002): 405–36; Raustiala, "States, NGOs, and International Environmental Institutions."

to enforcement capabilities.[24] The networked structure of global civil society also facilitates the spread of information from one NGO to another. This activity can tilt the cost-benefit analysis of states toward NGO preferences.[25] Recent scholarship also suggests that NGOs, like IGOs, can confer legitimacy upon certain types of regulatory standards through the deployment of supportive discourse and technical expertise. A comparative advantage in specialized and/ or local knowledge can make nonstate actors a useful tool in the management of existing standards regimes.[26] NGOs possess an edge over IGOs because of their perceived autonomy from state influences. Because global civil society is seen as independent, their imprimatur for a particular form of regulatory coordination is less likely to be challenged as beholden to powerful interests.

Despite these similarities, NGOs lack important capabilities that IGOs possess, even in the use of normative power. Unlike international governmental organizations, nongovernmental organizations cannot create any formal legal obligation—an important element in using the logic of appropriateness. Nonstate actors can try to cajole states into agreeing to codified standards, but cannot create what states think of as law without their assent. NGOs also face a much greater difficulty engaging in collective action. International governmental organizations are purposefully designed to facilitate the collective action of member governments.[27] To be sure, an NGO's mere existence demonstrates that social movements can surmount the collective action problems of individuals. However, the greater number of actors within global civil society poses greater coordination problems among nonstate actors. Combine the collective action problem with the reluctance of NGOs to compromise on even a mild heterogeneity of preferences, and the barriers to coordinated action among global civil society begin to look even more formidable.[28]

[24] Raustiala, "States, NGOs, and International Environmental Institutions." See also Matthew McCubbins and Thomas Schwartz, "Congressional Oversight Overlooked: Police Patrols versus Fire Alarms," *American Journal of Political Science* 28 (February 1984): 165–79; Kal Raustiala, "Police Patrols, Fire Alarms, and the Structure of Information in International Agreements," paper presented at the University of Chicago's Program on International Politics, Economics, and Security, Chicago, IL, October 2003.

[25] Emily Meierding, "Transnational Advocates and the International Regulatory Process," paper presented at the University of Chicago's Program on International Political Economy and Security, Chicago, IL, May 2005.

[26] For a first-person account of how this works for environmental regimes, see Mostafa Tolba, *Global Environmental Diplomacy* (Cambridge, MA: MIT Press, 1998).

[27] Robert Keohane, *After Hegemony* (Princeton, NJ: Princeton University Press, 1984); Abbott and Snidal, "Why States Act through Formal International Organizations."

[28] The networked structure of global civil society can exacerbate collective action problems. Social theory suggests that networks function more efficiently when key nodes can properly function as focal points. However, as more actors become involved in a network, and as the heterogeneity of preferences increases, it becomes more difficult for those nodes to function properly. See Ronald S. Burt, "Models of Social Structure," *Annual Review of Sociology* 6 (1980): 79–141, and Robert Sugden, "A Theory of Focal Points," *Economic Journal* 105 (May 1995): 533–50.

More significant is the fact that NGOs lack the hard power resources that even IGOs possess to some degree. NGOs have limited budgets, small staffs, and have no ability to compel state action. While elements of global civil society can call for consumer boycotts or other forms of social action, these campaigns have a limited material impact. Nongovernmental organizations rely much more on the use of soft power rather than hard power.[29]

Like domestic actors referenced in the previous chapter, NGOs can try to exercise political voice as a means to lobby national governments. However, that chapter also argued that governments respond in a more concerted fashion when the use of political voice signals economic as well as political costs from pursuing a particular course of action. Unless global civil society is capable of highlighting the material costs from changing a set of standards, their use of political voice does not pack the same punch as actors with large asset-specific investments in the status quo.[30] Unless NGOs succeed in altering the normative discourse to the point where policy change becomes taboo for an overwhelming majority of the selectorate, their use of political voice should not be expected to succeed.

From this brief précis, it is straightforward to derive the following assumptions about NGO preferences strategies and constraints: (a) NGOs are assumed *ceteris paribus* to prefer more stringent social and business regulation over international economic activity; (b) NGOs will rely on the logic of appropriateness to affect global governance processes and outcomes; (c) NGO activities can be parsed into advocacy and service functions; (d) the influence of global civil society will be diluted when its members fail to overcome collective action problems.

A TYPOLOGY OF GLOBAL GOVERNANCE PROCESSES

What happens when regulatory coordination is contemplated in a world of many states, many IGOs, and global civil society? This section uses the theoretical findings from the last chapter as a starting point and then folds in the additional nonstate actors discussed in this chapter. The result is a 2X2 typology of four possible processes of regulatory coordination (see table 3.1): harmonized standards, club standards, rival standards, and sham standards. They are discussed in turn:

---

[29] Joseph Nye, *Soft Power: The Means to Success in World Politics* (New York: Public Affairs, 2004).

[30] Ironically, the existence of direct economic costs undercuts the normative power of the NGO. If a nongovernmental organization is perceived as acting in a self-interested manner, then any claim of acting altruistically is undercut. This is one reason why labor unions are not conventionally thought of as falling into the same category as labor rights NGOs such as Human Rights Watch.

TABLE 3.1
A Typology of Regulatory
Coordination

		Divergence of interests between great powers and other international actors	
		High conflict	*Low conflict*
Divergence of interests among great powers	*High conflict*	Sham standards	Rival standards
	Low conflict	Club standards	Harmonized standards

Harmonized Standards

In a harmonizing equilibrium, great powers and other governments expect to reap significant public benefits from coordination while incurring minimal adjustment costs. Because of the similarity of government preferences, the harmonization of domestic regulations is the most probable outcome. This situation requires little distributional bargaining to achieve regulatory coordination. When current distributional concerns are at a minimum, the paramount concerns in the creation of any global governance structure are maximizing efficiency and retaining influence in any proposed change in the rules.[31]

Because of the lack of distributional conflict among national governments, universal IGOs would appear to be the likeliest forum for the creation and management of a harmonized regime. These organizations help to maximize the number of states formally willing to cooperate, and the legitimacy derived from their membership size increases the social costs of defection for potentially recalcitrant states. At a minimum, one would expect to see a universal IGO provide political and rhetorical support for the regulatory regime.

---

[31] When there is significant uncertainty about future gains, it is likely that regimes will be created that allow for the adjustment of rules in the near future. Barbara Koremenos, "Contracting around International Uncertainty," *American Political Science Review* 99 (November 2005): 549–65.

However, while universal-membership IGOs may play a role in legitimating the regime, it is likely that great powers will prefer to delegate regime management to nonstate actors. Harmonized standards will therefore lead to a "regime complex" consisting of universal IGOs and private or quasi-private orders.[32] This is partly for functional reasons; NGOs plugged into public policy networks can have a comparative advantage in gathering information and developing the requisite technical expertise.[33] Another reason for delegation to nonstate orders is cost minimization. States will be eager to exploit the service functions of NGOs when they suit government purposes. As Kal Raustiala observes, "The chief result of the plethora of NGOs providing policy information and evaluation is that states can maximize policy information and research while minimizing expenditures. . . . By providing extensive information, evaluations, and legal opinions, NGO policy research permits governments to redirect scarce resources elsewhere."[34]

Most importantly, however, the delegation to nonstate actors also provides great powers a less public way of ensuring control over the regime's governance structure.[35] Even if there is a rough consensus among governments about the preferred regulatory standard today, that could change in the future. Exogenous shocks—rapid technological innovation, market dislocations, wars, or natural disasters—could affect the costs and benefits of a given standard. Changing the rules in a universal IGO is difficult, however, because of the transaction costs involved in managing the interstate consensus. Private or quasi-private orders offer another comparative advantage to great powers—a lack of transparency. Because these institutions are not accountable to home populations, they are less likely to have all of their activities publicly observed. This allows governments to make policy interventions behind the scenes. Great power governments can act like a board of directors: states devolve regime management to an NGO, while still ensuring that they can influence any renegotiation of the rules of the game.

There are a number of issue areas where nonstate actors supply the dominant global governance structure. The International Organization for Standardization is responsible for the promulgation of a large number of technical standards to ensure the interoperability of recondite equipment across borders.

[32] See Raustiala and Victor, "The Regime Complex for Plant Genetic Resources," for more on this term.

[33] Mitchell, "Sources of Transparency: Information Systems in International Regimes"; Wolfgang Reinicke, *Global Public Policy: Governing without Government?* (Washington, DC: Brookings Institution Press, 1998).

[34] Raustiala, "States, NGOs, and International Environmental Institutions."

[35] This parallels the argument in American politics that regulatory agencies will be designed so that the designers can maintain their influence even in the face of exogenous shocks. See Terry Moe, "The Politics of Structural Choice: Towards a Theory of Public Bureaucracy," in *Organization Theory*, ed. Oliver Williamson (New York: Oxford University Press, 1990).

Although the ISO is a private body of national standard-setting institutions, both the United States and the European Union have exerted their influence in order to steer ISO outcomes toward their preferred outcomes.[36] Similarly, the International Accounting Standards Committee (IASC) is a private sector body, sponsored by private national accounting associations. Its objective is the harmonization of accounting principles used by business and other organizations for financial reporting around the world. Toward this end, the IASC promulgates the International Accounting Standards. While ostensibly a non-political organization, the IASC standards reflect established best practices in the United States and Europe.[37]

A similar kind of governance comes from international commercial arbitration (ICA). The legal basis for the ICA regime comes from a universal IGO: the 1958 New York Convention on the Recognition and Enforcement of Foreign Arbitral Awards is a United Nations product. A significant fraction of states have ratified the 1958 treaty during the current era of globalization—approximately 45 percent of the 134 signatories have joined since 1989.[38] The governance structure of ICA resides in private arbitration bodies such as the International Court of Arbitration of the International Chamber of Commerce.[39] In the past five years alone, the demand for private arbitration has increased by over 25 percent.[40] The governance structure of modern-day arbitration echoes the Lex Mercatoria—a private order from the Middle Ages.[41] As in the other examples, states have assented to NGO management of the regime, while making sure they can influence outcomes at the appropriate time.[42]

[36] Walter Mattli and Tim Büthe, "Setting International Standards: Technological Rationality or Primacy of Power?" *World Politics* 56 (October 2003): 1–42; Jennifer Clapp, "The Privatization of Global Environmental Governance: ISO 14000 and the Developing World," *Global Governance* 4 (June 1998): 295–316.

[37] Leonardo Martinez-Diaz, "Strategic Experts and Improvising Regulators: Explaining the IASC's Rise to Global Influence, 1973–2001," *Business and Politics* 7 (December 2005): Article 3; Sarah B. Eaton, "Crisis and the Consolidation of International Accounting Standards: Enron, the IASB, and America," *Business and Politics* 7 (December 2005): Article 4; Beth Simmons, "The International Politics of Harmonization: The Case of Capital Market Integration," *International Organization* 55 (Summer 2001): 589–620.

[38] Data available from http://www.uncitral.org/uncitral/en/about/origin_faq.html#members, accessed May 3, 2006.

[39] Walter Mattli, "Private Justice in a Global Economy: From Litigation to Arbitration," *International Organization* 55 (Fall 2001): 921.

[40] Jennifer Hughes, "Businesses Adopt New Ways to Resolve Disputes," *Financial Times*, June 22, 2004.

[41] See Paul Milgrom, Douglass North, and Barry Weingast, "The Role of Institutions in the Revival of Trade: The Law Merchant, Private Judges, and the Champagne Fairs," *Economics and Politics* 2 (1991): 1–23.

[42] A. Claire Cutler, *Private Power and Global Authority* (Cambridge: Cambridge University Press, 2003); Amy Shalakany, "Arbitration and the Third World," *Harvard International Law Journal* 41 (2000): 419–68.

Club Standards

When the great powers face low adjustment costs but other countries have higher adjustment costs, the likely route to coordination is through club standards. From the analysis in chapter 2, we can infer that a great power concert will generate enough market power to lock in the concert's preferred set of regulatory standards. The combined market size of a great power concert will induce most recalcitrant states into shifting their standards. However, states with severe adjustment costs will still resist, and the Prisoner's Dilemma aspect of enforcement can tempt some governments into noncompliance; under this constellation of interests, the enforcement of standards becomes an issue. The crucial step for coordination to take place is a coalition of the willing among the great powers.

Again, the first-best option for great power governments would be to use universal-membership IGOs with strong enforcement mechanisms. As previously noted, however, opposition from the mass of states that prefer different standards diminishes the chances for effective governance in those fora.[43] Because international governmental organizations are employed for different purposes in maintaining club standards than harmonized standards, different IGOs are used to manage this regime. The distribution of actor interests in this case suggests that powerful states will rely on club IGOs. Stringent membership and accession criteria permit great powers to act in concert while limiting participation in rule formation to like-minded countries. The mere creation of a club can sufficiently alter market payoffs to nonmembers such that they want to join, even if they were better off under the status quo prior to the creation of a club.[44]

Club membership organizations can enhance the logic of consequences by coordinating monitoring and enforcement activities. Membership in a club raises the political costs of defection for members. In dealing with nonmembers, a club IGO can encourage the pooling of resources to induce outsiders into agreeing to the core's regulatory regime. Material inducements, such as aid or technical assistance, can encourage peripheral states to accept the imposed standard. Small country leaders that are sympathetic to the core position can also use pressure from an international organization to bypass entrenched domestic interests and other institutional roadblocks. For the most recalcitrant states, a club IGO greatly enhances the utility of multilateral coercion.[45] Once

[43] This is particularly true if the IGO operates on a one-country, one-vote principle. See Stephen D. Krasner, *Structural Conflict* (Berkeley: University of California Press, 1985).

[44] Lloyd Gruber, *Ruling the World: Power Politics and the Rise of Supranational Institutions* (Princeton, NJ: Princeton University Press, 2000).

[45] Martin, *Coercive Cooperation*; Daniel W. Drezner, "Bargaining, Enforcement, and Multilateral Economic Sanctions: When Is Cooperation Counterproductive?" *International Organization* 54 (Winter 2000): 73–102.

they join, they then have an incentive to pressure other governments into altering their regulatory standards.[46] This dynamic produces a cascade effect in which a club IGO expands to near-universal size.[47] Effective enforcement, as well as an expanding membership, allows a club IGO to use the logic of appropriateness as well as the logic of consequences.

NGOs play a less significant role in this equilibrium outcome, because the great powers are acting in concert and will rely on a club IGO to create, promote, and enforce the regime. If NGOs agree with the regulatory standard set by the core, the great powers will be happy to exploit the advocacy functions of NGOs and facilitate their role as proselytizers, promoting the merits of regulatory coordination to recalcitrant members of the periphery. This type of activity can allow the core to rely on persuasion rather than coercion to ensure global participation. If NGOs oppose the regulatory standard, they will be excluded from substantive access to the club IGO. In this scenario, NGOs can act as protestors, rallying popular support for states excluded from the club. In either case, their actual influence is marginal. NGOs will simply lack the material resources to successfully oppose a great power concert. They will also lack the ability to connect their political voice to economic costs that would dissuade the great powers from pursuing their plan of action. Even coordinated GCS efforts to alter global norms will not produce much in the way of altering club standards.

A recent example of club standards comes from the development of anticorruption standards. The growth of foreign direct investment created the prospect of multinational corporations bribing officials in host country governments to secure preferential access to markets and resources. The incentive for making bribes was so strong that in several European countries, a firm could deduct bribes from their tax obligations. Corrupt officials in developing countries were the most obvious beneficiaries of the status quo.

In the wake of several corruption scandals, the United States outlawed the bribery of foreign officials with the 1977 Foreign Corrupt Practices Act, but found it difficult to export that standard. Because repealing the law was a political nonstarter, U.S.-based multinationals like General Electric started to lobby for internationalizing the standard. GE was uncomfortable with some units of the firm operating under a different set of ethical standards.[48] EU

---

[46] See Gregory Shaffer, "Power, Nested Governance, and the WTO: A Comparative Institutional Approach," paper presented at the University of Chicago's Program on International Politics, Economics and Security, Chicago, IL, January 2004; Elizabeth DeSombre, "Baptists and Bootleggers for the Environment: Explaining the Origins of United States Unilateral Sanctions," *Journal of Environment and Development* 4 (January 1995): 53–75.

[47] The growth in membership of the WTO, as well as the international financial institutions, can be thought of in this way.

[48] Kenneth Abbott and Duncan Snidal, "Values and Interests: Rational Choice and the Use of International Legalization to Fight Corruption," paper prepared for a conference on "Rational Choice and International Law," University of Chicago Law School, April 27–28, 2001.

members were initially reluctant, but by the mid-1990s the combination of economic globalization, domestic corruption scandals, and U.S. diplomacy altered EU preferences.[49]

Initial efforts to draft an anticorruption treaty in the United Nations failed miserably, because of the diverging preferences of developing country governments.[50] Efforts at the OECD proved more fruitful, however, as a nonbinding 1994 recommendation was quickly transformed into the 1997 OECD Anti-Bribery Convention, which came into force in 1999.[51] The convention required states to outlaw most forms of bribery, as well as eliminate the tax deduction for such practices. The initial signatories included all thirty OECD members plus Argentina, Brazil, Chile, and Bulgaria.

The United States and European Union used a mixture of cajoling and coercion to export the standards contained in the OECD Convention. The OECD held a number of workshops for developing countries interested in participating. The United States and European Union worked to develop similar anti-bribery treaties in their neighborhoods, and to create incentives for participation. While negotiating the Anti-Bribery Convention, the United States also secured the Inter-American Convention against Corruption in 1996.[52] The United States also predicated access to aid from the Millennium Challenge Corporation on anticorruption measures.[53] Similarly, the Council of Europe produced a Civil Law Convention for its members. The European Union included anticorruption legislation in its *acquis communautaire* for countries interested in accession.[54] This led to a proliferation of these conventions across the globe.[55]

On the coercion side of the equation, there were different policies for signatories and nonsignatories. For the former, two phases of peer review were

---

[49] Wayne Sandholtz and Mark Gray, "International Integration and National Corruption," *International Organization* 57 (Fall 2003): 761–800; Kenneth Abbott and Duncan Snidal, "Values and Interests: International Legalization in the Fight against Corruption," *Journal of Legal Studies* 31 (January 2002): S141–S178; Kimberly Elliott, ed., *Corruption and the Global Economy* (Washington, DC: Institute for International Economics, 1997).

[50] John Braithwaite and Peter Drahos, *Global Business Regulation* (Cambridge: Cambridge University Press, 1999), 191–94; A. Timothy Martin, "The Development of International Bribery Law," *Natural Resources and Environment* 13 (Fall 1999).

[51] The text is available at http://www.oecd.org/document/21/0,2340,en_2649_34859_2017813_1_1_1_1,00.html, accessed March 2006.

[52] Sheila Lakhani and Bruce Zagaris, "The Emergence of an International Enforcement Regime on Transnational Corruption in the Americas," *Law and Policy in International Business* 30 (January 1999): 53–73.

[53] Steve Radelet, "Governance, Corruption, and the Millennium Challenge Account," in *Global Corruption Report 2004* (Washington, DC: Transparency International, 2004).

[54] Quentin Reed, "Corruption and the EU Accession Process: Who is Better Prepared?" in *Global Corruption Report 2004*.

[55] Peter Schroth, "The African Union Convention on Preventing and Combating Corruption," *Journal of African Law* 49 (January 2005): 24–38.

designed to ensure compliance; by 2005 all G-7 members had undergone both phases of review. For nonsignatories, the International Monetary Fund, World Bank, and regional development banks all began to attach anticorruption conditions to their loans. The World Bank in particular demonstrated a willingness to cancel loans if corruption was deemed to be a problem.[56] NGOs also acted as cheerleaders on the coercion side. Transparency International's development of a corruption index helped to focus global attention on the issue, naming and shaming the worst offenders.[57] The International Chamber of Commerce developed its own Rules of Conduct as well.

A decade after the initial push to develop a global standard, there have been some notable successes in the coordination of antibribery standards. All of the signatories to the OECD Convention have passed the necessary implementing legislation and undergone peer review.[58] The countries responsible for more than 80 percent of all foreign direct investment are signatories. Implementation has not been perfect by any means, and it is always difficult to measure changes in illicit activity. That said, scholarly analyses suggest that the club standard has had a pronounced impact on the behavior of multinational corporations and public officials alike.[59]

Rival Standards

When great powers lack a bargaining core among each other but can strike bargains with other countries, the outcome is one of rival standards. From the previous chapter, we know that when great powers have different starting points for regulatory standards, high adjustment costs can make cooperation impossible. Furthermore, great powers are less susceptible to economic coercion. They can thwart any organized multilateral attempt at pressure, and ad hoc pressure coalitions have a low probability of success.[60]

---

[56] Martin, "The Development of International Bribery Law"; Sebastian Mallaby, *The World's Banker: A Story of Failed States, Financial Crises, and the Wealth and Poverty of Nations* (New York: Penguin, 2004), chap. 7.

[57] Available at http://www.transparency.org/policy_and_research/surveys_indices/cpi, accessed March 2006.

[58] "The OECD Anti-Bribery Convention: Does It Work?' available at http://www.oecd.org/dataoecd/43/8/34107314.pdf, accessed March 2006.

[59] Carl Pacini, Judyth Swingen, and Hudson Rogers, "The Role of the OECD and EU Conventions in Combating Bribery of Foreign Public Officials," *Journal of Business Ethics* 37 (June 2002): 385–405; Jeremy Carver, "Combating Corruption: The Emergence of New International Law," *Forum du Droit International* 5 (2003): 119–23; Sandholtz and Gray, "International Integration and National Corruption." For a dissenting view, see Daniel Tarullo, "The Limits of Institutional Design: Implementing the OECD Anti-Bribery Convention," *Virginia Journal of International Law* 44 (March 2004).

[60] Drezner, "Bargaining, Enforcement, and Multilateral Economic Sanctions."

There remains the possibility, however, that if a great power amasses as many allies as possible to its preferred set of regulations, the combined market power of such a coalition could cross the tipping point and induce rival states to switch standards. Of course, all great powers have an incentive to adopt this strategy. The result is a competition to establish and expand regulatory blocs. Because economic coercion is more effective against small allied governments, rival regulatory spheres of influence will be created.

In terms of the governance process, great powers will choose international bargaining fora where the membership and the governance structure benefits their position. If possible, they will try to expand the membership of their preferred international body with members of the periphery that share their preferences.[61] The outcome is therefore one of rival standards. Different groups of countries will generate alternative sets of regulatory standards, while trying to weaken the legitimacy of competing standards.

International governmental organizations will therefore play a contested role in this scenario. Powerful states will forum-shop among IGOs with overlapping mandates until they find a situation where their preferences are likely to prevail. Great powers will want to ensure a friendly fora, so they are likely to seek as many allies as possible as a way to enhance the legitimacy and bargaining power of their preferred set of regulatory standards. At the same time, great powers will opt out, bypass, obstruct or simply ignore fora when they are on the losing side of a regulatory arrangement. IGOs of all stripes will be used, but great power conflicts will curtail their effectiveness. Rival standards show repeated cycles of bargaining, contestation, and conflict, creating the (accurate) appearance of a dysfunctional regime complex.

The rival standards scenario gives nonstate actors a theoretical opportunity to advance their own preferences. If NGOs are in sufficient agreement to form transnational activist networks, public policy networks or epistemic communities, they can act as consensus-builders.[62] Experts can lobby government bureaucrats, IGO secretariats, and corporate leaders as a way of building bottom-up support for their preferred position. Governments that face a combination of external pressure from other states and internal pressure from an array of domestic interests may alter their preference ordering to stay in power.[63] If peak elements of global civil society are successful, they can end the cycle of

---

[61] This is similar to Schattschneider's concept of audience expansion. E. E. Schattschneider, *The Semisovereign People* (New York: Holt, Rinehart and Winston, 1960).

[62] On transnational activist networks, see Margaret Keck and Kathryn Sikkink, *Activists beyond Borders* (Ithaca, NY: Cornell University Press, 1998); on public policy networks, see Reinicke, *Global Public Policy*, and Anne-Marie Slaughter, "The *Real* New World Order," *Foreign Affairs* 76 (September/October 1997): 183–97; on epistemic communities, see Peter Haas, "Introduction: Epistemic Communities and International Policy Coordination," *International Organization* 46 (Spring 1992): 1–35.

[63] Audie Klotz, *Norms in International Relations* (Ithaca, NY: Cornell University Press, 1995).

bargaining, defection, and conflict, converting an unstable equilibrium of rival standards into a more robust equilibrium of harmonized standards.

However, as previously noted, there are reasons to doubt that this theoretical possibility will be realized in most situations. The absence of a bargaining core among the great powers is a function of the adjustment costs faced by salient private actors in these countries. The groups that would lose out from any regulatory coordination proposed by global civil society have an obvious and strong incentive to create their own advocacy networks to counter global civil society. Great powers have an incentive to aid nonstate actors sympathetic to their position. Multinational corporations with an investment in the status quo have similar incentives to fund friendly NGOs. These counter-coalitions can constrain the ability of global civil society to rely on the logic of appropriateness to alter national preferences. For global civil society groups to triumph, they would have to be able to generate a substantive policy consensus in spite of the rhetorical and material resources of these groups. The conditions under which this could happen are extremely rare.

One example of the rival standards outcome is the international whaling regime. The United States supports a ban on the commercial hunting of all whales to protect the endangered species. Because of their politically powerful whaling industries—and consumer preferences for whale meat—Japan and several EU member states prefer reversing the ban. This conflict has played itself out repeatedly in the International Whaling Commission (IWC). Since 1986 a ban on commercial whaling has been in effect. Japan has tried to circumvent this rule by authorizing the hunting of more than five hundred whales in the North Pacific, ostensibly for scientific research—but much of the whale meat harvested from these scientific hunts has found its way into commercial restaurants.[64] In an effort to alter the status quo, Japan has attempted to pack the IWC membership with loyal votes, paying membership dues so microstates such as Dominica, Grenada, and the Solomon Islands can join. These countries have consistently supported Japan's position in return for large dollops of official development assistance, preventing the creation of new sanctuaries for whales in the South Pacific.[65] Environmental NGO support of the whaling ban has helped to solidify the antiwhaling coalition within the IWC. Furthermore, countries flatly opposed to the ban—such as Iceland and Norway—operate outside IWC strictures, making enforcement a problem. In June 2006, a razor-thin majority of IWC members voted in favor of lifting the ban on commercial

[64] Joshua Kurlantzick, "Kill Willy," *The New Republic* Online, August 3, 2004. Available at http://www.tnr.com/doc.mhtml?i=express&s=kurlantzick080304, accessed May 3, 2006.

[65] Mark Fineman, "Dominica's Support of Whaling Is No Fluke," *Los Angeles Times*, December 9, 1997, A1; Canute James, "Islands Wooed in Battle for Whale Sanctuary," *Financial Times*, May 24, 2001; "Six Caribbean Countries Are Still Unlikely to Support South Pacific Whale Sanctuary," Associated Press, July 22, 2001.

hunting—but fell short of the 75 percent support needed to reverse the moratorium. Thus, while the ban remains in effect, it remains an unstable equilibrium position, as the persistent conflict threatens to rupture the IWC.[66]

Sham Standards

The final category is the one least likely to lead to substantial coordination. In this scenario, minimal benefits from coordination or high adjustment costs leave great powers without a bargaining core between each other as well as other countries. In this situation, adjustment costs for all states are very high, constraining the ability of powerful states to attract allies.

One obvious outcome is the simple absence of any international regime, and therefore no global standard. Another possible outcome is the creation of sham standards. Governments will agree to a notional set of global standards with weak or nonexistent monitoring or enforcement schemes. Sham standards are useful to states of all stripes, because they permit governments to claim the de jure existence of regulatory coordination, even in the absence of effective enforcement. These standards act to relieve or redirect any domestic or civil society pressure for significant global regulations. They also create path dependencies in governance institutions that cast a shadow over future governance efforts.[67]

The absence of enforceable global standards does not mean that great powers will refrain from advancing their interests through other fora. They will use coercion to advance their regulatory preferences in a sham standards outcome, but its effect will be limited. Unilateral pressure can be effective if applied against a dependent ally, or against firms rather than states. Asymmetrically dependent states in the periphery will be willing to acquiesce because they care more about maintaining the trading relationship than the distributional implications of any concession.[68] Similarly, firms dependent on a great power market will acquiesce to coercive pressure.[69] Through these tactics, great powers will generate their own spheres of influence where their regulatory preferences hold.

---

[66] See the *Economist*, "Sharpening their Harpoons," July 27, 2001, at http://www.economist.com/agenda/displayStory.cfm?Story_ID=717306, accessed March 2006; Jennifer Bailey, "Arrested Development: 'The Prohibition of Commercial Whaling' as a Case of Failed Norm Change," paper presented at the International Studies Association annual meeting, San Diego, CA, March 2006.

[67] Douglass North, *Institutions, Institutional Change, and Economic Performance* (New York: Cambridge University Press, 1990); Raustiala and Victor, "The Regime Complex for Plant Genetic Resources."

[68] Drezner, *The Sanctions Paradox*; Drezner, "Outside the Box."

[69] George Shambaugh, *States, Firms, and Power* (Albany: State University of New York Press, 1999).

Two types of IGOs will be involved in the "management" of this type of regime complex. Universal IGOs will be the creators and stewards of any sham standards. At the same time, the absence of any interstate consensus will prevent any real enforcement from taking place. Great powers will also exploit neighborhood IGOs to expand the domain of their regulatory standards. Regional allies will be most vulnerable to coercive tactics, and the creation of regional standards increases a regional hegemon's bargaining leverage in any future global negotiations.[70]

Due to the absence of interstate consensus on regulatory coordination, NGOs have several possible roles to play in this type of international regime. In the absence of genuine international cooperation, NGOs will deploy both their service and advocacy capabilities to advance their regulatory preferences. First, they can try to enhance the legitimacy of sham standards by acting as an imperfect enforcement substitute. Enforcement activities could include "naming and shaming" exercises directed against firms concerned with brand image, the sponsoring of consumer boycotts, and direct action against noncompliant actors.[71] If successful, states and/or firms pay a price for violating these standards, in the form of a tainted political image or bad public relations. Second, NGOs can generate their own "voluntary" codes and standards and apply consumer pressure on multinational corporations to adhere to them. If efforts at enforcement fail, they can at least act as monitors and publicizers of corporate and state behavior. Third, NGOs can act as domestic lobbyists, cajoling great powers into narrowing their set of preferences so that interstate coordination is possible. As previously discussed in the section on rival standards, however, the presence of high adjustment costs make it unlikely that NGOs would succeed in substantially altering domestic preferences.

The international regime for labor standards represents an empirical example of this type of governance structure. Developing states adamantly oppose the strict enforcement of any global labor standard, fearing that they would act as a smokescreen for trade protectionism. The great powers are also far apart on the appropriate international standard. The U.S. government has historically pushed for the vigorous enforcement of minimal labor conditions, but does not want any harmonization of labor laws beyond those core standards. Some continental European states prefer more stringent rules regarding the minimum wage, guaranteed health benefits, and the power of peak union

---

[70] See the citations in the last two footnotes, as well as Edward Mansfield and Helen Milner, eds., *The Political Economy of Regionalism* (New York: Columbia University Press, 1997).

[71] For why the former strategies may work, see the *Economist*, "Brands: Who's Wearing the Trousers?" September 8, 2001; Deborah Spar, "The Spotlight and the Bottom Line," *Foreign Affairs* 77 (March/April 1998). For an example of direct action, see Jack Hitt, "Eco-Mercenaries," *New York Times Magazine*, August 4, 2002.

associations. Great Britain, however, has been particularly leery of any measure to enforce labor standards.[72]

Because of the lack of agreement within the core and the periphery, the international regime governing labor standards is weak. Several countries, trade unions, and human rights NGOs have lobbied forcefully to add labor regulation onto the WTO agenda. To date these efforts have been unsuccessful. The 1996 Singapore Ministerial meetings discussed whether the enforcement of core labor standards should be integrated into WTO decision-making.[73] Despite American efforts, opposition from developing countries and principal EU members stymied any attempt to formalize a WTO role in labor standards. The Ministerial Declaration that year rejected that outcome, instead reaffirming that "The International Labour Organization (ILO) is the competent body to set and deal with these standards." The only affirmative action was a commitment for the secretariats of the WTO and ILO to "continue their existing collaboration."[74] U.S. efforts to reintroduce the issue at the 1999 Seattle Ministerial also failed. Nearly a decade later, a Consultative Board report for the WTO's director-general candidly described the extent of cooperation between the two bodies as "loose."[75]

Attempts to enforce labor regulation through human rights treaties have also generated meager results. Since the end of the Second World War the United Nations has advanced a series of human rights treaties, ranging from the Universal Declaration of Human Rights to the International Covenant on Civil and Political Rights to the conventions on the treatment of migrant workers.[76] Several United Nations agencies are committed to the promulgation and oversight of these treaties. Both statistical analyses and comparative case studies, however, have demonstrated these treaties are a classic example of sham standards. They have no substantive effect on human rights practices—or, in some cases, a negative effect.[77] Oona Hathaway concludes, "because human rights treaties are

---

[72] Robert O'Brien, Anne Marie Goetz, Jan Aart Scholte, and Marc Williams, *Contesting Global Governance* (Cambridge: Cambridge University Press, 2000), chap. 3; Steve Charnovitz, "The Influence of International Labour Standards on the World Trading System: A Historical Overview," *International Labour Review* 126 (Winter 1987): 565–84; Charnovitz, "Promoting Higher Labor Standards," *The Washington Quarterly* 18 (Summer 1995): 167–90; interviews with ILO officials.

[73] O'Brien et al., *Contesting Global Governance*, chap. 3.

[74] World Trade Organization, Singapore Ministerial Declaration, December 12, 1996, paragraph 4, available at http://www.wto.org/English/thewto_e/minist_e/min96_e/wtodec_e.htm, accessed March 2006.

[75] Peter Sutherland et al., *The Future of the WTO: Addressing Institutional Challenges in the New Millennium* (Geneva: World Trade Organization, 2005), 36.

[76] For a complete list of UN human rights treaties, see the UN Office of the High Commissioner for Human Rights, "International Human Rights Instruments," at http://www.unhchr.ch/html/intlinst.htm, accessed March 2006.

[77] See Goldsmith and Posner, *The Limits of International Law*, chap. 4; Ellen Lutz and Kathryn Sikkink, "International Human Rights Law and Practice in Latin America," *International Organi-*

generally only minimally monitored and enforced, there is little incentive for ratifying countries to make the costly changes in actual policy that would be necessary to meet their treaty commitments." Jack Goldsmith and Eric Posner concur, noting that "modern multilateral human rights treaties have little exogenous influence on state behavior." They conclude: "most human rights practices are explained by coercion or coincidence of interest."[78]

The International Labor Organization has issued over a hundred conventions governing labor standards. In 1998, the ILO members agreed to a set of core labor standards—prohibition against abusive child labor, forced labor, discrimination in hiring practices, and the right to collective bargaining—requiring the adherence of all its members.[79] Compliance with these conventions has been erratic at best, however. ILO efforts to enforce core labor standards against even the worst offenders—like Myanmar—have proven to be ineffective at best and counterproductive at worst. More than a third of ILO members have not honored their reporting requirements.[80]

The weak global regime has led to a plethora of regional and private sets of standards. The European Union requires new entrants to adhere to a panoply of labor regulations contained in its *acquis communitaire*. The United States required Mexico to agree to enforce its own labor standards before joining NAFTA. The United States has also been willing to unilaterally coerce developing states into ratcheting up their labor standards.[81] Both the United States and the European Union have insisted on inserting and enforcing labor standards in their trade agreements with developing countries. These great power efforts have generated some policy successes directly correlated to the rigor with which labor standards are linked to trade access.[82]

At the same time, NGOs have tried to apply pressure on multinational firms to commit to voluntary sets of labor standards.[83] The most visible face of this

---

zation 54 (Summer 2000): 633–59; Oona Hathaway, "Do Human Rights Treaties Make a Difference?" *Yale Law Journal* 111 (June 2002): 1935–2042; Emilie Hafner-Burton, "Globalizing Human Rights? How Preferential Trade Agreements Shape Government Repression, 1972–2000" (PhD diss., University of Wisconsin, Madison, June 2003).

[78] Hathaway, "Do Human Rights Treaties Make a Difference?" 2020; Goldsmith and Posner, *The Limits of International Law*, 108, 134.

[79] OECD, *International Trade and Core Labour Standards* (Paris: OECD, 2000), part I.

[80] Kimberly Ann Elliott and Richard Freeman, *Can Labor Standards Improve under Globalization?* (Washington, DC: Institute for International Economics, 2003), 98–106; Associated Press, "SE Asian Labor Ministers Urge ILO to 'Understand' Myanmar," May 10, 2001.

[81] Peter Dorman, *Worker Rights and U.S. Trade Policy* (Washington, DC: U.S. Department of Labor, 1989); Kimberly Ann Elliott, "Preferences for Workers? Worker Rights and the U.S. Generalized System of Preferences," Working Paper, Institute for International Economics, May 2000.

[82] Emilie Hafner-Burton, "Trading Human Rights: How Preferential Trade Agreements Influence Government Repression," *International Organization* 59 (July 2005): 593–629.

[83] Gary Gereffi, Ronie Garcia-Johnson, and Erika Sasser, "The NGO-Industrial Complex," *Foreign Policy* 125 (July/August 2001): 56–65.

TABLE 3.2
Attributes of Different Global Governance Processes

	Sham Standards	Rival Standards	Club Standards	Harmonized Standards
State strategies	Unilateral coercion and inducements	Competing standards; Schatt-schneider-style expansion of audience if losing	Great power concert; multilateral coercion and inducements	Functional optimization, delegation
Predicted solution	Weakly enforced standards; repeated conflict	Competing standards in multiple fora; great power opt-outs; unstable equilibria	Concert-created and concert-imposed standards	Technical standards
IGO role	Political cover; regional bodies significant	Competing arenas for bargaining	Coalition-building, standard-setting, strong monitoring/ enforcement role	Legitimation
NGO role	Lobbyists; norm promoters; substitute enforcers	Consensus-builders	Proselytizers; protestors	Standard-setters

effort has been the attempt to highlight the use of sweatshop labor by multinational corporations such as Nike, or brands linked to celebrities such as Kathie Lee Gifford. These efforts have certainly led to patchwork progress, including changes in Nike's subcontracting operations and the creation of the UN's Global Compact as a way to improve labor conditions in emerging markets. However, these NGO campaigns have been less efficacious when the target has been subcontractors based in the Pacific Rim. The global coordination of labor standards remains weak.

The Role of Nonstate Actors in the Revisionist Model

Table 3.2 summarizes the principal traits of the various outcomes. The table illustrates the variety of IGOs employed in managing global regulations. One clear conclusion to draw is that the effectiveness of IGOs declines as great power disagreements rise. If a great power concert exists, then either club IGOs or universal IGOs are seen as critical actors in the coordination process. However, if no bargaining core among the powerful actors exists, then these same IGOs will experience intractable deadlocks, inconsistent articulations of policy, and weak enforcement. While one rationale for IGOs is their ability to increase the likelihood of effective multilateral cooperation, these abilities are irrelevant if the distribution of interests is sufficiently diverse.[84] The role and influence of nonstate actors varies widely from quadrant to quadrant, ranging from regime management to powerlessness in the face of a great power concert. However, there is an inverse correlation between NGO influence and the public visibility of these actors. The least powerful outcome for NGOs occurs when they rely on their advocacy capabilities to act as protestors in a club standards outcome. This is also the activity that generates the most attention, however. Similarly, "naming and shaming" activities, as well as consumer boycotts, feed off of publicity. However, material constraints hinder the ability of these actors to provide effective global governance on their own. And since these activities are likely to take place when great power preferences strongly diverge, the probability of these actors to affect intergovernmental cooperation is low. The service functions of NGOs are a vital part of global governance structures; the advocacy functions are peripheral.

The salience of great power preferences remains constant. The presence of a bargaining core among the great powers is a necessary and sufficient condition for effective global governance.[85] If these governments act in concert, the outcome is effective policy coordination regardless of the preferences or strategies of other actors. If these states have divergent preferences, then effective policy coordination is next to impossible.

Employing the concept of substitutability also makes it easier to understand the methodological and conceptual confusion in the literature on the relative power and influence of various actors, structures, and processes in an era of globalization. Past scholarship focusing on IGOs in global economic governance tended to treat all such organizations as the same type of actor. This overlooks the extent to which IGOs differ by membership and organizational structure. Furthermore, as Kal Raustiala and David Victor point out about the preexisting literature, "most empirical studies focus on the development of a single regime, usually centered on a core international agreement and administered by a discrete organization."[86] This overlooks the extent to which governance structures can act as substitutes. Ironically, liberal institutionalists have focused so much on demonstrating the existence of functional regimes that they have ignored the realpolitik implication of the growing thickness of international economic institutions; great powers will engage in forum-shopping to select the optimal IGO to advance their preferences. Activities by nonstate

---

[84] James Morrow, "Modeling the Forms of International Cooperation: Distribution versus Information," *International Organization* 48 (Summer 1994): 387–423.

[85] On the distinction between necessary and sufficient conditions in substitutability theory, see Gary Goertz, "Monitoring and Sanctioning in International Institutions: Nonsubstitutability and the Production of International Collective Goods," paper presented at the workshop on Substitutability and World Politics, Penn State University, State College, PA, June 2002.

[86] Raustiala and Victor, "The Regime Complex for Plant Genetic Resources," 278.

TABLE 3.3
Possible Case Structures and Outcomes

Standards Situation	Prominent Role for Great Powers Governments?	Prominent IGO Role?	Prominent NGO Role?	Effective Global Governance?
Harmonized	NO	NO	YES	YES
Harmonized	NO	YES	YES	YES
Core	YES	YES	NO	YES
Core	YES	YES	YES	YES
Rival	YES	YES	YES	NO
Rival	YES	NO	YES	NO
Sham	NO	YES	YES	NO
Sham	YES	NO	YES	NO

actors may be relevant to the regulatory process, but are epiphenomenal to the regulatory outcome.

The failure to recognize the substitutability of governance structures, and the presence of a bargaining core among the great powers as a necessary condition for regulatory coordination to take place, also explains the murky empirical work on global governance. Table 3.3 shows a variety of possible case structures consistent with the model developed here. If a researcher focused primarily on IGO or NGO activity as their independent variable, it would be possible to show instances in which these actors are effective, and instances in which they are not. Unless the distribution of interests and the substitutability of governance structures are taken into account, it would be impossible to develop a model that garners significant empirical support. Once NGOs and IGOs are reconceived as intervening processes rather than governance outcomes, their roles and varying effectiveness make much more sense.

CONCLUSIONS

Significant empirical work remains to substantiate the theoretical propositions made in this chapter and the previous one. Nevertheless, this model does suggest some intriguing conclusions for international relations theory in an era of globalization—particularly the relationship between states, IGOs, and nonstate actors. The debate about the relevance of nonstate actors is not a recent one, but globalization has intensified the argument. Some scholars exaggerate the impotence of the state, interpreting a failure to perfectly regulate a sphere of social life as an example of a general retreat of the Westphalian system. However, statists commit the same error, highlighting the vast areas of world politics where nonstate actors have minimal influence. Both sides generalize from their most favorable cases.

The role and effectiveness of both NGOs and IGOs must be viewed in the context of state power and preferences. NGOs can range from playing a paramount role in regime management (harmonized standards) to cheerleading on the sidelines (club standards) to acting as imperfect substitutes for state action (sham standards). The typology of regulatory coordination proposed here could prove useful in explaining when, rather than if, NGOs will play an important role in international affairs. Similarly, this theory demonstrates the extent to which great powers will engage in forum-shopping to match the proper IGO to the proper political environment. Each type of IGO proves useful for different constellations of state interests. Club IGOs are most prominent when great powers are in agreement but smaller states experience high adjustment costs. Neighborhood or regional IGOs prove useful as a means for powerful states to develop regulatory spheres of influence. Universal IGOs will have a spotty track record of success. In the case of harmonized standards, these organizations will play a legitimating role. In the case of sham standards, these IGOs will be set up to fail.

This chapter also has implications for the scholarly debate about the extent to which international agreements require enforcement. For some cases, such as harmonized standards, coordination requires little enforcement, which is consistent with the management approach to international compliance.[87] However, for the other quadrants, cooperation will be difficult to achieve, and in the cases of club standards, disagreement will often involve threats of coercion. This is consistent with arguments that effective cooperation only occurs under a limited set of circumstances.[88]

The revisionist theory makes it clear that great powers are the key actors in determining the pattern of global regulatory regimes. If they can agree among themselves, coordination will occur regardless of NGO, IGO, and peripheral state preferences. Opposition from these actors affects the means of regulatory coordination, not the ultimate end. Furthermore, great powers will rely on nonstate actors for certain functional purposes. By giving the great powers pride of place in the global political economy, it is easier to understand how other actors can maximize their influence over the process of global economic governance.

---

[87] Abram Chayes and Antonia Handler Chayes, "On Compliance," *International Organization* 47 (Spring 1993): 175–206.

[88] George Downs, David Rocke, and Peter Barsoom, "Is the Good News about Compliance Good News about Cooperation?" *International Organization* 50 (Summer 1996): 379–406.

PART II • PRACTICE

CHAPTER FOUR

The Global Governance of the Internet

THE SCHOLARLY RESEARCH on the Internet encapsulates all of the theoretical problems with the literature on globalization and global governance, only in a more concentrated form. For many international relations theorists, *the* defining feature of the Internet is that it "overcomes all barriers of territorial distance and borders."[1] Because the costs of communication are so low on the Internet, nonstate actors can coordinate their activities to a much more sophisticated degree than in the past. Internet sites can be located anywhere in the globe, making it theoretically possible for business and individuals to bypass bothersome regulations. It seems difficult to reconcile state regulations with the decentralized structure of the computer network.[2] In the place of the state, cyber-analysts posit a governance structure with more emphasis on direct democracy and open debate, guided by an epistemic community of cyber-enthusiasts that embrace a libertarian creed of no state interference.[3] If globalization has altered international regulatory regimes, its effects should be most pronounced in the regulation of the Internet itself.

This chapter examines the global governance of the Internet more closely to see if the theory presented in the previous section can explain the variation in governance process and outcomes. The international regulation of the Internet provides a fertile testing ground for these arguments. Prior analysis on regulating the Internet has been less than enlightening, due in part to the assumption that all Internet-related activity can be defined along a single policy dimension. In fact, the Internet has generated multiple regulatory issue areas, including the development of technical protocols, content restrictions, e-taxation, intellectual property, and privacy rights. For many of these issue areas, states express divergent interests, halt cross-border online transactions that contradict their preferences, and use international governmental organizations and treaties to advance their preferences. Even on issues in which there are large zones of agreement, such as the standardization of technical proto-

---

[1] Jan Aart Scholte, *Globalization: A Critical Introduction* (New York: St. Martin's Press, 2000), 75. See also Stephen Kobrin, "Territoriality and the Governance of Cyberspace," *Journal of International Business Studies* 32 (Fall 2001): 687–704.

[2] Virginia Haufler, *A Public Role for the Private Sector* (Washington, DC: Carnegie Endowment for International Peace, 2001), 82.

[3] John Perry Barlow, "A Declaration of the Independence of Cyberspace," http://www.islandone.org/Politics/DeclarationOfIndependance.html, September 2, 1996, accessed March 2006.

cols, great powers will manipulate private forms of authority to achieve their desired ends.

These cases also make clear that the substitutability principle is essential to understanding the process of global governance. States can and will substitute different governance structures within a common regime complex, and they will substitute different policy tools to create those structures, depending on the constellation of great power interests. Because scholars have failed to consider the delegation strategy as a conscious state choice, they have misinterpreted the state's role in the global governance of the Internet.[4]

This chapter is divided into seven sections. The next section briefly reviews the existing arguments on the Internet and international relations, and contrasts those predictions with the revisionist model. The third section surveys the state of play on the regulation of Internet content, and finds that it fits the sham standards outcome. The fourth section examines how intellectual property rights are enforced in e-commerce; consistent with the distribution of interests across states, the process and outcome closely match the club standards template. The fifth section looks at data privacy as an example of rival standards. The sixth section reviews the international regimes regulating the technical protocols that form the backbone of the Internet. This section confirms that even when states agree about regulatory outcomes, great powers will delegate regime management to nonstate actors, where their influence still dominates the outcome. There is a common denominator in the behavior of states in all of these issue areas—governments acting decisively to protect their interests. The final section considers the ramifications for the study of globalization and global governance.

Globalization and the Internet: The Accepted Wisdom

As noted in chapter 1, two themes run through much of the globalization discourse. The first is that globalization undercuts state sovereignty, weakening a government's ability to effectively regulate its domestic affairs. The second is that as state power has waned, globalization simultaneously enhances the power of nonstate actors via the reduction of transaction costs across borders. Ronnie Lipschultz and Cathleen Fogel encapsulate this view when they write, "The 'fluidization' of regulatory space is a feature arising from globalization, the declining authority of the state, and the growing tendency of individuals and organizations to act outside traditional roles and frameworks."[5] Interna-

---

[4] For an exception, see Christoph Knill and Dirk Lehmkuhl, "Private Actors and the State: Internationalization and Changing Patterns of Governance," *Governance* 15 (January 2002): 41–63.

[5] Ronnie D. Lipschultz and Cathleen Fogel, "Regulation for the Rest of Us?" in *The Emergence of Private Authority in Global Governance*, ed. Rodney Bruce Hall and Thomas J. Biersteker (Cambridge: Cambridge University Press, 2002), 122.

tional relations theorists, public intellectuals, and cyber-enthusiasts agree that the Internet greatly enhances these effects of globalization.

Regarding state power, Viktor Mayer-Schönberger and Deborah Hurley observe, "Governance based on geographic proximity, territorial location and exclusivity of membership to such physical communities will be fundamentally challenged by the advent of numerous non-proximity based, overlapping virtual communities."[6] David Post and David Johnson assert, "The volume of electronic communications crossing territorial boundaries is just too great in relation to the resources available to government authorities."[7] Frances Cairncross notes, "Government jurisdictions are geographic. The Internet knows few boundaries. The clash between the two will reduce what individual countries can do. Government sovereignty, already eroded by forces such as trade liberalization, will diminish further. . . . *One result: no longer will governments be able to set the tax rates or other standards they want.*"[8] Cyber-guru John Perry Barlow opined that, "By creating a seamless global economic zone, borderless and unregulatable, the Internet calls into question the very idea of the nation-state."[9]

There is also general agreement that the Internet enhances the power of nonstate actors, permitting them to network at an ever-increasing level of sophistication. Ronald Deibert argues: "What the Internet has generated is indeed a new 'species'—a cross-national network of citizen activists linked by electronic mailing lists and World-Wide Web home pages that vibrate with activity, monitoring the global political economy like a virtual watchdog."[10] Craig Warkentin and Karen Mingst reach a similar conclusion: "the nature and possibilities of the World Wide Web combined with those of an emergent global civil society . . . create a new international political environment, one in which state sovereignty was constrained and NGOs—as key actors in civil society—were able to work in novel and notably effective ways."[11] The in-

---

[6] Viktor Mayer-Schönberger and Deborah Hurley, "Globalization of Communication," in *Governance in a Globalizing World*, ed. Joseph S. Nye and John Donahue (Washington, DC: Brookings Institution, 2000), 23. See also Geoffrey Herrera, "The Politics of Bandwidth: International Political Implications of a Global Digital Information Network," *Review of International Studies* 28 (January 2002): 93–122; and Richard Latham, "Information Technology and Social Transformation," *International Studies Review* 4 (Spring 2002): 101–15.

[7] David Johnson and David Post, "The Rise of Law in Cyberspace," *Stanford Law Review* (1996): 1372.

[8] Frances Cairncross, *The Death of Distance*, 2nd ed. (Cambridge, MA: Harvard Business School Press, 2000), 177 (emphasis is added).

[9] John Perry Barlow, "Thinking Locally, Acting Globally," *Time*, January 15, 1996, 76.

[10] Ronald Deibert, "International Plug 'n' Play? Citizen Activism, the Internet, and Global Public Policy," *International Studies Perspectives* 1 (July 2000): 264. See also Stephen M. Kobrin, "Economic Governance in an Electronically Networked Society," in *The Emergence of Private Authority in Global Governance*, ed. Rodney Bruce Hall and Thomas J. Biersteker (Cambridge: Cambridge University Press, 2002).

[11] Craig Warkentin and Karen Mingst, "International Institutions, the State, and Global Civil Society in the Age of the World Wide Web," *Global Governance* 6 (June 2000): 1.

creased coordination of protests at venues like Seattle, Prague, Genoa, and Barcelona speaks to the sophistication of nonstate actors in the Internet age.[12]

Following these arguments to their logical conclusion, the effects of globalization should be at their most concentrated when the object of regulation is the Internet itself. Internet governance should see states at their most enfeebled and nonstate actors at their most powerful. This is certainly the conclusion of most international relations scholars who study the Internet. Deborah Spar observes, "International organizations lack the power to police cyberspace; national governments lack the authority; and the slow pace of interstate agreement is no match for the rapid-fire rate of technological change."[13] Virginia Haufler concurs, noting, "The decentralized, open, global character of . . . the Internet makes it difficult to design and implement effective regulations through top-down, government-by-government approaches."[14]

Cyber-enthusiasts concur with this assessment. Nicholas Negroponte, the cofounder of MIT's Media Lab, states: "The Internet cannot be regulated. It's not that laws aren't relevant, it's that the nation-state is not relevant."[15] A joint study commissioned for the Defense Department in 1998 observed:

> [I]t may be that the real problem created for governments by the proliferation of the Internet (and other IT-enhanced communications media) is not the proliferation of information so much as the proliferation of actors on the governmental and diplomatic stages. Organized groups and individuals can build, and in fact are building, coalitions, both domestic and international, that can bring unprecedented pressure to bear on national governments regarding virtually any activity or area of interest. These groups may in fact create *faits accomplis* that require no more action of governments than to accept what has already been accomplished. This raises the question of whether the nature of sovereignty has changed in the area of instant and ubiquitous communications and, if so, how.[16]

Indeed, a cursory review of the nonstate actors involved in the regulation of the Internet—the Global Business Dialogue on e-Commerce (GBDe), Internet

[12] The coordination of worldwide protests that took place in the run-up to the Second Gulf War would seem to be further evidence of this phenomenon. See, for example, George Packer, "Smart-Mobbing the War," *New York Times Magazine*, March 9, 2003.

[13] Deborah Spar, "Lost in (Cyber)space: The Private Rules of Online Commerce," in *Private Authority and International Affairs*, ed. A. Claire Cutler, Tony Porter, and Virginia Haufler (Albany: State University of New York Press, 1999), 47. Spar refined this view in *Ruling the Waves* (New York: Harcourt Brace, 2001).

[14] Haufler, *A Public Role for the Private Sector*, 82.

[15] Quoted in Andrew Higgins and Azeem Azhar, "China Begins to Erect Second Great Wall in Cyberspace," *The Guardian*, February 5, 1996.

[16] Seymour E. Goodman et al., *The Global Diffusion of the Internet Project: An Initial Inductive Study* (Washington, DC: The MOSAIC Group, 1998), 21, quoted in Helen Milner, "The Digital Divide: The Role of Political Institutions in Technology Diffusion," paper presented at the American Political Science Association annual meeting, Philadelphia, PA, August 2003.

Engineering Task Force (IETF), Internet Society (ISOC), and Internet Corporation for Assigned Names and Numbers (ICANN)—suggests the existence of a strong, coherent epistemic community on these issues. Examining Internet regulation is a tough test for any theory of international regulatory regimes that gives pride of place to nation-states.

Content Regulation: When States Disagree

Countries have wildly divergent preferences over the extent to which Internet content should be regulated. A Bertelsmann Foundation—sponsored study concluded, "It is not possible to arrive at a general definition of offensive or undesirable Internet content. Internet users' moral sensitivity is determined, *inter alia*, by national, cultural, religious, and political views and beliefs."[17] At the governmental level, these preferences are clearly a function of regime type and cultural history. Nondemocratic regimes must balance the potential economic gains from an unfettered Internet with the loss of power that status quo rulers inevitably face when confronted with an important technological innovation. Individual autocratic governments will place different weights on these issues. Totalitarian governments such as Cuba, Myanmar, or Saudi Arabia want absolute control over citizen access to the Internet. Authoritarian governments such as Singapore or China want to exploit the Internet's commercial opportunities while restricting use of the Internet for political criticism.

This does not mean that liberal democracies are in agreement on content regulation. Although these governments are not worried about the Internet as a source for violent regime change, liberal democracies may wish to place restrictions on what are considered to be "offensive" forms of content. Not surprisingly, tastes on what is offensive vary across countries—even among OECD members. As Amitai Etzioni concludes, "the Internet carries harmful messages—racist, violent, pornographic, and damaging to children—but so far we have not formed a shared moral sense about whether free speech in cyberspace should trump all other normative considerations."[18] For this issue, there is no bargaining core among governments. The predicted outcome would be the unilateral use of national regulation to bar undesired content, and the creation of sham standards at the global level.

Internet enthusiasts have long dismissed the ability of states to block specific kinds of Internet content. In 1993 John Gilmore, a cofounder of the Electronic Frontier Foundation, famously concluded: "The Net interprets censorship as damage and routes around it." More recently, New York Times columnists Nich-

---

[17] Marcel Machill, Thomas Hart, and Bettina Kaltenhäuser, "Structural Development of Internet Self-Regulation," *Info* 4 (September/October 2002): 45.

[18] Amitai Etzioni, *From Empire to Community* (New York: Palgrave Macmillan, 2004), 7.

olas Kristoff and Thomas Friedman argued that the Internet enervates authoritarian regimes, with Friedman asserting that, "the Internet and globalization are acting like nutcrackers to open societies."[19] However, the evidence strongly suggests that states can regulate Internet content when they so desire. Technological measures include the creation of firewalls, proxy servers, routers, and software filters to block content labeled as undesirable. Nontechnological measures include the imprisonment of relevant individuals, active policing, high taxation, and pressuring Internet service providers (ISPs).[20] Even if these measures are not 100 percent effective, their enactment affects the cost/benefit analysis of individuals seeking to use the Internet as a means of acquiring officially frowned-upon content. As Jack Goldsmith observes: "If governments can raise the cost of Net transactions, they can regulate Net transactions."[21] Combined, these steps can block undesired content, as well as retard Internet use.

The result has been effective government regulation of Internet content across a wide range of countries. For totalitarian states, the modes of regulation have been crude but effective. Cuba simply outlawed the sale of personal computers to individuals; until 2002, Myanmar outlawed personal ownership of modems.[22] Middle Eastern countries have been especially vigilant in blocking undesirable content. Iranian president Mohammad Khatami said in December 2003 that, "We are exerting control over pornographic and immoral websites that are not compatible with Islam." In the fall of 2004 the government went further, blocking hundreds of prodemocracy Web sites and weblogs. The Syrian government arrested numerous citizens for using the Internet to send information about government demonstrations.[23] Saudi Arabia censors the Internet by requiring all Web access to be routed through a proxy server that the government edits for content, blocking access to pornographic, religious, and politically sensitive material.[24] One assessment of the Saudi filtering system

---

[19] Quoted in Jack Goldsmith and Timothy Wu, *Who Controls the Internet? Illusions of a Borderless World* (New York: Oxford University Press, 2006), 89.

[20] Jesse Scanlon, "7 Ways to Squelch the Net," *Wired*, August 2003. Available at http://www.wired.com/wired/archive/11.08/start.html?pg=5, accessed March 2006.

[21] Jack Goldsmith, "Regulation of the Internet: Three Persistent Fallacies," *Chicago-Kent Law Review* 73 (December 1998): 1123.

[22] Robert Lebowitz, "Cuba Prohibits Computer Sales," Digital Freedom Network, http://dfn.org/news/somalia/sparse-internet.htm, March 26, 2002, accessed May 28, 2002. Associated Press, "Internet Remains Prohibited in Myanmar," May 3, 2000. Myanmar's expansion of Internet access was strictly regulated to screen out any politically sensitive material. See Amy Kazmin, "Burmese get Glimpse of Superhighway," *Financial Times*, April 25, 2002.

[23] *BBC News*, "Iran's President Defends Web Control," December 12, 2003; Nazila Fathi, "Iran Jails More Journalists and Blocks Web Sites," *New York Times*, November 8, 2004; Lillian Swift, "Iran's War on Weblogs," *Daily Telegraph*, November 28, 2005; *BBC News*, "Syrian Jailed for Internet Usage," June 21, 2004.

[24] Khalid Al-Tawil, "The Internet in Saudi Arabia," *Telecommunications Policy* 25 (September 2001): 625–32.

concluded that substantial amounts of Web content are "effectively inaccessible" from Saudi Arabia.[25]

Authoritarian states with a greater interest in exploiting the Internet to boost economic growth have succeeded in restricting political content on the Internet without sacrificing its commercial possibilities. The model for this sort of regulatory effort is Singapore. The government has been eager to attract investment in information technologies. Nevertheless, Singapore regulates the Internet the same way it regulates print or broadcast media, effectively deleting what the government considers to be offensive or subversive material. As information minister George Yeo explained in 1995: "Censorship can no longer be 100 percent effective, but even if it is only 20 percent effective, we should not stop censoring."[26] The evidence suggests that the government has been far more successful than 20 percent. A 1996 law required all political parties, religious organizations, and any individuals with Web pages discussing either religion or politics to register with the Singapore Broadcasting authority. Gerry Rodan, reviewing the government's efforts to control Internet content, concludes, "When the political will to obstruct certain information and views is coupled with such variables as an efficient and technically competent bureaucracy, an established regime of political intimidation and surveillance, and embedded corporatist structures facilitating cooperation between state officials and administrators across the public and private sectors, you have a formidable mix."[27]

Singapore's approach has been the model for many East Asian governments, including China.[28] Starting in 2000, China passed a series of laws criminalizing the production or consumption of "unauthorized" political content.[29] In July 2002, China was able to persuade more than three hundred Internet service providers and Web portals, including Yahoo!, to sign a voluntary pledge refraining from "producing, posting, or disseminating pernicious information that may jeopardize state security and disrupt social stability."[30] The central government also rerouted attempts to access search engines like Google to search engines owned or regulated by the government, and ordered equipment

[25] Jonathan Zittrain and Benjamin Edelman, "Documentation of Internet Filtering in Saudi Arabia," Berkmen Center for Internet and Society, Harvard University, http://cyber.law .harvard.edu/filtering/saudiarabia/, July 2002, accessed March 2006.

[26] Quoted in Garry Rodan, "The Internet and Political Control in Singapore," *Political Science Quarterly* 113 (Spring 1998): 80.

[27] Ibid., 88.

[28] Ibid.; Georgette Wang, "Regulating Network Communication in Asia," *Telecommunications Policy* 23 (April 1999): 277–87; Shanthi Kalathil, "China's Dot-Communism," *Foreign Policy* 122 (January/February 2001): 74–75.

[29] Ethan Gutmann, "Who Lost China's Internet?" *The Weekly Standard*, February 25, 2002. See, more generally, Goldsmith and Wu, *Who Controls the Internet?*, chap. 6.

[30] Christopher Bodeen, "Web Portals Sign China Content Pact," Associated Press, July 15, 2002.

from Cisco to automatically block undesirable Web pages.[31] By 2005, China had required bloggers to register with the government and was increasing its crackdown on cyber-dissidents.[32] In January 2006 Google agreed to create a China-based search engine that complied with the government's censorship policy. Google's acquiescence epitomizes the eagerness of multinational corporations to comply with Beijing's demands in order to access the Chinese marketplace.[33]

Nondemocratic regimes have taken pains to regulate Internet content; have they been successful? One obvious way to measure this is the extent to which Internet access is limited in these countries. Cross-national studies provide strong support for the argument that authoritarian and totalitarian regimes have been successful in blunting the spread of the Internet. One 2001 study found that the combined Internet bandwidth used by eight Arab countries was roughly equal to five hundred cable modem subscribers in the United States.[34] Richard Beilock and Daniela Dimitrova found that countries with lower Freedom House scores for civil liberties had significantly lower Internet usage—even after controlling for economic development.[35] Helen Milner's research into Internet diffusion generated similar results. Time series cross-sectional regressions using multiple measures of regime type demonstrate that, *ceteris paribus*, democracies permit much greater access, both in terms of Internet users per capita and Internet hosts per capita.[36]

This does not mean that the European Union and United States see eye to eye on content regulation. Public opinion polls reveal sharp divergences over which content is so offensive that it merits blocking. On the one hand, in one poll 58 percent of Germans favored the restriction of extreme left-wing or right-wing political rhetoric on the Internet—as opposed to 28 percent of Americans. On the other hand, 43 percent of Americans favored blocking Web

---

[31] Joseph Kahn, "China Toughens Obstacles to Internet Searches," *New York Times*, September 12, 2002.

[32] Howard French, "China Tightens Restrictions on Bloggers and Web Owners," *New York Times*, June 8, 2005; Paul Mooney, "China Wages a New War on Academic Dissent," *Chronicle of Higher Education*, June 17, 2005.

[33] Anne Applebaum, "Let a Thousand Filters Bloom," *Washington Post*, July 20, 2005; Evan Osmos, "Global Pursuits Leave Web Firms in Quandary," *Chicago Tribune*, September 12, 2005; David Barboza, "Version of Google in China Won't Offer E-Mail or Blogs," *New York Times*, January 24, 2006; Adam Penenberg, "Search Engine Diplomacy," *Slate*, January 31, 2006.

[34] ClickZ Stats, "Arab World Suffering from Bandwidth Drought," September 6, 2001, available at http://www.clickz.com/stats/big_picture/geographics/print.php/879641, accessed March 2006.

[35] Richard Beilock and Daniela Dimitrova, "An Exploratory Model of Inter-Country Internet Diffusion," *Telecommunications Policy* 27 (April/May 2003): 237–52.

[36] Milner, "The Digital Divide." See also Shanthi Kalathil and Taylor C. Boas, *Open Networks, Closed Regimes: The Impact of the Internet on Authoritarian Rule* (Washington, DC: Carnegie Endowment for International Peace, 2003).

sites with nudity—in contrast to only 13 percent of Germans.[37] While some areas—such as child pornography—generate a greater consensus among the great powers, material labeled as offensive by one government is often tolerated by other governments.

In Europe, the strong preference for the regulation of hate speech on the Internet has translated into laws outlawing such content on the Internet.[38] The most notorious example is the French success in legal efforts to get Yahoo! to drop Nazi paraphernalia from its auction site. Because of the number of "mirror" servers that target Web sites to particular geographic areas, governments have developed the means to censor the national content of the Web without globally censoring the distribution of information.[39] An EU Commerce Directive requires local ISPs to screen out any illegal content—and this directive has been met with general compliance.[40] Unilateral content regulation has succeeded despite the strong normative consensus among Internet enthusiasts against such regulation.[41]

The 9/11 terrorist attacks, and the use of the Internet by the terrorists to communicate with one another, only accelerated the pace of content regulation in the developed world. In September 2002, one advocacy group concerned with press freedom noted, "The United States, Britain, France, Germany, Spain, Italy, Denmark, the European Parliament, the Council of Europe and the G8 nations have all challenged cyber-freedoms over the past year."[42]

Human rights NGOs and other elements of global civil society have protested these disparate national efforts to curb Internet content, but this has not led to the creation of any effective system of global governance on the matter. International governmental organizations have been largely hamstrung by the extreme distribution of state preferences over content regulation. This was reflected in the first meeting of the World Summit for the Information Society (WSIS), held in December 2003. One of the key sticking points at the WSIS was the language regarding the extent to which any agreement would affect the regulation of speech on the Internet. China in

---

[37] Polling data from Machill, Hart, and Kaltenhäuser, "Structural Development of Internet Self-Regulation," 39–55.

[38] See, for example, Wendy McAuliffe, "Europe Hopes to Outlaw Hate Speech Online," CNET News.com, November 12, 2001, available at http://news.com.com/2102-1023-275708.html, accessed November 20, 2002; Declan McCullagh, "U.S. Won't Support Net 'Hate Speech' Ban," CNET News.com, November 15, 2002, available at http://news.com.com/2102-1023-956983.html, accessed November 20, 2002.

[39] Goldsmith and Wu, *Who Controls the Internet?*, chap. 1.

[40] Ibid., 73.

[41] Human Rights Watch, "Free Expression on the Internet," http://www.hrw.org/advocacy/internet/, accessed May 25, 2002.

[42] Reporters without Borders, "The Internet on Probation," http://www.rsf.fr/IMG/doc-1274.pdf, September 2002, accessed September 6, 2002.

particular protested the U.S.-inspired text regarding press freedoms. As a result, although language was inserted into the Declaration of Principles that specifically addressed press freedoms, it was watered down. Language reaffirming state sovereignty was also added.[43] The Plan of Action also committed governments to "Take appropriate measures—consistent with freedom of expression—to combat illegal and harmful content in media content."[44] Outside observers agreed that the language papered over irreconcilable differences about content regulation, and that the plan of action provided little guidance for the future.[45]

The absence of any interstate coordination does not mean that there have been no efforts to create global governance structures to regulate content. In 1999, a group of nonprofit organizations and multinational corporations formed the Internet Content Rating Association (ICRA) to devise a means of letting users filter offensive content.[46] Not surprisingly, the ICRA regime is incomplete and unenforceable. A key component of the ICRA regime is for companies to self-categorize their online content according to ICRA's schema. Outside observers agree that although the regime is well intentioned, it is "hardly conceivable" to expect voluntary compliance by a significant fraction of online content providers—especially those with potentially offensive content.[47]

The regulation of Internet content neatly fits the outcome of sham standards. There has been no consensus among governments on what material is suitable for regulation. The nascent international regimes designed to tackle this issue have promulgated either an unenforceable or a voluntary sham standard. Two key facts about these issues are particularly salient. First, nonstate actors have been unable to influence government preferences on this issue. Second, when necessary, governments of every stripe have been willing to disrupt or sever Internet traffic in order to ensure their ends are achieved. Given the high adjustment costs that all governments would face on this issue, the likelihood of a bargaining core in the future is equally unlikely. Thomas Hart and Gerhard Rolletschek conclude, "There is little chance to enforce the same standard throughout the globe—be it the most liberal or the most repres-

---

[43] World Summit on the Information Society Declaration of Principles, Document WSIS-03/GENEVA/DOC/4-E, December 12, 2003, paragraph 18. The document can be accessed at http://www.itu.int/wsis/. On the debate over the language, see Kieren McCarthy, "Internet Showdown Side-Stepped in Geneva," *The Register Newsletter*, December 8, 2003.

[44] World Summit on the Information Society Plan of Action, Document WSIS-03/GENEVA/DOC/5-E, December 12, 2003, paragraph 24c. The document can be accessed at http://www.itu.int/wsis/.

[45] David Souter, "The View from the Summit: A Report on the Outcomes of the World Summit on the Information Society," *Info* 6 (January/February 2004): 6–11. Souter also observes that a key flaw of the WSIS process was a failure in any of the relevant documents to provide a clear definition of the "information society."

[46] Available at http://www.icra.org.

[47] Machill, Hart, and Kaltenhäuser, "Structural Development of Internet Self-Regulation," 50.

sive. . . . The problems posed by regulating Web content will never find uniform solutions throughout the globe."[48] Furthermore, from the perspective of governments, this outcome is the most efficient one; any real policy coordination on this issue would harm one government or another.

Intellectual Property Rights and E-Commerce

The best example of a club standards outcome for Internet issues concerns intellectual property rights (IPR), particularly copyright and trademark protection. Developed and developing countries have divergent preferences on this issue—in part because the degree of asset-specific investment in intellectual property varies according to development. The United States and the European Union have a clear incentive for stringent IPR protections. Most online goods and services are created in the advanced industrialized states. According to UNESCO, the advanced industrialized states are responsible for more than 70 percent of the world's "cultural output."[49] For Internet-related goods, the figure is higher.

The ease of replication, transmission, and alteration of Internet content poses significant challenges to the traditional foundations of copyright and trademark protection.[50] At the domestic level, the American and European response has been to enact stringent protections against copyright or trademark infringement—if anything, the rise of the Internet accelerated the ratcheting up of regulatory standards.[51] Furthermore, the sectors affected by these regulatory standards—computer software, entertainment, and financial services—all require high degrees of asset-specific investment prior to the generation of revenue. The costs to these firms of adjusting to lax IPR standards is formidable. Not surprisingly, these sectors have exercised considerable voice in pushing both the U.S. government and the European Commission to internationalize their preferences.[52]

[48] Thomas Hart and Gerhard Rolletschek, "The Challenges of Regulating the Web," *Info* 5 (September/October 2003): 15.

[49] Cited in Jagdish Bhagwati, *In Defense of Globalization* (New York: Oxford University Press, 204), 111.

[50] For an early primer, see Pamela Samuelson, "Digital Media and the Law," *Communication of the ACM* 34 (October 1991): 23–28. For a more recent case study, see John Meisel and Timothy Sullivan, "The Impact of the Internet on the Law and Economics of the Music Industry," *Info* 4 (March/April 2002): 16–22.

[51] Lawrence Lessig, *Free Culture: How Big Media Uses Technology and the Law to Lock Down Culture and Control Creativity* (New York: Penguin, 2004); Goldsmith and Wu, *Who Controls the Internet?*, chap. 5. For the European Union in particular, see Leigh Phillips, "Europe Passes Intellectual Property Rights Directive," DMEurope.com, March 10, 2004, available at http://www.dmeurope.com/default.asp?ArticleID=1169, accessed July 15, 2004.

[52] For one example, see the Motion Picture Association of America's campaign to combat movie piracy at http://www.mpaa.org/Campaign/, accessed July 15, 2004.

For several reasons, the less developed countries (LDCs) have a different set of preferences on intellectual property rights. Because—to date—these countries do not produce much original content for the Internet, their material reward for stringent IPR protection appears to be weak. Economically, these governments prefer lax standards as a way of accelerating the transfer of technology and lowering the cost of acquiring new innovations and ideas.[53] Politically, developing-country governments that accept tougher IPR standards have the unenviable task of enforcing them. For LDC governments, this requires the investment of scarce fiscal and manpower resources.

Despite the clear conflict between developed and developing countries on intellectual property rights, the emerging international regulatory regime mirrors great power preferences. In 1996, the World Intellectual Property Organization negotiated two treaties—one on copyrights and one on performances and phonograms—to cover online IPR. Experts agree that these treaties provided "strong" IPR protection.[54] Furthermore, the key negotiating parties behind the Uruguay round of the General Agreements on Tariffs and Trade (GATT)— the "quad" of the United States, Japan, Canada, and the European Union— strengthened the IPR regime by permitting member countries to use the WTO dispute settlement system mechanism to enforce trade-related intellectual property rights.[55]

These efforts came in the wake of American and European efforts to apply economic pressure against countries with lax IPR regimes. As Susan Sell documents, the United States aggressively deployed section 301 of U.S. trade law— and the threat of suspending Generalized System of Preferences treatment—to coerce developing countries into promulgating new laws strengthening IPR.[56] European Union preferences mirrored American preferences on this issue.[57]

The incentive for private actors in developing countries to evade this kind of stringent regulatory standard is quite high.[58] Despite that incentive, there is

---

[53] Susan Sell, *Power and Ideas: North-South Politics of Intellectual Property and Antitrust* (Albany: State University of New York Press, 1998). One factor that might alter developing country attitudes over time has been the increase in offshore outsourcing of high-tech services. This presents a significant opportunity for developing countries to expand economic growth and technology transfer. However, surveys repeatedly show that the biggest hesitation first-world CEOs have is the loss of intellectual property that could come with offshoring. See Don Durfee and Kate O'Sullivan, "Offshoring by the Numbers," *CFO Magazine*, June 1, 2004.

[54] Catherine Mann, Sue Eckert, and Sarah Cleeland Knight, *Global Electronic Commerce: A Policy Primer* (Washington, DC: Institute for International Economics, 2000), 118.

[55] Jeffrey Schott, *The Uruguay Round: An Assessment* (Washington, DC: Institute for International Economics, 1994), 115.

[56] Sell, *Power and Ideas*, chap. 6. For a complete listing of section 301 disputes, see http://www.ustr.gov/assets/Trade_Agreements/Monitoring_Enforcement/asset_upload_file985_6885.pdf, accessed May 3, 2006.

[57] Hadewych Hazelzet, *Carrots or Sticks? E.U. and U.S. Reactions to Human Rights Violations,* draft manuscript, Brussels, 2002.

[58] The incentive for firms in developed countries to enforce this kind of regulation is equally strong. See Knill and Lehmkuhl, "Private Actors and the State," 60.

evidence to suggest that in the face of combined U.S.-EU pressure, even powerful developing countries have signed onto the rigorous set of property rights standards. For example, China is one of the largest sources of digital piracy, responsible for $4 billion in losses for the software industry. However, in response to U.S. and EU pressure, the Chinese government ratcheted up its legal prohibitions to TRIPS levels. The Beijing government criminalized even the purchase, as well as the production, of illegally copied goods—making their laws tougher than either Japan or Taiwan. Enforcement of these rules has been haphazard but increasing—prosecutions for copyright infringement increased sharply in recent years. At least one reason for the imperfect nature of enforcement has been a lack of sufficient capabilities as opposed to a conscious effort to defect from the global rules.[59]

Statistical analyses demonstrate that the threat of WTO sanctions had a significant effect on copyright enforcement. Between 1995 and 2000, software piracy declined by nearly 20 percent in developing countries.[60] This has not eliminated private actor defections from stringent sets of regulatory standards, particularly as entertainment media becomes increasingly accessible over the Internet.[61] However, the WTO, reflecting great power preferences on the matter, has made it clear that the growth of the Internet will not alter its enforcement of copyright protection: "The basic notions and principles of intellectual property have survived over a century of rapid economic, social, and technological change. The traditional objectives of the system as reflected in the current international norms are valid even in 'cyberspace.'"[62]

DATA PRIVACY AND RIVAL STANDARDS

The regulation of data privacy is a good example of the rival standards outcome. Businesses have an incentive to acquire as much information about their customers as possible. This information-gathering facilitates marketing and sales strategies. Firms may also have an incentive to sell their customer database to third parties interested in like-minded consumers. As more commerce is transacted over the Internet, there is increased concern

[59] State Council of the People's Republic of China, "New Progress in China's Protection of Intellectual Property Rights," Beijing, China, April 2005, available at http://english.gov.cn/official/2005-07/28/content_18131.htm, accessed January 2006; Lisa Movius, "Imitation Nation," *Salon*, July 8, 2002, available at http://www.salon.com/tech/feature/2002/07/08/imintation_nation/print.html, accessed July 8, 2002. On the lack of capabilities for enforcement, see Abram Chayes and Antonia Handler Chayes, "On Compliance," *International Organization* 47 (Spring 1993): 175–206.

[60] Kenneth Shadlen, Andrew Schrank, and Marcus Kurtz, "The Political Economy of Intellectual Property Protection," *International Studies Quarterly* 49 (March 2005): 45–71.

[61] *Australian IT*, "Broadband Drives Movie Piracy," July 12, 2004.

[62] WTO secretariat, *Electronic Commerce and the Role of the WTO* (Geneva: World Trade Organization, 1998), 61.

about firms or governments taking advantage of the personal information of online consumers. Opinion polls show that privacy is the biggest concern of Internet users.[63]

The European Union and the United States adopted different stances on the data privacy issue. The U.S. attitude toward privacy rights is based on freedom *from* state intervention. As a result, the push in the United States for comprehensive state regulation of data privacy has been modest. As Rändi Bessette and Virginia Haufler observe, "The United States prefers a more market-oriented approach to data collection."[64] President Clinton's principal advisor for e-commerce, Ira Magaziner, stated his preference that, "if the privacy protections by the private sector can be spread internationally, that will become the *de facto* way privacy is protected."[65]

In Europe, privacy is considered a fundamental right to be protected *by* the state. Bessette and Haufler point out, "Because of historical abuses of privacy by government, European nations in particular have established strong privacy protections, defining privacy as a human right."[66] In 1995, the European Union passed a sweeping Data Protection Directive that set clear guidance and enforcement mechanisms for European firms. The Directive was to take effect in late 1998, and to ensure that firms did not evade the law by carrying out operations beyond the EU jurisdiction, the export of EU citizens' personal data to third countries with inadequate protection was banned.[67]

This threat proved sufficiently potent for Australia, Canada, and Eastern European countries to revise their own laws in an attempt to comply with EU preferences. However, the U.S. response was to encourage American multinationals to establish self-regulatory mechanisms that would meet EU standards. Sets of voluntary principles, such as those provided by TRUSTe and BBBOnline, were developed.

The Clinton administration also engaged in repeated negotiations with the EU Directorate General V to try and resolve the issue before sanctions kicked in. As Bessette and Haufler observe, these negotiations made little headway: "the United States steadfastly argued that personal information transferred to the United States would be adequately protected by industry self-regulation. The European Union consistently refused to accept the U.S. system as provid-

[63] Haufler, *A Public Role for the Private Sector*, 84.

[64] Rändi Bessette and Virginia Haufler, "Against All Odds: Why There Is No International Information Regime," *International Studies Perspectives* 2 (February 2001): 71.

[65] Henry Farrell, "Constructing the International Foundations of E-Commerce," *International Organization* 57 (Spring 2003): 303.

[66] Bessette and Haufler, "Against All Odds," 74.

[67] William J. Long and Marc Pang Quek, "Personal Data Privacy Protection in an Age of Globalization: The U.S.-EU Safe Harbor Compromise," *Journal of European Public Policy* 9 (June 2002): 325–44.

ing adequate privacy protections under the Data Directive."[68] Henry Farrell's assessment of the situation perfectly characterizes the bargaining involved in a rival standards outcome: "Both the US and EU sought to preserve and extend their domestic systems of privacy protection. Each sought, in effect, to dictate the terms under which privacy would be protected in the burgeoning sphere of international e-commerce."[69]

Several nonstate actors tried to mediate a solution on the issue, with no success. Human rights groups lobbied the U.S. government position to accept the EU regulatory outcome, because it represented more stringent protection of consumers.[70] A transnational business group, the Global Business Dialogue on e-commerce (GBDe), attempted to develop a common voluntary framework on data privacy. This effort failed miserably, with both U.S. and EU officials criticizing the final product.[71]

At the same time, American and European negotiators agreed to a "safe harbor" compromise.[72] The underlying premise of safe harbor was simple: the European Union would not impose sanctions against American firms that adhered to a voluntary standard consistent with the Data Protection Directive. The safe harbor compromise immediately ran into opposition from global civil society. The Transatlantic Consumer Dialogue asserted that the safe harbor regime provided inadequate enforcement of the rules, and placed unreasonable burden on consumers.[73] Despite this protest, however, both the United States and European Union accepted the deal.

The safe harbor compromise went into effect in November 2000, but the EU (state-directed) and U.S. (self-regulation) approaches remained rival standards. Both TRUSTe and BBBOnline took steps to become transnational certifiers. Farrell argues that the agreement was an example of communicative action triumphing over the divergence of preferences: "If actors representing different systems wish to avoid mutually destructive stalemate, and to identify potential solutions, they typically must engage in dialogue with each other. . . . Safe Harbor shows that efforts to resolve interdependence can involve just such dialogue."[74]

However, Farrell's conclusion is open to interpretation. U.S. compliance with the EU Directive remains uncertain at best. Even before safe harbor kicked

[68] Bessette and Haufler, "Against All Odds," 81.

[69] Farrell, "Constructing the International Foundations of E-Commerce," 19.

[70] Gregory Shaffer, "Globalization and Social Protection: The Impact of EU and International Rules in the Ratcheting Up of U.S. Privacy Standards," *Yale Journal of International Law* 25 (Winter 2000): 1–88.

[71] Maria Green Cowles, "Who Writes the Rules of E-Commerce?" AICGS Policy Paper No. 14, Johns Hopkins University, Baltimore, MD, 2001, 24.

[72] Dorothee Heisenberg, *Negotiating Privacy: The European Union, the United States and Personal Data Protection* (Boulder, CO: Lynne Reinner, 2005), chap. 4.

[73] Bessette and Haufler, "Against All Odds," 81–82.

[74] Farrell, "Constructing the International Foundations of E-Commerce," 301.

in, Federal Trade Commission studies showed that U.S. firms did not enforce their own privacy principles.[75] In one study conducted the summer after safe harbor kicked in, none of the seventy-five companies studied had met the requisite privacy standards; furthermore, only 5 percent of the surveyed firms had established mechanisms for ensuring compliance with the EU guidelines.[76] Few companies registered for the safe harbor in the year after the agreement went into effect. In the pharmaceutical sector, very few U.S. firms were certified under the safe harbor agreement in its first three years of existence.[77] Even for those firms that sought certification, it remains unclear whether there has been any impact on corporate practices. For example, when Yahoo! altered its privacy preferences for customers without their consent, TRUSTe did not revoke the firm's "trustmark."[78] Two years after safe harbor went into effect, the security chief at Reuters said that the accord was "not working as claimed."[79]

Although the European Commission launched an investigation to see whether Microsoft's .NET passport system was in compliance with the directive,[80] the European Union's response to the lax U.S. enforcement has been relatively mild. A 2004 report funded by the Commission found significant problems with implementation in the United States. The Commission, however, downplayed the report—in part because of the limited leverage it could repeatedly apply to American firms.[81] Bessette and Haufler conclude, "All sides appear to be disappointed with the results so far. . . . The safe-harbor proposal for privacy issues is not widely accepted yet, and we can expect many challenges to it."[82]

The Global Governance of Internet Technical Protocols

The economics of technical standards on the Internet are a classic example of network externalities at work, in that a standard's utility directly corresponds

[75] Marcus Franda, *Governing the Internet* (Boulder, CO: Lynne Reinner, 2001), 159.

[76] Michael Mahone, "U.S. Businesses Fail 'Safe Harbor' Data Privacy Test," *E-Commerce Times,* August 17, 2001.

[77] *Washington Drug Letter,* "Drug Firms Shy Away from Data-Privacy Certification," February 9, 2004.

[78] Zoë Baird, "Governing the Internet," *Foreign Affairs* 81 (November/December 2002): 20.

[79] Quoted in John Riley, "Reuters: Safe Harbor not Working," *Computer Weekly,* October 14, 2003. See also Aaron Lukas, "Safe Harbor or Stormy Waters? Living with the EU Data Protection Directive," Trade Policy Analysis No. 16, Cato Institute, Washington, DC, October 2001, 2. For a contrary view, see Dorothee Heisenberg and Marie-Helene Fandel, "Projecting EU Regimes Abroad: The EU Data Protection Directive as Global Standard," paper presented at the American Political Science Association annual meeting, Boston, August 29–September 1, 2002.

[80] Francesco Guerrera, "Microsoft Faces Brussels Privacy Inquiry," *Financial Times,* May 28, 2002.

[81] Heisenberg, *Negotiating Privacy,* 130–31.

[82] Bessette and Haufler, "Against All Odds," 89.

to the number of consumers using it. For the Internet to be useful for informational and commercial purposes, producers need to agree on the technical protocols that permit users to successfully transmit and access data. Although common protocols create obvious public goods, such standards can also reap disproportionate benefits for actors that either own the standards in a proprietary fashion or have first-mover advantages in exploiting those standards.[83] Because of the huge network externalities that are evident in the Internet, however, one would expect a large bargaining core among states, leading to a harmonized standards outcome.

Popular and scholarly histories of the Internet argue that the technical protocols were created by an epistemic community of computer experts that constituted the Internet Engineering Task Force (IETF), and more recently the World Wide Web consortium (W3C), and that no government could thwart this outcome.[84] A closer look at the origins of these protocols, and the regimes for managing them, suggests a rather different picture. At two crucial junctures in the growth of the Internet—the acceptance of the TCP/IP protocol for exchanging information across disparate computer networks, and the creation of the ICANN regime for governing the Internet domain name system—governments took active steps to ensure that the outcome serviced their interests and that the management regime remained private but amenable to state interests.[85] In the first episode, great power governments acted in concert to prevent firms from acquiring too much influence over the setting of standards; in the second episode, they acted to prevent particular NGOs and IGOs from acquiring too much influence.

TCP/IP was developed between 1973 and 1978 by members of ARPANET, the Defense Department's network that connected civilian and military research complexes. The protocols were designed so as to permit interoperability between disparate hardware systems. TCP is short for Transmission Control Protocol; IP is short for Internet Protocol. TCP is responsible for packing and unpacking data such that they can be transferred from one computer to another; IP is responsible for ensuring that the data are routed to the appropriate recipients. To use a postal analogy, TCP is the functional equivalent of the envelope, and IP is the functional equivalent of the mailing address on the envelope.

---

[83] Carl Shapiro and Hal Varian, *Information Rules* (Cambridge, MA: Harvard Business School Press, 1999), 174.

[84] Katie Hafner and Matthew Lyon, *Where Wizards Stay Up Late* (New York: Simon and Schuster, 1996); Mayer-Schönberger and Hurley, "Globalization of Communication."

[85] This is not to deny that the epistemic communities of the IETF and W3C wield considerable authority over some technical features of the Internet and World Wide Web. My point, rather, is that when these nongovernmental regimes have deviated from great power preferences, governments have intervened to insure their preferred regulatory outcome. For more on the IETF and W3C regimes, see Hart and Rolletschek, "The Challenges of Regulating the Web," 10–12.

TCP/IP placed minimal code demands on new entrants to the network, which was consistent with the research community's norm of open access.[86] However, this was also consistent with U.S. government preferences. According to Marcus Franda, the Defense Department embraced TCP/IP because "it lengthened the odds that when networks were less reliable (under conditions of war, for example), they might still be functional using TCP/IP."[87]

Although the Defense Department and ARPANET constituents favored the TCP/IP protocol, other networks did not rely on it. The actors behind these alternative networks had different motivations. Companies with investments in computer networks preferred developing their own proprietary standards, so as to reap the pecuniary rewards of managing their own networks.[88] By the mid-1970s, Xerox was pushing XNS, Digital was marketing DECNET, and IBM was promoting SNA to its government buyers. As Ben Segal describes the environment, "The variety of different techniques, media and protocols was staggering; open warfare existed between many manufacturers' proprietary systems, various home-made systems, and the then rudimentary efforts at defining open or international standards."[89] In other words, TCP/IP was far from the de facto benchmark when the standards debate of the 1970s started. An open, nonproprietary standard faced strong opposition from corporate actors.

The major economic powers clearly feared the prospect of being held hostage to a firm's ownership of the dominant network protocol. This was particularly true for states with government monopolies of the telecommunications sector. This concern was not unfounded. In 1975, IBM refused a Canadian government request to develop a protocol that could interface with non-IBM hardware systems. Instead the corporation urged Canada to accept IBM's proprietary SNA network protocol. In 1978, the French government issued a report warning other European governments: "If IBM became master of the network market, it would have a share—willingly or unwillingly—of the world power structure."[90]

There were two international responses to this threat. The first was a concerted effort by Canada, Britain, and France to develop a nonproprietary standard, called Recommendation X.25, for the Consultative Committee on International Telegraphy and Telephony (CCITT) of the International Telecommunications Union (ITU), a universal-membership IGO. Created in fewer than six months, X.25 was designed as a public standard freely available

[86] Will Foster, Anthony Rutkowski, and Seymour Goodman, "Who Governs the Internet?" *Communications of the ACM* 40 (August 1997): 17–18.

[87] Franda, *Governing the Internet*, 23.

[88] Ibid, 24; David Passmore, "The Networking Standards Collision," *Datamation* 31 (February 1985): 105.

[89] Ben Segal, "A Short History of Internet Protocols at CERN," http://wwwinfo.cern.ch/pdp/ns/ben/TCPHIST.html, April 1995, accessed May 2, 2002.

[90] Janet Abbate, *Inventing the Internet* (Cambridge, MA: MIT Press, 1999), 153 and 172.

to all private firms. The ITU approved the standard in 1976; the French, Japanese, and British governments immediately adopted X.25 as the standard for their government networks. Because of the significance of these government procurement markets for producers, IBM, Digital, and Honeywell reluctantly agreed to offer X.25-compatible software on their computers in addition to their own proprietary standards. As Janet Abbate concludes: "X.25 was explicitly designed to alter the balance of power . . . and in this it succeeded. Public data networks did not have to depend on proprietary network systems from IBM or any other company."[91]

The CCITT initiative was a successful holding action that prevented the emergence of a norm for proprietary standards. The second and more significant initiative was the push by the United States, United Kingdom, France, Canada, and Japan to have the International Organization for Standardization—a nongovernmental organization of technical standard-setters—develop compatible network standards for both private and public uses. This push was unusual, in that ordinarily the ISO declared an official standard only after there was a rough consensus among producers. In advocating a role for the ISO at an earlier stage, the major economic powers were clearly trying to accelerate the creation of an international regime consistent with their preferences.

This initiative resulted in the 1978 creation of the Open Systems Interconnection (OSI) model. OSI is not a standard so much as a metastandard, a minimal architecture through which disparate network protocols could communicate with one another. Abbate summarizes OSI's qualities and purpose: "The OSI standards would be publicly specified and nonproprietary, so that anyone would be free to use them; the system would be designed to work with generic components, rather than a specific manufacturer's products; and changes to the standards would be made by a public standards organization, not by a private company."[92]

The creation of OSI had two significant effects on the development of common standards. First, because of the wide ISO membership and the rapid acceptance of its standards, it became prohibitively expensive for any state or firm to create a protocol that was incompatible with OSI. The great powers were particularly enthusiastic about OSI. European governments liked it because it gave their computer producers a chance to compete with IBM, Digital, and other American producers.[93] The United States government liked OSI because it was consistent with its preferences for nonproprietary, open source coding.[94]

[91] Ibid, 166–67.

[92] Janet Abbate, "Government, Business, and the Making of the Internet," *Business History Review* 75 (Spring 2001): 163.

[93] Franda, *Governing the Internet*, 39.

[94] Hafner and Lyon, *Where Wizards Stay Up Late*, 236–37.

Second, because OSI stressed openness and accessibility, the TCP/IP code fit more seamlessly with the OSI framework than with other proposed protocols, including X.25. Furthermore, with the ISO as the location for managing network standards, the U.S. government strongly encouraged ARPANET participants to actively participate in ISO committees and meetings, in order to get the TCP/IP protocol accepted as consistent with the OSI framework.[95] By 1984, the ISO had officially recognized TCP/IP as consistent with OSI principles. Because by that juncture TCP/IP was already widely used and considered reliable, it became the de facto standard as the Internet grew in size, a classic example of historical "lock-in."[96]

Members of the Internet community often argue that the failure of X.25 or OSI to replace TCP/IP is an example of states being unable to regulate cyberspace.[97] This argument is factually correct but conceptually incomplete, in that it misses the primary motivation of both ventures. The chief concern of both the CCITT and ISO initiatives was not to replace TCP/IP, but to ward off corporate attempts to lock in a dominant proprietary standard for network protocols. If governments had not intervened, the probable outcome would have been a system of proprietary network protocols. The actual outcome—an open, nonproprietary set of network protocols—reflected the preferences of governments. Furthermore, consistent with the model presented here, states relied on a universal-membership IGO to boost legitimacy, and delegated to a nonstate actor to manage the actual standards.

The second government intervention over technical protocols came two decades later. As the commercial possibilities of the Internet and World Wide Web emerged in the early 1990s, all of the relevant actors recognized the need to create a more robust regime to manage the Domain Name System (DNS) for unique Internet addresses. The DNS is responsible for creating unique identifiers for each individual Internet address. This includes, among others, the valued generic Top Level Domains (gTLDs) such as .com, .org, or .net, as well as the country code Top Level Domains (ccTLDs) such as .de or .uk.

There were three reasons for concern about DNS management. First, Internet commentators agreed that the DNS system represented an excellent focal point through which an actor could control access to the Internet.[98] Second, actors with valued trademarks were concerned about the possibility of "cyber-squatters" acquiring valuable addresses such as www.toyota.com or

---

[95] Abbate, *Inventing the Internet*, 174–78.

[96] W. Brian Arthur, "Competing Technologies, Increasing Returns, and Lock-In by Historical Events," *Economic Journal* 99 (March 1989): 116–31.

[97] Martin Libicki et al., *Scaffolding the New Web: Standards and Standards Policy for the Digital Economy* (Arlington, VA: RAND Corporation, 2000).

[98] Lawrence Lessig, *Code and Other Laws of Cyberspace* (New York: Basic Books, 1999). See also Rajiv Shah and Kay Kesan, "Manipulating the Governance Characteristics of Code," *Info* 4 (September/October 2003): 3–9.

www.nike.com.[99] Third, there were significant commercial opportunities in managing the DNS system. Between 1994 and 1998 the U.S. government contracted the DNS registry to Network Solutions Incorporated (NSI). That monopoly was estimated in 1996 to be worth $1 billion to NSI.[100]

The first efforts to develop an international regime to reform the DNS system came from nonstate actors, particularly the Internet Society (ISOC), a network of researchers responsible for developing and managing the original ARPANET. After repeated false starts, ISOC formed the International Ad Hoc Committee (IAHC) to develop a proposal to manage domain names in lieu of NSI. The IAHC was an eminent persons group with representatives from ISOC, the International Trademark Association, WIPO, and the ITU. The ITU secretariat was particularly eager to be involved, and viewed itself as the natural location for an international regime to manage these issues.[101]

The result of this process was a memorandum of understanding among the IAHC parties on generic Top Level Domains (gTLD-MOU). The gTLD-MOU proposed assigning governance functions to an entity housed in the ITU, with representation from business interests, IGOs, and ISOC. The ITU arranged a "formal" signing ceremony in Geneva in March 1997, to give the agreement the trappings of an international treaty. This process neatly fits the definition of an epistemic community.[102] The actors involved in the creation of the gTLD-MOU—international governmental organizations, business constituencies, and technical experts—are precisely the actors emphasized in the globalization literature on how the Internet would affect global governance.

The gTLD-MOU immediately ran into opposition from two groups. Governments—particularly great power governments—strongly protested the agreement. The U.S. Secretary of State wrote a memo blasting the ITU secretariat for acting "without authorization of member governments" and "concluding with a quote international agreement unquote."[103] Ironically, EU governments opposed the agreement because it was deemed too U.S.-centric. The proposal also ran into opposition from a significant fraction of Internet enthusiasts. They criticized the proposed governance structure as lacking in democratic accountability, and as too solicitous of corporate concerns.

The IAHC proposal spurred President Clinton to issue a July 1, 1997, Executive Order authorizing the commerce secretary to "support efforts to make the

---

[99] Even if a corporation was able to wrest control of its .com name, a related concern was that cyber-squatters would simply migrate to the identical name with a different gTLD—such as www.nike.org instead of www.nike.com.

[100] Franda, *Governing the Internet*, 49.

[101] Milton Mueller, "ICANN and Internet Governance," *Info* 1 (December 1999): 501; see also Hart and Rolletschek, "The Challenges of Regulating the Web," 6–24.

[102] Renee Marlin-Bennett, "ICANN and the Global Digital Divide," paper presented at the International Studies Association annual meeting, Chicago, IL, February 2001, 4.

[103] Quoted in Mueller, "ICANN and Internet Governance," 502.

governance of the domain name system private and competitive."[104] Presidential advisor Magaziner was put in charge of the initiative, underscoring the high priority the United States gave to settling the issue. U.S. preferences on the issue were clear: to have a nonstate actor—rather than a universal-membership IGO such as the ITU—manage the DNS regime. Magaziner stated publicly: "As the Internet grows up and becomes more international, these technical management questions should be privatized, and there should be a stakeholder-based, *private international organization* set up for that technical management. In the allocation of domain names, we should, where it is possible, create a competitive marketplace to replace the monopoly that now exists."[105]

Given the ITU's one nation, one vote structure, and the secretariat's eagerness to independently manage the issue area, it is not surprising that the United States wanted to switch fora. Historically, the United States has shifted governance of new issue areas away from the ITU in order to lock in its own preferences.[106] Magaziner made the U.S. opposition to an ITU role quite explicit when he stated, "Technical management certainly should not be controlled by an intergovernmental organization or international telecommunications union."[107]

The European Union wanted three significant changes to the IAHC proposal. The EU Commission insisted that WIPO be involved in any governance structure on settling trademark disputes. This was a hedge against U.S. trademark law being imposed by fiat. The Europeans agreed with the U.S. government that the NSI monopoly of the gTLD registries had to be broken up. The European motivation for this, however, was preventing total U.S. dominance of the Internet.[108] Finally, there was a desire for a formal governmental channel between any private order and governments. This was considered especially relevant to the management of the ccTLDs. The United States was sensitive to these concerns, and because Magaziner needed European cooperation, promised there would be a significant number of Europeans on any Internet governance board.[109]

In June 1998, the Commerce Department issued a white paper that officially rejected the gTLD-MOU process and advocated privatization of the DNS system based on four principles: stability, competition, private bottom-up

---

[104] Ibid.

[105] Ira Magaziner, "Creating a Framework for Global Electronic Commerce," http://www.pff.org/ira_magaziner.htm, July 1999, accessed June 10, 2002 (my italics).

[106] Stephen D. Krasner, "Global Communications and National Power: Life on the Pareto Frontier," *World Politics* 43 (April 1991): 336–66.

[107] Magaziner, "Creating a Framework for Global Electronic Commerce," 13.

[108] European Commission, "Reply of the European Community and Its Member States to the US Green Paper," March 16, 1998, available at http://europa.eu.int/ISPO/eif/InternetPoliciesSite/InternetGovernance/Main.html, accessed July 7, 2004.

[109] Mueller, "ICANN and Internet Governance," 505.

coordination, and representation.[110] There were two reactions to the White paper. Among Internet enthusiasts, a series of self-organized conferences, called the International Forum on the White Paper (IFWP) were held, with the idea of providing citizen feedback to the U.S. proposal.[111] Many people dubbed the IFWP as an Internet "constitutional convention." Although U.S. government representatives attended IFWP meetings, there is considerable evidence demonstrating that the IFWP process had no effect on the policy outcome.[112] This was because ISOC, European Union, and American officials were simultaneously negotiating the exact contours of what a private Internet regime would look like.

The result was the Internet Corporation of Assigned Names and Numbers. While ICANN was incorporated by key members of ISOC, the resulting governance structure accommodated both U.S. and EU concerns. A Government Advisory Committee (GAC) was created to act as a conduit for government concerns. The European Commission reported that the GAC adopted operating rules "consistent with the objectives initially envisaged for this body by the EU."[113] The Commission also manages and houses the GAC's secretariat.[114] The NSI monopoly of gTLDs was broken, and the ITU was given only a peripheral role in the new regime. A significant fraction of ICANN's governing board consisted of non-Americans. Renee Marlin-Bennett summarizes the outcome in the following way: "In the creation of ICANN, the United States government clearly indicated that it did not wish the International Telecommunications Union to be that source of governance. But neither did the US government take responsibility for it itself. What resulted was a particularly unusual international organization: a private entity designed to make rules for a global Internet."[115]

While ISOC's wish to manage the DNS system was granted after a fashion, the negotiating history of ICANN shows that the key actors were the great powers.[116] It was the U.S. government that rejected the IAHC process, shut out

[110] "Management of Internet Names and Addresses (White Paper)," *Federal Register* 111, no. 63, http://www.ntia.gov/ntiahome/domainname/6_5_98dns.htm, accessed May 20, 2002.

[111] Available at http://www.domainhandbook.com/ifwp.html, accessed June 7, 2002.

[112] Mueller, "ICANN and Internet Governance," 506–8; Mueller, *Ruling the Root*; Franda, *Governing the Internet*, 53–55.

[113] European Commission, "The Organisation and Management of the Internet: International and European Policy Issues 1998–2000," communication from the Commission to the Council and the European Parliament, 8.

[114] Hart and Rolletschek, "The Challenges of Regulating the Web," 8.

[115] Marlin-Bennett, "ICANN and the Global Digital Divide," 5. See also Goldsmith and Wu, *Who Controls the Internet?*, 168–69.

[116] One question is why ISOC members were given such a prominent role in the ICANN regime, given their prominence in the gTLD-MOU fiasco. One answer is that Magaziner respected ISOC and IETF's prior background in developing technical standards. Between ISOC's proven ability

the ITU from the process, and ensured the creation of a private order to manage the policy issue.[117] The European Union, acting in concert with the Japanese and Australian governments, ensured that the eventual regime would not be dominated by the United States. The key governments vetted the initial roster of ICANN's governing board. In contrast, elements of global civil society were largely shut out of the process. Milton Mueller concludes, "The process of forming ICANN has been mired in so much factionalism and political controversy that references to 'consensus-based' self-regulation are laughable."[118] Indeed, efforts by individual ISOC members to technically constrain the power of the U.S. government in this area were met with effective threats of coercion.[119]

ICANN's history since its 1998 creation only underscores these conclusions. Nonstate actors out of the ISOC loop have vigorously protested ICANN's governance structure and lack of openness to outside input. In contrast to claims that the Internet would foster greater democratic participation, many individuals protested about the travel costs of attending ICANN's meetings. Meetings are not widely available on the Web. More generally, its detractors label ICANN as undemocratic and unresponsive, and a threat to the more decentralized culture of the Internet.[120]

Key governments have been consistent in ensuring their influence and in preferring stability over representation. A year after granting DNS governance to ICANN, the U.S. government publicly stated: "The Department of Commerce has no plans to transfer to any entity its policy authority to direct the authoritative root server."[121] In April 2002, a Commerce official explained the U.S. government's influence over ICANN in this way: "We do have a contractual relationship with them, which we have the ability to modify, or, if we want, terminate. That is how our input comes into the process."[122] In June 2005, the United States refused to relinquish control over the authoritative root server to ICANN as originally planned.

At the same time, U.S. and European preferences on the matter were carried out. ICANN's adoption of the Uniform Dispute Resolution Policy drastically reduced the transaction costs of resolving trademark disputes for domain names.[123] Despite numerous denial-of-service attacks, the Internet has yet to

---

to develop successful standards and ISOC's critics, who had no such experience, Magaziner went with ISOC. See Farrell, "Constructing the International Foundations of E-Commerce," 289–90.

[117] A. Michael Froomkin, "Wrong Turn in Cyberspace: Using ICANN to Route Around the APA and the Constitution," *Duke Law Journal* 50 (2000): 17–184.

[118] Mueller, "ICANN and Internet Governance," 498. See, more generally, Mueller, *Ruling the Root: Internet Governance and the Taming of Cyberspace* (Cambridge, MA: MIT Press, 2002).

[119] Goldsmith and Wu, *Who Controls the Internet?*, chap. 3.

[120] See www.ICANNwatch.org for a Web site devoted to these criticisms.

[121] Quoted in Mueller, "ICANN and Internet Governance," 515.

[122] Quoted in Susan Stellen, "Plan to Change Internet Group Is Criticized as Inadequate," *New York Times*, April 1, 2002.

[123] Hart and Rolletschek, "The Challenges of Regulating the Web," 16.

suffer a systemic failure at the architectural level. Since ICANN's creation, competition to provide domain name services has increased and prices have fallen.[124] In July 2004, the OECD issued a report evaluating ICANN's performance. The authors concluded, "ICANN's reform of the market structure for the registration of generic Top Level Domain names has been very successful. The division between registry and registrar functions has created a competitive market that has lowered prices and encouraged innovation."[125] Another clue to ICANN's success was the decline of cyber-squatting or speculation in Internet domain names. By June 2004, 72 percent of all registered domain names were attached to active Internet sites; only two years previously, that figure was 55 percent.[126]

ICANN's own governing body also indicated its eagerness to cater more to government preferences. ICANN currently lists as one of its core values: "Act with sensitivity to the public interest and related governmental concerns, so that *the need for direct governmental action is minimized.*"[127] In February 2002, ICANN's president, Stuart Lynn, proposed reforming its structure by having national governments explicitly nominate five members of ICANN's governing board. In defending the proposal against charges from critics, Lynn commented, "Our mission is not to run an exercise in global democracy. I happen to think we need to be a private organization."[128] Most of Lynn's proposals were approved in June 2002, which provoked complaints from outside groups about ICANN's transparency.[129]

ICANN and its great power patrons also successfully blocked other actors—including private firms, smaller states, and other IGOs—from encroaching on its governance turf. In September 2003, VeriSign—the successor to NSI and still in charge of the .com and .net registries—launched its Site Finder technology. Site Finder redirected Internet users who entered unregistered Web addresses ending with .com or .net to a Web site owned and operated by VeriSign, as opposed to the standard DNS resolution failure message. ICANN responded by ordering VeriSign a month later to discontinue the service, later arguing that

[124] Lisa M. Bowman, "ICANN Comes under Fire—Again," Cnet News.com, http://news.zdnet .co.uk, April 1, 2002, accessed April 2, 2002; Mueller, *Ruling the Root*, 188.

[125] Sam Paltridge and Masayuki Matsui, "Generic Top Level Domain Names: Market Development and Allocation Issues," Organization for Economic Cooperation and Development (DSTI/ ICCP/TISP(2004)2/FINAL), Paris, July 13, 2004.

[126] Ibid; David McGuire, "Web Address Sales Hit Record High," *washingtonpost.com*, June 8, 2004, available at http://www.washingtonpost.com/ac2/wp-dyn/A23803-2004Jun8?language= printer, accessed July 14, 2004; Leslie Walker, "Web Addresses Extending Their Global Domain," *Washington Post*, June 17, 2004, E1.

[127] Committee on ICANN Evolution and Reform, "ICANN: A Blueprint for Reform," http:// www.icann.org/committees/evol-reform/blueprint-20jun02.htm, June 20, 2002, accessed September 10, 2002 (emphasis added).

[128] Quoted in Bowman, "ICANN Comes under Fire—Again."

[129] Susan Stellin, "Internet Address Group Approves Overhaul," *New York Times*, June 29, 2002. On the transparency objections, see Baird, "Governing the Internet."

Site Finder was guilty of violating "fundamental architecture principles." The firm complied but sued ICANN for antitrust violations. In response, ICANN contemplated an auction for the .net registry when VeriSign's contract expired in 2005.[130] In October 2005, the two parties reached an agreement; VeriSign removed Site Finder and promised to submit any other innovations for ICANN approval—in return for five more years operating the .com registry.[131]

On a different front, ICANN and the great powers blocked an attempt at the December 2003, WSIS summit to transfer some of ICANN's authority to the ITU. Some smaller governments registered their uneasiness with ICANN's lack of transparency and close relationship with the U.S. and EU governments. As an Argentinean delegate phrased it, "How a government deals with ICANN is not the same for the United States as for Mali. There should be an entity where all governments have the same rights somewhere inside the U.N." UN and ITU officials also acknowledged some interest in such a forum shift. However, the United States and European Union were able to prevent such a proposal from being expressed in either the WSIS Declaration of Principles or the Plan of Action. ICANN's president stated at the time that he found the language "very pleasing."[132]

Prior to the 2005 WSIS meeting in Tunis, there was a flurry of more contentious diplomatic actions that only partially conformed to the revisionist model. As previously noted, the United States had refused to relinquish control over the authoritative root server to ICANN as originally planned. Other governments—including EU members—protested over the American refusal to budge, proposing a multilateral IGO to replace the United States as the overseer of the root server. Most authoritarian governments sided with the European Union. The United States resisted efforts at forum-shifting. A State Department spokesman said, "We will not agree to the UN taking over management of the Internet. Some countries want that. We think that's unacceptable."[133]

In the run-up to Tunis, however, a face-saving compromise set up a nonbinding intergovernmental forum to discuss the issue.[134] The puzzle for the revisionist model is why the European Commission acted the way it did, when a universal IGO would not have served its interests on this issue. Press reports and expert analysts provide two explanations for this anomalous behavior.

---

[130] Quotation from Graeme Wearden, "ICANN Roundly Condemns VeriSign's Site Finder," *ZDNet UK*, July 13, 2004. See also Robert Lemos, "VeriSign Relents on Browser 'Hijack,'" CNET news.com, October 6, 2003; Jennifer Schenker, "Control over .net Could Change in 2005," *International Herald-Tribune*, July 14, 2004.

[131] Associated Press, "ICANN, VeriSign Reach Accord," October 25, 2005. ICANN later revised the agreement to lower prices for .com registration. Anne Broache, "Price Hikes for .com Could Be Curbed," CNET News.com, January 31, 2006.

[132] Both quotations from John Zaracostas, "U.N. Control of Web Rejected," *Washington Times*, December 8, 2003. See also David McGuire, "U.N. Summit to Focus on Internet," *Washington Post*, December 5, 2003; Souter, "The View from the Summit."

[133] Quoted in Goldsmith and Wu, *Who Controls the Internet?*, 171.

[134] BBC News, "US Retains Hold of the Internet," November 16, 2005.

First, the European Commission saw the dispute as a way to stand up to the Bush administration's unilateralist foreign policy.[135] Second, and related, the EU Commissioner in charge of the ICANN portfolio was inexperienced and eager to politicize the dispute.[136] On the substance, Lawrence Lessig asserted that, "it's not really a cyberlaw problem."[137] These exceptional circumstances explain the public nature of the transatlantic dispute—but the revisionist model explains the absence of any change in the status quo.

Stepping back, had the great powers not intervened in the late 1990s the outcome in this case would have been significantly different from ICANN. The Internet Society initially wanted to expand the number of gTLDs to fifty. The management of the DNS system would have been housed in the ITU, a one-country, one-vote universal membership IGO, rather than a private nonprofit organization. This case demonstrates that nonstate actors have some agenda-setting powers. However, once an issue comes to the attention of states, the outcome will reflect great power preferences. Even as LDC government preferences have shifted over time, the United States' and European Union's conscious delegation of the domain name system to ICANN locked in the regime that favored the great powers.

In both the protocol wars of the 1970s and the creation of ICANN in the 1990s, government preferences were consistent. The great powers repeatedly acted to ensure that the Internet would be governed so as to maximize efficiency, without abrogating monopoly power to any one actor, be it a multinational firm, a nonstate organization, or an IGO secretariat. In the 1970s, governments acted with Internet enthusiasts to ensure that multinational firms would not develop their own proprietary network protocols. In the 1990s, governments acted in concert with multinational firms to prevent NGOs and IGOs from overstepping their policy authority. In both instances, governments delegated regime management to nongovernmental international organizations—ISO and ICANN—to ensure efficient outcomes and to retain their influence over future policy shifts.

Rethinking the Internet's Effect on World Politics

The globalization literature frequently argues that the exponential growth of the Internet empowers networked nonstate actors and weakens the state's role in global governance. The globalization literature is wrong; states, particularly great power governments, remain the primary actors in fashioning interna-

---

[135] Lawrence Lessig, "Battling for Control of the Internet," ForeignPolicy.com, November 2005, available at www.foreignpolicy.com/story/cms.php?story_id=3306, accessed March 2006; Kenneth Neil Cukier, "Who Will Control the Internet?" *Foreign Affairs* 84 (November/December 2005): 7–13; Adam Penenberg, "Who Controls the Internet?" *Slate*, November 29, 2005.

[136] Frederick Kempe, "How the Web Was Run," *Wall Street Journal*, October 25, 2005.

[137] Lessig, "Battling for Control of the Internet."

tional regulatory regimes. When great power governments saw significant benefits and low adjustment costs from coordination, the likelihood of effective global governance of Internet-related issues was high. When questions about Internet governance intersected with larger questions of public policy—such as the right to privacy or the freedom of speech—adjustment costs for all governments dramatically increased. In the absence of a great power concert, governments used all of the tools of statecraft at their disposal to protect their preferred set of regulatory standards—even if such a decision heavily restricted Internet use.

In focusing on the binary question of state power versus nonstate power, these globalization scholars have glossed over the diversity of governance relationships that can exist among heterogeneous actors in world politics. Recognition of the substitutability of global governance structures gives us a more powerful lens to understand the ramifications of globalization. A review of Internet governance demonstrates that even when states prefer to let private actors take the governance lead, they will intervene at crucial junctures to advance their desired ends.

States may be the primary actors, but they are not the only actors. The case studies clearly show that nonstate actors can affect governance processes through their technical expertise and agenda-setting abilities. However, only by giving the great powers pride of place is it possible to ascertain the conditions under which nonstate actors will exercise their influence. This finding is consistent with previous work that suggests the provision of collective goods at the national or local level involves a complex distribution of governance functions among actors representing the state, the market, and civil society.[138]

The implications for scholars of international relations and globalization are significant. The Internet could be safely described as a tough test for state-centric theories of international relations, and an easy test for global civil society arguments.[139] If states are found to be the key actors for Internet-related issues, the globalization literature will need to reconsider the relationship between states and nonstate actors. The evidence presented here suggests that both international governmental organizations and nongovernmental organizations have roles to play in global governance. At times they can act as independent agenda-setters and advocates, but they become more important when they provide services as the agents of state interests.

---

[138] Elinor Ostrom, *Governing the Commons: The Evolution of Institutions for Collective Action* (Cambridge: Cambridge University Press, 1990).

[139] On case selection, see Harry Eckstein, "Case Study and Theory in Political Science," in *Handbook of Political Science, Volume 7*, ed. Fred Greenstein and Nelson Polsby (Reading, MA: Addison-Wesley, 1975).

CHAPTER FIVE

Club Standards and International Finance

GLOBALIZATION DRAMATICALLY increased the size and depth of international capital markets. From 1994 to 2002, the valuation of all international debt securities almost quadrupled, from $2.3 trillion to $8.3 trillion. Over the past twenty years, the size of all banks' cross-border positions increased from $1.4 trillion to $12.7 trillion.[1] The renaissance of global finance led to a concomitant rise in global financial instability:[2] the frequency of banking and currency crises rose to a level unseen since the interwar years.[3] The fallout from these shocks in Latin America, East Asia, Russia, and Turkey triggered fresh demands to strengthen the "international financial architecture."[4] That term refers to the set of governance structures that manage international monetary and financial affairs.

The focus of this chapter will be on the governance of the international financial system—the set of rules, resources, and institutions designed to ensure the solvency of financial institutions against the vicissitudes of global finance.[5] In the wake of the financial crises of the 1990s, most of the proposals

---

[1] International Monetary Fund, *Global Financial Stability Report—Statistical Appendix*, March 2003, 120; Bank of International Settlements, "External positions of banks in individual reporting countries," http://www.bis.org/publ/qcsv0303/anx2a.csv, accessed April 25, 2003.

[2] There have been previous areas of financial globalization. See Kevin O'Rourke and Jeffrey Williamson, *Globalization and History* (Cambridge, MA: MIT Press, 1999).

[3] Michael Bordo, Barry Eichengreen, Daniela Klingebiel, and Maria Soledad Martinez-Peria, "Is the Crisis Problem Growing More Severe?" *Economic Policy* 32 (April 2001): 51–83.

[4] Jose De Gregorio, Barry Eichengreen, Takatoshi Ito, and Charles Wyplosz, *An Independent and Accountable IMF.* (London: Centre for Economic Policy Research, 1999); Council on Foreign Relations, *Safeguarding Prosperity in a Global Financial System: The Future International Financial Architecture* (New York: Council on Foreign Relations, 1999); Montek Ahluwalia, "The IMF and the World Bank in the New Financial Architecture," in *International Monetary and Financial Issues for the 1990s* (New York and Geneva: United Nations, 1999); Barry Eichengreen, *Toward a New International Financial Architecture* (Washington, DC: Institute for International Economics, 1999); Stanley Fischer, "On the Need for an International Lender of Last Resort." *Journal of Economic Perspectives* 13 (Fall 1999): 85–104; International Financial Institution Advisory Commission, *Report of the International Financial Institution Advisory Commission* (Washington, DC: United States Congress, 2000); Overseas Development Council, *The Future Role of the IMF in Development* (Washington, DC: Overseas Development Council, 2000); John Williamson, "The Role of the IMF: A Guide to the Reports," Institute for International Economics Policy Brief 00-5. Washington, DC, May 2000.

[5] In focusing on financial matters, I am excluding a discussion of the regulation of the international monetary system, which focuses more on the coordination of exchange-rate regimes and

for strengthening financial regulation focused on the international financial institutions (IFIs)—the International Monetary Fund (IMF) and the World Bank. They implicitly or explicitly assumed that these institutions would remain the focal point for global financial governance, and either belittled or ignored reform efforts made outside these fora.

In the early half of this decade, many commentators believed that progress on this front had been minimal.[6] However, this overlooks the development of more rigorous financial codes and standards across a range of issues, including banking supervision, insurance, auditing, securities, and data transparency. In recent years several international financial bodies have increased their surveillance of emerging economies to ensure adherence to these standards. Moreover, these codes and standards were developed and selected outside the IFI's purview, in a newly created venue—the Financial Stability Forum (FSF). Preliminary evidence suggests that the new coordination of financial codes and standards—and the monitoring and enforcement that goes with them—have helped to reduce financial instability and increased the flow of salient information to capital markets.[7]

The myriad arguments contained within the globalization and global governance literature are hard-pressed to explain both this process and outcome. The most obvious arguments made—race-to-the-bottom arguments[8] or capital dominance arguments[9]—emphasize structural economic forces. These pressures are theorized to force states to lower their regulatory standards. With regard to financial regulation, however, the race-to-the-bottom hypothesis cannot explain the ratcheting up of regulatory stringency that has taken place over the past five years. Anne-Marie Slaughter and Wolfgang Reinicke argue that

---

monetary policies. See Kenneth Dam, *The Rules of the Global Game* (Chicago: University of Chicago Press, 2001), chaps. 11 and 12, on the distinction between financial and monetary regulation. However, Michael Webb examines coordination on monetary regulation in *The Political Economy of Policy Coordination: International Adjustment since 1945* (Ithaca, NY: Cornell University Press, 1995), and reaches conclusions similar to those developed here.

[6] Peter Kenen, *The International Financial Architecture* (Washington, DC: Institute for International Economics, 2001); Joseph Stiglitz, *Globalization and Its Discontents* (New York: Norton, 2002); Thomas Willett, "Why Is There So Much Disagreement about the IMF and Reform of the International Financial Architecture?" paper prepared for the IMF Seminar on Current Developments in Monetary and Financial Law, Washington, DC, 2002.

[7] Barry Eichengreen, "Strengthening the International Financial Architecture, 2004," plenary address to 3rd Annual PECC Finance Conference, Santiago, Chile, June 2004, 6–7; John Cady, "Does SDDS Subscription Reduce Borrowing Costs for Emerging Market Economies?" IMF Working Paper No. 04/58, Washington, DC, April 2004.

[8] Richard Falk, "State of Siege: Will Globalization Win Out?" *International Affairs* 73 (January 1997): 123–36; Philip Cerny, "Paradoxes of the Competition State: The Dynamics of Political Globalization," *Government and Opposition* 36 (Spring 1997): 251–74.

[9] John Goodman and Louis Pauly, "The Obsolescence of Capital Controls?" *World Politics* 46 (October 1993): 50–82; Sebastian Edwards, "How Effective are Capital Controls?" *Journal of Economic Perspectives* 13 (Fall 1999): 65–84.

regulatory outcomes can be explained by the preexisting strength of transnational public policy networks embedded in regional and international governmental organizations.[10] However, the key codes and standards govern issue areas with wildly divergent levels of prior networking. In the area of banking supervision, for example, strong transnational ties existed among the relevant groups and institutions. However, in other areas, like securities regulation, transnational ties and preexisting governance mechanisms were much weaker.[11]

Beth Simmons provides an explanation of harmonization in capital market regulation that relies on hegemonic state power.[12] As noted in chapter 1, however, this characterization does not jibe with the actual distribution of financial power. John Braithwaite and Peter Drahos have challenged this broad-based characterization of the international financial sector, observing, "These days no one state really leads the globalization of banking regulation . . . the hegemony of the US in international monetary relations has no counterpart in banking regulation."[13] Examining transatlantic negotiations over financial regulation, Elliott Posner found that the European Commission possessed equal bargaining power vis-à-vis the United States.[14]

Ideational approaches have stressed the ways in which the emergence of shared causal beliefs can lead to significant policy change.[15] In recent years, variations of this argument have been used to explain aspects of global financial governance.[16] According to these approaches, the variation in global financial governance can be explained by the variation in ideational consensus on the extant issues. The problem with this explanation of events is that while

---

[10] Anne-Marie Slaughter, "The *Real* New World Order," *Foreign Affairs* 76 (September/October 1997): 183–97; Wolfgang Reinicke, *Global Public Policy: Governing without Government?* (Washington, DC: Brookings Institution Press, 1998); David Bach, "Varieties of Cooperation: Domestic Politics and Transnational Market Governance," paper presented at the American Political Science Association annual meeting, Philadelphia, PA, August 2003; and Tony Porter, "Technical Collaboration and Political Conflict in the Emerging Regime for International Financial Regulation," *Review of International Political Economy* 10 (August 2003): 520–51.

[11] Beth Simmons, "The International Politics of Harmonization: The Case of Capital Market Regulation," *International Organization* 55 (Summer 2001): 589–620.

[12] Ibid.

[13] John Braithwaite and Peter Drahos, *Global Business Regulation* (Cambridge: Cambridge University Press, 1999), 113.

[14] Elliott Posner, "Market Power without a Single Market: The New Transatlantic Relations in Financial Services," in *The Future of Transatlantic Economic Relations*, ed. David Andrews et al. (Florence: European University Institute, 2005), 234–36.

[15] Judith Goldstein and Robert Keohane, eds., *Ideas and Foreign Policy* (Ithaca, NY: Cornell University Press, 1993).

[16] Jeffrey M. Chwieroth, "Neoliberalism's Role in Capital Account Liberalization in Emerging Markets," paper presented at the 2002 American Political Science Association annual meeting, Boston, August 29–September 1, 2002; Kathleen McNamara, "Consensus and Constraint: Ideas and Capital Mobility in European Monetary Integration," *Journal of Common Market Studies* 37 (September 1999): 455–77.

an expert consensus existed on financial standards, it also existed across the entire range of architecture issues, including the role of IMF conditionality, the division of labor between the IFIs, and transparency issues.[17] Progress was made only on the issue of standards, and much of that progress took place outside the purview of the IFIs.[18]

The revisionist model can explain this outcome as a classic case of club standards. Until the crises of the mid-1990s, the perceived benefits from regulatory coordination were not thought to be significant, and as a result there was little impetus for global financial regulation. In the aftermath of the crisis, however, both the United States and European Union preferred to see a ratcheting up of financial codes and standards in order to reduce financial instability, protect domestic investors, and improve the functioning of capital markets. The primary cleavage of interests among the relevant actors in global finance was between the developed and developing countries. In the financial realm, both of the great powers were developed countries with comparatively high levels of income per capita. The great powers, as developed economies, derived significant benefits from coordination at a stringent level of regulation. In contrast, the distributional implications among these states were small. The preferences of developing countries diverged from the great powers. For states with unregulated or repressed financial sectors, the benefits of coordination at a high level were more uncertain, while the short-term costs were significant.

Because of this distribution of interests, the United States and European Union chose to use club IGOs as the primary fora to establish global financial regulations. Universal-membership international governmental organizations were an inhospitable environment for creating financial regulation, because the majority of developing countries held different preferences. Even the IFIs, with their weighted voting schemes, proved difficult, because of their strong norm of consensus decision-making. Therefore, the great powers relied on club IGOs to promulgate common regulatory standards. This preference for club IGOs also explains the lack of progress made on the other aspects of the architecture exercise. Most of the proposed reforms entailed the husbanding of governance within the IFIs. Despite the considerable influence the great powers possess in these institutions, their control of the IFI agendas was less certain than in club fora like the Basle Committee on Banking Supervision or the Financial Action Task Force on Money Laundering. Furthermore, many of the proposed changes would have diluted the influence of the great powers. It should therefore not be surprising that reform efforts in other areas of the international financial architecture stalled out.

---

[17] Williamson, "The Role of the IMF"; Willett, "Why Is There So Much Disagreement about the IMF and Reform of the International Financial Architecture?"

[18] On the lack of progress in transparency, see Robert O'Brien, Anne Marie Goetz, Jan Aart Scholte, and Marc Williams, *Contesting Global Governance* (Cambridge: Cambridge University

The chapter is divided into seven sections. The next section discusses why the primary cleavage of interests in the establishment of international financial regulation was between developed and developing countries—which leads to a prediction of club standards. From this distribution of interests, one would predict great power forum-shopping and a reliance on club IGOs. The third and fourth sections trace the development of global financial codes and standards following the Mexican and Asian crises. The fifth section examines great power efforts to enforce these standards at the global level. The sixth section considers alternative case-specific explanations and examines other initiatives to reform the global financial architecture and why they failed. The final section summarizes and concludes.

National Preferences for Global Finance

From 1995 onward, the great powers in the financial realm have been the United States and the principal members of the European Union. As previously noted, these jurisdictions possess the two largest capital markets, as measured by bonds, equities, and bank assets.[19] Only the United States and the European Union have capital markets larger than $50 trillion—more than double the next largest market.[20] There was also a large gap between the great powers and the rest of the world in terms of financial strength. In percentage terms, Moody's weighted average of bank financial strength for the United States and principal EU countries was 75 percent and 70 percent; the average figure for the rest of the world was 28 percent.[21]

There are several reasons to believe that with regard to the international financial architecture, the primary cleavage in the distribution of state preferences would have been between developed and developing countries. For developed countries, the benefits of global financial regulatory coordination at stringent levels of regulation were significant, while the adjustment costs were relatively minimal. For developing countries, the benefits of such coordination were somewhat less tangible, while the adjustment costs were significant.

For developed countries, there are three distinct benefits of coordination above a minimum level of regulatory stringency. First, regulatory coordination lowers the transactions costs of transnational capital flows. When countries remove border-level barriers to exchange, regulatory frictions act as a residual obstruction to deeper market integration. A lowering of such costs improves

Press, 2000). On the IMF's defense of conditionality, see Kenneth Rogoff, "The IMF Strikes Back," *Foreign Policy* 134 (January/February 2003): 38–47.

[19] *IMF Global Financial Stability Report Statistical Appendix*, Fall 2003, table 3.

[20] The value of Japanese bank, bond, and equities markets totals $21.6 trillion (ibid.).

[21] Ibid., table 25.

both the static and dynamic efficiency of capital markets.[22] With segmented capital markets, the rate of investment is constrained by national savings. As capital markets become more integrated, individual countries are able to escape constraints on the magnitude of aggregate investment. The removal of national savings as a constraint on investment increases the balance of payments flexibility for developed governments.[23] Access to global capital markets also increases competition among financial institutions, lowering the cost of capital and thereby facilitating new firm creation and greater technological innovation.[24]

Second, the coordination of national financial regulation protects developed financial sectors from losing business due to lower profit rates. Regulatory stringency reduces the rate of return for financial institutions by imposing compliance costs. For banks, adherence to stringent regulations can come in the form of higher capital adequacy ratios or implementing know-your-customer regulations.[25] Because of the high costs of regulatory compliance, firms with mobile assets have an incentive to engage in regulatory arbitrage. Internationally, lax regulation in developing countries—in the form of lower standards *and* weaker enforcement—can act as a magnet for profit-maximizing firms.

Offshore financial centers (OFCs) represent the extreme version of this problem. OFCs are jurisdictions that have large numbers of financial institutions geared to perform services for nonresidents. The comparative advantage of OFCs in international finance is their inviting tax and regulatory structures. OFCs have encouraged the creation of international business companies and other offshore vehicles. These financial innovations facilitate the management of investment funds without close scrutiny, and lower the costs of exit for the financial sector. When successful, OFCs amass external assets and liabilities far out of proportion to domestic financial intermediation.[26] Between 1990 and 2000, cross-border lending to OFCs doubled to $850 billion, approximately 8

---

[22] Raghuram Rajan and Luigi Zingales, *Saving Capitalism from the Capitalists* (New York: Crown Business Books, 2003); Barry Eichengreen, "Financial Instability," Copenhagen Consensus Challenge Paper, Berkeley, CA, April 2004, available at http://copenhagenconsensus.com/Files/Filer/CC/Papers/Financial_Instability_160404.pdf, accessed October 27, 2004.

[23] Martin Feldstein and Charles Horioka, "Domestic Savings and International Capital Flows," *Economic Journal* 90 (June 1980): 314–29. The United States' ability to sustain such a massive current account deficit as a percentage of GDP in recent years is one obvious example of this benefit.

[24] Eichengreen, "Financial Instability," 3.

[25] Ethan Kapstein, "Resolving the Regulator's Dilemma: International Coordination of Banking Regulations," *International Organization* 43 (Spring 1989): 323–47; Ann Florini, "Does the Invisible Hand Need a Transparent Glove? The Politics of Transparency," paper prepared for annual World Bank Conference on Development Economics, Washington, DC, April 28–30, 1999.

[26] International Monetary Fund, "Offshore Financial Centers," IMF Background Paper, available at http://www.imf.org/external/np/mae/oshore/2000/eng/back.htm, accessed June 12, 2002.

percent of all reported claims.[27] While financial institutions based in the developed world can open up operations in these countries, developed-country governments suffer from the transfer of capital to OFCs in two ways. First, significant amounts of tax revenue are lost. Second, the integration of OFCs into the global financial system increases systemic vulnerability to financial crises in offshore centers.[28]

The final benefit of global financial regulation is the protection offered to domestic investors holding overseas assets.[29] As the source for global liquidity, investors in these countries have incurred significant losses from financial crises triggered by inadequate financial regulation. According to the Institute for International Finance, private investors lost approximately $225 billion during the Asian financial crisis and some $100 billion when Russia defaulted on its debt in August 1998.[30] Critics argue that these investors are the prime beneficiaries of any IMF-funded bailout. However, even if these critics are correct, such bailouts only mitigate the financial losses—they do not erase them. From the perspective of the great powers, it is far more cost effective to coordinate prudential regulation across countries than to cover private sector losses from financial crises after the fact.

For the developed economies, the costs of adjustment to ensure regulatory coordination would be expected to be small—but not nonexistent. Differences between the United States and the European Union in the policy content of financial regulation have narrowed over the past twenty-five years.[31] This does not mean changes in the regulatory environment would be free. The first cost that could emerge is the tradeoff between stringent regulation and financial innovation. Overly strict regulatory intervention raises the costs of creating new financial instruments. In the case of financial derivatives, for example, extensive European regulation shifted the growth of these instruments to offshore markets.[32] Measuring the opportunity costs of lost innovation is an impossible counterfactual to calculate. Finance ministry officials on both sides of the Atlantic were cognizant of this tradeoff but still believed that coordination provided positive value-added.

Another adjustment cost to global regulatory standards is specific to federal states, where much financial regulation is managed at the subnational level. States that delegate significant policymaking autonomy in financial regulation

---

[27] Liz Dixon, "Financial Flows Via Offshore Financial Centers as Part of the International Financial System," *Financial Stability Review* 12 (June 2001): 105.

[28] William Wechsler, "Follow the Money," *Foreign Affairs* 80 (July/August 2001): 40–57.

[29] Kenneth Rogoff, "International Institutions for Reducing Global Financial Instability," *Journal of Economic Perspectives* 13 (Autumn 1999): 21–42.

[30] Cited in Rogoff, "The IMF Strikes Back."

[31] Andreas Busch, "Divergence or Convergence? The Example of State Regulation of the Banking Sector," Working Paper, St. Antony's College, University of Oxford, November 2002, 11.

[32] Braithwaite and Drahos, *Global Business Regulation*, chap. 8.

to local governments would have to bear the political burden of reallocating such authority back to the central government. For example, unitary states such as France would have little trouble altering their corporate governance regulations at the national level. Such an enterprise would be much more difficult in the United States, where corporate governance is the realm of state-level regulation. Some states—Delaware in particular—and the corporations headquartered in those states benefit disproportionately from the federal system of regulation on this topic.[33] International regulatory coordination triggers costs in the form of the political battles necessary to superimpose global standards on top of subnational regulation.

For less developed countries (LDCs), the benefits of regulatory coordination can be appreciable but outweighed by the significant adjustment costs. The clearest benefit from regulatory coordination at stringent levels is the potential to maintain open capital markets. For countries and societies determined to maximize economic growth, maintaining an open capital account is a sizeable benefit.[34] As Stanley Fischer observes:

> What can be done to reduce the volatility of capital flows to emerging market countries? The first response would be for countries to shut themselves off from international capital flows. It bears emphasis that *despite the crises, and the arguments of many critics of globalization, almost no country has taken this route; the revealed preference of the emerging market countries is to stay involved with the international financial system.*[35]

Regulatory coordination—particularly when it facilitates transparency—is likely to facilitate the development of capital markets while reducing financial instability and its attendant social and economic costs.[36]

However, it should be noted that the benefits of open capital markets for developing countries are more nuanced than neoclassical economic theory predicts. As Fischer notes, open capital markets lead to more growth, but also

---

[33] Because of Delaware's minimal standards for corporate governance, more than half of the Fortune 500 companies are headquartered in the state. See Jonathan Chait, "Rogue State," *The New Republic*, August 19, 2002.

[34] Peter Henry, "Stock Market Liberalization, Economic Reform, and Emerging Market Equity Price," *Journal of Finance* 55 (April 2000): 529–64; Geert Bekaert and Campbell Harvey, "Does Financial Liberalization Spur Growth?" NBER Working Paper No. w8245, April 2001; Dennis Quinn, A. Maria Toyoda, and Carla Inclan, "Does Capital Account Liberalization Lead to Economic Growth?: An Empirical Investigation," Working Paper, Georgetown University, Washington, DC, March 2002; Rajan and Zingales, *Saving Capitalism from the Capitalists*; Eichengreen, "Financial Instability."

[35] Stanley Fischer, "Globalization and Its Challenges," paper presented at the American Economic Association annual meeting, Washington, DC, January 2003, 20 (emphasis in original).

[36] James Barth, Gerard Caprio, and Ross Levine, *Rethinking Bank Regulation: Till Angels Govern* (Cambridge: Cambridge University Press, 2005). See also Frederic Mishkin, *The Next Great Globalization: How Disadvantaged Nations Can Harness Their Financial Systems to Get Rich* (Princeton: Princeton University Press, 2006).

lead to increased economic volatility. Several studies indicate that since the end of Bretton Woods, developing countries that remove capital controls are far more vulnerable to banking crises and twin crises of runs on banks and national currencies.[37] According to one estimate, over the past quarter-century financial instability reduced the incomes of developing countries by 25 percent.[38] Indonesia and Argentina suffered greater losses in output and real incomes from their recent financial crises than the United States incurred during the Great Depression.[39] Commentators across the political spectrum agree that the combination of liberalized capital markets and inadequate regulation of financial sectors was the chief cause of these crises.[40] In theory, stringent regulatory standards address this problem for less developed countries, but the empirical support for this claim remains murky.[41]

Another problem is the indirect quality of the perceived benefits. Open and well-regulated capital markets do lower the transaction costs of foreign direct investment (FDI)—in which foreign firms control physical facilities located in the host country. Open capital accounts permit multinational corporations to repatriate their profits across borders, which should encourage more FDI. However, the primary effect of regulatory coordination is to facilitate flows of foreign portfolio investment—in which investors purchase securitized assets in the home country without exercising direct control. Various empirical studies suggest that less developed countries benefit far more from foreign direct investment than portfolio investment.[42] Even Fischer acknowledges that "the relationship between capital account liberalization and growth is likely inherently weaker than that between current account liberalization and

---

[37] Jagdish Bhagwati, "The Capital Myth," *Foreign Affairs* 77 (May/June 1998): 7–12, and *In Defense of Globalization* (New York: Oxford University Press, 2004), chap. 13; Gerard Caprio and Patrick Honohan, "Restoring Banking Stability: Beyond Supervised Capital Requirements," *Journal of Economic Perspectives* 13 (Fall 1999): 43–64; Graciela Kaminsky and Carmen Reinhart, "The Twin Crises: The Causes of Banking and Balance of Payments Problems," *American Economic Review* 89 (June 1999): 473–500; Bordo et al., "Is the Crisis Problem Growing More Severe?" It should be observed that LDCs that maintain capital controls are less vulnerable to banking crises but more vulnerable to currency crises.

[38] Wendy Dobson and Gary Hufbauer, *World Capital Markets: Challenge to the G-10* (Washington, DC: Institute for International Economics, 2001), 44.

[39] Eichengreen, "Financial Instability," 10.

[40] Brink Lindsey, *Against the Dead Hand: The Uncertain Struggle for Global Capitalism* (New York: John Wiley, 2002); Stiglitz, *Globalization and Its Discontents*; Rajan and Zingales, *Saving Capitalism from the Capitalists*; Caprio and Honohan, "Restoring Banking Stability"; Dam, *Rules of the Global Game*, 215–18. Robert Rubin and Jacob Weisberg, *In an Uncertain World* (New York: Random House, 2003), 217.

[41] Carlos Arteta, Barry Eichengreen, and Charles Wyplosz, "When Does Capital Account Liberalization Help More Than It Hurts?" NBER Working Paper No. w8414, August 2001.

[42] Pierre-Richard Agénor, "Benefits and Costs of International Financial Integration: Theory and Facts," Working Paper No. 2699, Washington, DC: The World Bank, 2002; Eduardo Borensztein, José De Gregorio, and Jong Wha Lee, "How Does Foreign Direct Investment Affect Economic Growth?" *Journal of International Economics* 45 (June 1998): 115–35.

growth."[43] So, while open capital markets should benefit LDCs in principle, in practice the benefits are somewhat murkier.[44]

The political and economic costs to governments in emerging markets of regulatory coordination are considerable, although they vary based on the relative depth of the capital market. Governments with repressed capital markets incur political costs in the form of lost patronage power over the allocation of scarce finance. States with liberal capital markets incur economic costs in the form of a loss of comparative advantage relative to developed markets. Both types of countries also incur costs from implementing and enforcing the requisite financial regulation.

For countries with underdeveloped capital markets, the most obvious political cost of stringent regulation is the loss of the state's ability to allocate scarce finance to important political supporters.[45] Governments can exploit repressed capital markets and privileged access to scarce foreign exchange to reward favored interests and political supporters.[46] Leaders who want to stay in power will try to direct government benefits toward key backers. One of the most potent levers in less developed countries is access to government-owned or government-influenced financial institutions.

Stringent regulatory coordination undercuts this political lever in two ways. First, appropriate regulation creates oversight institutions to segment political actors from the financial sector. Properly enforced, stringent regulatory structures prevent clientilism in financial markets. At a minimum, regulatory oversight raises the political and economic costs of engaging in acts of favoritism. Second, regulatory coordination combined with access to foreign markets reduces the scarcity of capital in emerging markets. These institutions' ability to borrow from foreign sources dilutes the utility of the financial lever for political actors. Rewarding political allies with access to finance means less if capital is less scarce. This translates into high adjustment costs for any regulatory shift. A cosseted financial sector generates high exit barriers for both the financial sector and the government. One would therefore expect any proposed regulatory reform would generate the strong use of voice by both private- and public-sector officials.

For emerging markets with offshore financial centers, coordination raises the specter of losing their institutional comparative advantage. Less stringent

---

[43] Fischer, "Globalization and Its Challenges," 17.

[44] See, at more length, Jean-Pierre Gourinchas and Olivier Jeanne, "The Elusive Gains from International Financial Integration," NBER Working Paper No. w9684, May 2003.

[45] Lindsey, *Against the Dead Hand*; Rajan and Zingales, *Saving Capitalism from the Capitalists.*

[46] A rent-seeking narrative has a different logic but a similar conclusion. In this scenario, state leaders exploit their positions of power to direct finance toward their own enterprises as a way of enriching themselves. In either scenario, government officials redirect capital away from their most efficient location as a way of benefiting themselves.

regulations lower operating costs for financial institutions in OFCs, permitting them to undercut international competition in terms of price. Lax regulatory enforcement has a similar effect of lowering the financial sector's marginal costs. This effect would be particularly pronounced in the potential loss of illicit capital flows. A former president of the IMF estimates the size of illicit capital flows at approximately 2–5 percent of global GDP, or upwards of $2 trillion.[47] Emerging markets with offshore financial centers have fewer disclosure requirements for customers. This provides black market entrepreneurs—such as narcotics traffickers—the opportunity to insert assets into the global financial marketplace. Although there are long-term risks to reputation for the emerging markets, many of these governments operate on the principle of "any capital is good capital" and are therefore loath to displace such investments in the name of regulatory coordination.[48]

Finally, emerging markets must invest in the training and implementation necessary to enforce any newly adopted regulations. From the perspective of a developed economy, such an investment would appear to be minimal. However, the transaction costs of compliance with the rules of the global marketplace can be considerable for developing country bureaucracies.[49] This is particularly true when dealing with international economic institutions, because of the complexity of the rules involved. The effective regulation of sophisticated financial markets requires a great deal of human capital, a relatively scarce resource in emerging markets.

For developed country governments, the benefits to global regulatory coordination in an era of globalization are transparent. The distribution of costs among these governments is relatively even, with federal states incurring slightly greater costs. For developing countries, the benefits of regulatory coordination at stringent levels require a long-term time horizon, and appear to be indirect. The costs are short-term and significant for the governments in power. Given this distribution of preferences, one would predict global governance in financial matters to follow a club standards model. Attempts to harmonize international financial regulation should originate in club-based organizations dominated by the economic great powers—the United States and the European Union.

[47] Michel Camdessus, "Money Laundering: the Importance of International Countermeasures," speech delivered to the Financial Action Task Force, Paris, France, February 10, 1998.

[48] Peter Quirk, "Macroeconomic Implications of Money Laundering," IMF Working Paper 66, Washington, DC, 2002.

[49] Stiglitz, *Globalization and Its Discontents*, 227; Cally Jordan and Giovanni Majnoni, "Financial Regulatory Harmonization and the Globalization of Finance," World Bank Policy Research Working Paper 2919, Washington, DC, 2002; Eric Reinhardt, "Tying Hands without a Rope: Rational Domestic Response to International Institutional Constraints," in *Locating the Proper Authorities*, ed. Daniel W. Drezner (Ann Arbor: University of Michigan Press, 2003).

Forum Shopping after Financial Crises

Prior to the financial crises of the mid- to late 1990s, there was not a significant amount of global regulatory coordination of financial markets. Tony Porter surmises, "Before 1999, capacity for prudential regulation at the international level was fragmented."[50] What regulation existed focused primarily on banking among the developed countries, that is, the Basle Capital Accord and the Basle Concordat. These rules were not intended to affect developing countries. Efforts to expand regulatory coordination to such areas as securities markets or money laundering were ineffective.[51] *None* of the financial standards now considered to be important by the IFIs existed prior to 1996.[52]

This was due, in large part, to a lack of demand. Financial markets were thought to be so segmented that global regulatory coordination was unnecessary. Prior to the Mexican crisis, Richard Herring and Robert Litan observed:

> [R]egulation of financial activities and the institutions that conduct them continues to be carried out mostly by national, and in some countries subnational, governments. By the same token, the problems countries have experienced in financial institutions have so far been confined largely to national borders. The now infamous savings and loan debacle in the United States had essentially no international ramifications. The same is generally true for . . . the troubles of banks in Japan and the Scandinavian countries in the early 1990s.[53]

At the same time, the *costs* of any regulatory coordination were perceived to be too great as well, as Miles Kahler pointed out: "National regulatory regimes

[50] Tony Porter, "The Democratic Deficit in the Institutional Arrangements for Regulating Global Finance," *Global Governance* 7 (October–December 2001): 427–39.

[51] Miles Kahler, *International Institutions and the Political Economy of Integration* (Washington, DC: Brookings Institution, 1995); Tommaso Padoa-Schioppa and Fabrizio Saccomanni, "Managing a Market-Led Global Financial System," in *Managing the World Economy: Fifty Years after Bretton Woods*, ed. Peter Kenen (Washington, DC: Institute for International Economics, 1995); Braithwaite and Drahos, *Global Business Regulation*.

In the wake of the Herstatt banking crisis in 1974, the Group of Ten countries created what is now known as the Basle Committee on Banking Supervision, or Basle Committee, which was responsible for the Basle Concordat, an agreement to ensure that "no foreign banking establishment escaped adequate supervision," as well as the Basle Capital Accord. For more on this era of regulation, see Richard Herring and Robert Litan, *Financial Regulation in the Global Economy* (Washington, DC: Brookings Institution, 1995), 99, as well as Kapstein, "Resolving the Regulator's Dilemma."

[52] Among the codes and standards collected in the Financial Stability Forum's *Compendium of Standards*, eleven existed prior to 1996, and none of those are among the twelve "key standards." Sixty-nine standards were created between 1996 and 2002, including all of the twelve key standards. Some of these, however, do include elements devised prior to 1996. For example, the Basle Core Principles incorporate adherence to the 1988 Basle Capital Accord. See http://www.fsforum.org/compendium/compendium_of_standards_date_2002.html, accessed March 31, 2006.

[53] Herring and Litan, *Financial Regulation in the Global Economy*, 1. This observation also held for the crisis within the European exchange rate mechanism in the early 1990s.

in the financial sector are much more deeply embedded in political bargains ... internationally agreed changes are much more prone to pressures undermining their implementation."[54] Prior to the wave of financial turbulence starting in early 1995, the calculation of most analysts was that the costs of coordinating financial supervision and regulation exceeded the benefits. Because the international externalities of national financial crises were considered to be small, no bargaining core existed for enhanced coordination.

The financial crises that hit Latin America in 1994–95 and East Asia in 1997–98 dramatically altered these perceptions.[55] It became accepted wisdom that poor financial regulation contributed to the depth and breadth of these crises.[56] In the wake of the Mexican peso crisis, a Group of Seven background paper on the IFIs stressed the need for greater coordination of regulatory authorities:

> [W]ith today's highly integrated financial markets, there is a greater potential for the rapid transmission of financial disturbances. Close international cooperation in the regulation and supervision of markets is essential to the continued safeguarding of the financial system and to prevent erosion of necessary prudential standards. . . . In this context, we recognize the important initiatives being undertaken separately and jointly by various committees under the aegis of the BIS [Bank of International Settlements] and the International Commissions as well as by national authorities.[57]

A year later, at the 1996 Lyon summit, the G-7 statement focused more on the role that common financial codes and standards should play. The heads of state communiqué wanted "maximum progress" on "encouraging the adoption of strong prudential standards in emerging economies and increasing cooperation with their supervisory authorities; international financial institutions and bodies should increase their efforts to promote effective supervisory structures in these economies."[58] The intent of the G-7 was to raise the regulatory standards of developing countries to first-world levels.

The Asian financial crisis merely reinforced and expanded the great power demand for global regulatory coordination in financial matters. The Mexican crisis was largely a product of how the country's large current account deficit affected the government's ability to repay its sovereign debt. The Asian crisis,

---

[54] Kahler, *International Institutions and the Political Economy of Integration*, 71.

[55] An excellent summary of this period comes from Kenen, *The International Financial Architecture*, chap. 1, and Paul Blustein, *The Chastening* (Washington, DC: PublicAffairs, 2001).

[56] See the citations in footnote 40.

[57] Group of Seven Finance Ministers, "Review of the International Financial Institutions," 1995, available at http://www.g7.utoronto.ca/summit/1995halifax/financial/6.html, accessed March 31, 2006. All G-7 documents can be accessed at http://www.g7.utoronto.ca.

[58] Economic Communiqué, Lyon G-7 Summit, June 28, 1996, paragraph 11, available at http://www.g7.utoronto.ca/summit/1996lyon/communique/eco1.htm, accessed March 31, 2006.

in contrast, was worsened by a failure of these countries' financial sectors to efficiently allocate their access to cheap foreign capital, as Gerard Caprio and Patrick Honohan observe:

> As additional funds became available from abroad, banking systems across east Asia funneled that money into their respective economies, ramping up a boom in real estate and equity prices. The lack of reliable financial information and trustworthy mechanisms for enforcing contracts (including bankruptcy procedures) made for a situation where lending was happening without a clear sense of whether it would be repaid or what procedures would be followed in the case of bankruptcy.[59]

The close relationship between the large banks, the primary industrial groupings, and the political elites badly compromised regulatory and prudential supervision of the financial sector.[60] Even more than the peso crisis, the spread of the Asian crisis to Russia and Brazil exposed both the complex interdependence of financial markets and the poor regulation and supervision of financial sectors among emerging economies. U.S. Treasury secretary Robert Rubin concluded, "Better regulatory infrastructure and stronger financial institutions alongside more open capital markets would have reduced the potential for instability."[61]

At this juncture, a key question remained unanswered: which forum would decide the relevant financial codes and standards that merited global coordination? Although many considered the IMF to be a natural focal point for such a decision-making process, the great powers were exceedingly wary of using the IMF as the primary decision-making forum. The emphasis in the 1995 G-7 statement quoted above on the Bank of International Settlements (BIS) and its emanations is telling. Even before the Mexico crisis, some European officials had observed that club-based models of governance like the G-7, G-10, or the Basle Committee were better suited than the IMF to handle the regulation of financial matters.[62]

It could be argued that the IMF and World Bank were *already* clubs of the developed great powers, and therefore one would expect the IFIs to remain the principal foci of efforts to harmonize regulatory standards.[63] Indeed, the

---

[59] Caprio and Honohan, "Restoring Banking Stability," 46.

[60] Stijn Claessens, Simeon Djankov, Joseph Fan, and Larry Lang, "Corporate Diversification in East Asia: The Role of Ultimate Ownership and Group Affiliation," World Bank Policy Research Paper 2089, March 1999; Lindsey, *Against the Dead Hand*, chap. 7.

[61] Rubin and Weisberg, *In an Uncertain World*, 256.

[62] Padoa-Schioppa and Saccomanni, "Managing a Market-Led Global Financial System," 263–65. Even when the G-7 countries created the New Arrangements to Borrow at the IMF in the wake of the Mexico crisis, they insisted on retaining control for disbursement among the G-10 states (Kenen, *The International Financial Architecture*, 4).

[63] Stiglitz, *Globalization and Its Discontents*; Kimberly Ann Elliott, Debayani Kar, and J. David Richardson, "Assessing Globalization's Critics: 'Talkers Are No Good Doers?'" in *Challenges to*

IFIs, by operating as credit unions, are unique among universal IGOs in allocating voting rights by economic size rather than one country, one vote.[64] Over the fifty-year history of the institution, the salience of economic size has only increased in determining voting quotas.[65] Combined, the United States and European Union members controlled more than 45 percent of the voting power in the IMF Executive Board.[66] This leads to an obvious question: given the unequal distribution of voting power within the IFIs, why didn't the great powers simply formulate and implement their regulatory policies within these institutions?

First, despite the weighted voting structure, there remains a strong norm of consensual decision-making within Fund governance bodies. Rule C-10 of the IMF's Bylaws, Rules, and Regulations states that at IMF Executive Board meetings, "The Chairman shall ordinarily ascertain the sense of the meeting in lieu of a formal vote."[67] In April 1998, the U.S. executive director to the IMF testified before Congress that during her tenure she had recorded a formal vote in only twelve out of approximately two thousand IMF Executive Board decisions.[68] One career IMF bureaucrat, in discussing the decision-making procedures within the IMF, observes:

> On complex issues there is, generally, an understanding that "nothing will be decided until everything is agreed." This practice offers valuable protection to the developing countries because interrelated issues may well involve financial matters, such as the rate of charge or the rate of remuneration, or other issues requiring a special voting majority for decision making. It provides the developing countries as a group with a potential veto power to ensure that the package as a whole would be acceptable to them.[69]

A developing country executive director of the IMF concurs:

Globalization, ed. Robert E. Baldwin and L. Alan Winters, 17–62 (Chicago: University of Chicago Press, 2004).

[64] Since the early 1980s, the determinants of quota size include, "GNP, official reserves, current external payments and receipts, the variability of current receipts, and the ratio of current receipts to GNP." See Leo van Houtven, "Governance of the IMF," *IMF Pamphlet Series* 53, Washington, DC, 2002, 5. For more on the weighted voting concept, see Stephen Zamora, "Voting in International Economic Organizations," *American Journal of International Law* 74 (July 1980): 566–608.

[65] Ngaire Woods, "The Challenge of Good Governance for the IMF and the World Bank Themselves," *World Development* 28 (May 2000): 823–41; Woods, *The Globalizers: The IMF, the World Bank, and Their Borrowers* (Ithaca: Cornell University Press, 2006).

[66] For the allocation of voting rights, see IMF, "IMF Executive Directors and Voting Power," at http://www.imf.org/external/np/sec/memdir/eds.htm#1, and "IMF Members' Quotas and Voting Power," at http://www.imf.org/external/np/sec/memdir/members.htm#1, accessed March 31, 2006.

[67] Available at http://www.imf.org/external/pubs/ft/bl/rr03.htm#p3, accessed March 31, 2006.

[68] Quoted in Carol Welch, "The IMF and Good Governance," *Foreign Policy in Focus* 3 (October 1998): 3.

[69] Van Houtven, "Governance of the IMF," 24.

[T]he Board of this institution is democratic. I can not imagine another forum where the person with only 1 percent of the shares can take the floor and argue as long as the others. This has a moderating effect on the G-7.[70]

Subtle changes in the IMF's institutional structure created further difficulties for great power efforts at fostering consensus. In the 1970s, much of the Executive Board's policymaking power was delegated to an Interim Committee.[71] The memberships of the Executive Board and Interim Committee are equivalent, but the Committee does not have *any* formal voting rules—instead, the chair is expected to achieve a "sense of the meeting," and report on any minority viewpoints. These practices make the need for consensus even greater. Fully half of the membership consists of developing countries, making it difficult to foster a consensus on financial regulation.

The second constraint on great power influence is the size and professionalism of the IMF staff. Most international governmental organizations have small secretariats or are run by staff seconded from national governments. The IMF has a staff of approximately 2,650 individuals, attracting economists of the first rank into its organization.[72] The Fund has resident missions—its version of a diplomatic service—located in over seventy countries. The size, professionalism, and distribution of its staff provide the IMF leadership with independent sources of information. One U.S. Treasury official observed in an interview that although the United States wields considerable power in the IMF, "a strong staff can have influence and feel obligated to follow the consensus."[73] Michael Barnett and Martha Finnemore argue that the acknowledged expertise of the IMF's staff is an important source of the organization's legitimacy and agenda setting power.[74]

Critics of the IFIs are undeniably correct in pointing out that despite these mitigating circumstances, the underlying voting structure influences governance decisions. However, the important point is that *relative to club IGOs,*

---

[70] Quoted in Anne Bichsel, "The World Bank and the International Monetary Fund from the Perspective of the Executive Directors from Developing Countries," *Journal of World Trade* 28 (June 1994): 148.

[71] Available at http://www.imf.org/external/np/exr/facts/groups.htm#IC, accessed March 31, 2006. The Interim Committee was renamed the International Monetary and Financial Committee in September 1999. See http://www.imf.org/external/np/sec/pr/1999/PR9947.HTM, accessed March 31, 2006.

[72] Chwieroth, "Neoliberalism's Role in Capital Account Liberalization in Emerging Markets."

[73] Both of these constraints on great power influence are even more concentrated in the World Bank. The Bank, with approximately 10,000 employees, has a larger and more independent staff than the Fund. The norms of consensus carry greater weight in that institution as well. See Bischel, "The World Bank and the International Monetary Fund from the Perspective of the Executive Directors from Developing Countries"; Stiglitz, *Globalization and Its Discontents*; Sebastian Mallaby, *The World's Banker* (New York: Penguin Press, 2004).

[74] Michael Barnett and Martha Finnemore, *Rules for the World: International Organizations in Global Politics* (Ithaca: Cornell University Press, 2004), chapter 3.

the international financial institutions pose a more divergent set of actor preferences and greater transaction costs of decision-making. Even Ngaire Woods, a critic of the current IMF governance structure, acknowledges:

> The IMF and the World Bank enjoy a special place in the politics of international economic relations. Both organizations can claim a virtually universal membership and accountability to governments across the world. In this they are unlike most other international financial institutions, such as the Group of Seven (G-7), the Bank of International Settlements (BIS) the Group of Ten (G-10), and a host of other regulatory agencies. Indeed the claim to universal membership underpinned the IMF's recent insistence that deliberations on any reform of the global financial system should take place within the Fund's Interim Committee as opposed to any ad hoc or US-selected group of countries.[75]

As the next section demonstrates, however, the IMF's efforts to remain the focal point of reforming the international financial architecture did not succeed.

RATCHETING UP FINANCIAL CODES AND STANDARDS

By the summer of 1998, the Asian crisis was in full bloom. The G-7 recognized the need for further action, but was wary of giving the IMF too strong a role to play. The result was the creation of a new club IGO. The British finance minister and the U.S. undersecretary of the treasury for international affairs advocated for the creation of a new institution to coordinate the erection of a new financial architecture of regulatory standards.[76] In response, the G-7 finance ministers delegated Bundesbank president Hans Tietmeyer to develop recommendations for any new institutions to facilitate the "cooperation and coordination between the various international financial regulatory and supervisory bodies and the international financial institutions."[77] The resulting report led to the creation of the Financial Stability Forum (FSF), which was tasked with "strengthening and . . . encouraging the development and implementation of international best practices and standards."[78] As one veteran IMF

[75] Woods, "The Challenge of Good Governance for the IMF and the World Bank Themselves," 823.

[76] The British effort was public; the American effort was private. Interview with U.S. Treasury officials; Rubin and Weisberg, *In an Uncertain World*, 262.

[77] Statement by the G-7 Finance Ministers and Central Bank Governors, Washington DC, October 3, 1998, available at http://www.g7.utoronto.ca/finance/fm100398.htm, accessed June 12, 2003.

[78] Hans Tietmeyer, "International Cooperation and Coordination in the Area of Financial Market Supervision and Surveillance," report to the G-7 Ministers and Governors, February 11, 1999. The report is available at http://www.fsforum.org/publications/Tietmeyerreport.pdf.

official observed: "The Forum's responsibilities overlap in large part with the core financial tasks of the IMF."[79]

The FSF was constituted as a club of clubs, heavily tilted toward the representation of G-7 interests. At its inception, each G-7 member was assigned three members—one slot for a finance ministry official, one slot for a central bank official, and one slot for a financial regulatory authority. Three other countries—Hong Kong, Australia, and the Netherlands—had a total of five members. The remaining sixteen members consisted of representatives from the IFIs, the BIS and its emanations, and preexisting regulatory bodies. Six of those sixteen representatives came from club-based organizations, of which the G-7 were the principal members.[80] The first chair of the FSF was Andrew Crockett, general manager of the BIS. The headquarters and staff of the FSF were seconded from the BIS headquarters. Barry Eichengreen concludes, "The FSF was created very much in the image of the Basle Committee of Banking Supervision, but with a broader remit."[81]

The composition of the FSF—as well as the standards highlighted for global implementation—was designed to ensure G-7 control over the standard-setting process. In discussing the process, Yung Chul Park and Yunjong Wang conclude, "In most of the forums or agencies drawing up standards, EMEs [emerging market economies] and DCs [developing countries] are not included or, at best, are underrepresented."[82] Tony Porter reaches a similar conclusion: "Despite their increased enthusiasm for consultations, the OECD and the Basel Committee do not include the developing countries as members, and the inclusion of . . . Hong Kong in the FSF hardly makes it much more representative."[83]

The FSF commissioned a task force to draw up a list of codes and standards to be promulgated globally. While the committee made an effort at inclusion, G-10 representatives outnumbered developing country representatives, and club IGO representatives outnumbered universal IGO representatives.[84] The

[79] Van Houtven, "Governance of the IMF," 41.

[80] The full membership list is available at http://www.fsforum.org/about/who_we_are.html.

[81] Barry Eichengreen, "Governing Global Financial Markets: International Responses to the Hedge-Fund Problem," in *Governance in a Global Economy*, ed. Miles Kahler and David A. Lake (Princeton, NJ: Princeton University Press, 2003), 186. See also OxFam International, "The IMF and the Global Financial Architecture," Washington, DC, April 2000, available at http://www.oxfam.org.uk/what_we_do/issues/democracy_rights/downloads/imf_architecture.rtf, accessed January 2006.

[82] Yung Chul Park and Yunjong Wang, "What Kind of International Financial Architecture for an Integrated World Economy?" paper prepared for the Asian Economic Panel, Cambridge, MA, April 2001, 22.

[83] Porter, "The Democratic Deficit in the Institutional Arrangements for Regulating Global Finance," 438.

[84] The report and the list of members can be accessed at http://www.fsforum.org/publications/Issues_Paper_Standards00.pdf.

TABLE 5.1

The Twelve Key Financial Codes and Standards

Subject Area	Issuing Body	Membership Size (by country)	Type of Organization
Monetary policy transparency	International Monetary Fund	184	Universal IGO
Fiscal policy transparency	International Monetary Fund	184	Universal IGO
Data dissemination	International Monetary Fund	184	Universal IGO
Insolvency	World Bank	184	Universal IGO
Corporate governance	Organization for Economic Cooperation and Development	30	Club IGO
Accounting	International Accounting Standards Board	0	Private order
Auditing	International Federation of Accountants	0	Private order
Payment and settlements	Committee on Payments and Settlements Systems	11	Club IGO
Money laundering	Financial Action Task Force	29	Club IGO
Banking supervision	Basle Committee on Banking Supervision	13	Club IGO
Securities regulation	International Organization of Securities Commissions	102	Universal IGO
Insurance supervision	International Association of Insurance Supervisors	101	Universal IGO

IMF representative opposed the creation of any list of financial codes and standards, but was not able to prevent the FSF from agreeing upon a set of key standards.[85] In April 2000, the FSF promulgated what it considered the twelve key financial codes and standards for the international system.

Table 5.1 displays these standards as well as their creating organizations. Half of the standards emanated from club IGOs or private orders. Only one of the agreed-upon standards provided any differentiation for the country's stage of economic development.[86] These standards represented a significant ratcheting up of stringency for the developing economies. When originally

[85] Interview with U.S. Treasury official, August 2001.

[86] The IMF created two standards for data dissemination. The General standard for less developed countries, and the Special standard for developed economies.

promulgated, many of these club-based standards were designed to represent "best practices" for the advanced economies.[87]

The club IGOs that managed the establishment of global financial standards—the Bank of International Settlements and its emanations—were appreciated by the great powers precisely because of their club characteristics.[88] One committee of American experts observed:

> During its 70-year history the BIS has adapted well to large changes in the financial industry and central banking practices. *Its ability to adapt was due largely to its limited and homogeneous membership.* An example of such adaptation is the way the BIS quickly rose to the challenge of meeting regulatory deficiencies at the international level. The BIS has also demonstrated its ability to convince the most financially important countries to adopt its standards. . . .
>
> *The monthly meetings of central bankers are held behind closed doors. This is widely regarded as an advantage. It facilitates discussion and comments within the group.* The BIS keeps a low profile and is not well-known outside the circles of central bankers.[89]

It is noteworthy that the U.S. Treasury Department, in its reply to that report, concurred with this assessment, agreeing that "expansion of membership in the BIS should be judicious and deliberate."[90] Similarly, Rubin found the informal processes surrounding these G-7 creations quite useful in crafting policy.[91]

John Braithwaite and Peter Drahos record a similar assessment in comparing the Basle Committee—a BIS emanation—to the International Organization of Securities Commissions (IOSCO)—a universal IGO:

> During its first decade IOSCO's accomplishments were minimal assessed in terms of settled harmonizations. IOSCO compared unfavorably with the Basle Committee's accomplishments on the harmonization of banking standards during the same period. As one senior regulator who has been active in both IOSCO and the Basle Committee portrayed the difference: "Basle is an example of leadership; IOSCO is an example of democracy. IOSCO had democracy with no leadership."[92]

---

[87] Interviews with U.S. Treasury officials, August 2001.

[88] For one example of appreciation by G-7 officials, see Padoa-Schioppa and Saccomanni, "Managing a Market-Led Global Financial System."

[89] International Financial Institution Advisory Commission, *Report of the International Financial Institution Advisory Commission*, 100 (emphasis added).

[90] U.S. Treasury Department, "Response to the Report of the International Financial Institution Advisory Commission," June 8, 2000, 42.

[91] Rubin and Weisberg, *In an Uncertain World*, 224.

[92] Braithwaite and Drahos, *Global Business Regulation*, 156. See also Simmons, "The International Politics of Harmonization," on IOSCO's weakness, though Braithwaite and Drahos (p. 158) suggest that its influence has grown in recent years.

ENFORCEMENT OF GLOBAL FINANCIAL STANDARDS

With the publication of the FSF's *Compendium of Standards*, the process of devising the relevant financial codes and standards clearly took place within a club IGO. However, the question of enforcement in the face of potential LDC resistance remained an issue. The great powers pursued a three-track policy on this issue. The first track was to link access to IFI resources to compliance with the twelve key codes and standards. The second track was to rely on club IGOs in lieu of the IFIs to coordinate sanctions against noncompliant countries. The final track was to rely on market-led enforcement, by communicating/publicizing national compliance with the relevant standards and codes to private sector financial institutions and rating agencies.[93]

On access to IFI resources, Mario Lamonte notes: "The G-7 seems to follow a hard-line approach."[94] In September 1999, the G-7 finance ministers initially argued that, "Countries should be encouraged to demonstrate their commitment to making rapid progress towards full compliance with existing international codes as part of IMF and World Bank conditionality when the IFIs extend loans or credits."[95] However, resistance from LDCs and the IMF staff made this issue a contentious one. The consensus decision-making structure of the IFIs rendered the G-7 unable to force through explicit conditionality between compliance and access to the preexisting range of IMF resources. The G-7 was able to link compliance with some of the key codes and standards to the new Contingency Credit Line, envisioned to assist countries with sound financial sectors but threatened by financial contagion.[96] However, this proved to be a dubious achievement, as no country opted for the new credit line.[97]

The G-7 countries pushed harder to have the twelve key standards incorporated into the IMF's surveillance function.[98] This move also met significant

[93] Morris Goldstein, "Strengthening the International Financial Architecture: Where Do We Stand?" Institute for International Economics Working Paper 00-8, Washington DC, 2000, and Porter, "The Democratic Deficit in the Institutional Arrangements for Regulating Global Finance," 433. See Layna Mosley, "Attempting Global Standards: National Governments, International Finance, and the IMF's Data Regime," *Review of International Political Economy* 10 (May): 331–62, for a skeptical appraisal of market-led enforcement. For a more positive assessment, see Helmut Reisen "Standards and Codes in the Global Financial Architecture," Paris: OECD Development Center, April 2002.

[94] Mario B. Lamonte, "Reforming the International Financial Architecture: The East Asian View," Philippine Institute for Development Studies Discussion Paper Series 2000-37, Makati City, Philippines, 2000, 15.

[95] G-7 Statement of Finance Ministers and Central Bank Governors, September 25, 1999, available at http://www.g7.utoronto.ca/finance/fm992509state.htm.

[96] In particular, adherence to the IMF's Data Dissemination Standard and the Basle Core Principles are prerequisites for access.

[97] Kenen, *The International Financial Architecture*, 126–27.

[98] Statement of G-7 Finance Ministers and Central Bank Governors, Washington, DC, April 16, 2000, available at http://www.g7.utoronto.ca/finance/fm001604.htm. See also the statements

resistance from the developing country members of the IMF's key decision-making body, the International Monetary and Finance Committee. Their primary concern was the adjustment costs to LDC governments:

Russian IMFC representative: "[W]e oppose hasty decisions to include the assessment of observance of standards and codes in the practice of the Fund's surveillance activities. . . . their implementation by certain countries requires substantial effort and/or outside technical assistance."[99]

South African representative: "[U]niversal application requires to be implemented with due flexibility. We urge the Fund to take greater cognisance of the different levels of development among members seeking to implement and to comply with the wide new range of elements of strengthened surveillance."[100]

Indian representative: "I must also add, however, that the plethora of these codes, standards and principles are overwhelming and highly demanding of manpower and financial resources. Not only do these involve avoidable micromanagement but they also have a potential to become overly intrusive vis-à-vis national authorities."[101]

The IMF staff concurred with this assessment.[102] Stanley Fischer, the IMF's deputy managing director at the time, observed in June 2000: "There is a concern in some countries that the Fund is pushing too hard for the implementation of these standards. Maybe it is true that we sometimes risk overburdening their absorptive capacity."[103]

These objections managed to delay but not prevent the IMF from agreeing to expand its surveillance activities to match the codes and standards highlighted by the FSF. By acting as a great power-endorsed focal point, the FSF *Compendium of Standards* prevented any alternative set of standards or ideas from acquiring significant support.[104] In 2000, the IFIs agreed to expand their Reports on the Observance of Standards and Codes (ROSC). One victory for the developing countries came in the decision to make the ROSC "modules" voluntary rather than mandatory. However, this was only a nominal success. One U.S. Treasury official pointed out in an interview that an LDC government

---

of the G-7 finance ministers to the IMF's International Financial and Monetary Committee—especially those by U.S. Treasury Secretary Lawrence Summers and French Finance Minister Laurent Fabius—at http://www.imf.org/external/spring/2000/imfc/, accessed March 31, 2006.

[99] Available at http://www.imf.org/external/spring/2000/imfc/rus.htm.

[100] Available at http://www.imf.org/external/spring/2000/imfc/zaf.htm.

[101] Available at http://www.imf.org/external/spring/2000/imfc/ind.htm.

[102] Van Houtven, "Governance of the IMF," 54–55.

[103] Stanley Fischer, "The IMF and the Financial Sector," speech given at the Seminar on Financial Risks, System Stability, and Economic Globalization, Washington DC, June 5, 2000.

[104] Thomas Schelling, *The Strategy of Conflict* (Cambridge, MA: Harvard University Press, 1960); Geoffrey Garrett and Barry Weingast, "Ideas, Interests, and Institutions: Constructing the European Community's Common Market," in *Ideas and Foreign Policy*, ed. Judith Goldstein and Robert Keohane (Ithaca, NY: Cornell University Press, 1993).

decision *not* to release its IMF assessments publicly would in and of itself "raise eyebrows" in financial markets. Even if there was no explicit linkage between compliance and conditionality, the developing countries sensed an implied threat of coercion. As one OECD economist pointed out: "how 'voluntary' is the adherence to standards if there is an implicit link to IMF lending programmes?"[105] In its first two years of operation, more than 70 percent of the ROSC modules were made publicly available on the IMF's Web site.

A year into the ROSC process, the IMF staff reported the following reactions from developing country participants:

> Participants remarked on the shift in attitude that had taken place on this point over the past two years. Participants noted that a striking sign of progress was that the value of international standards is now taken as given, and is no longer a subject for debate.

> However, concerns were also expressed. The major concern of some country authorities was for greater participation by developing and emerging market countries in the development of international standards. While some standard-setting bodies already have wide membership or conduct consultation with non-member countries, participants at the Conference agreed that more should be done to reflect the views and needs of developing and emerging market countries.[106]

Developing country officials and economists also voiced concerns about the implementation costs of the new set of financial standards.[107]

By November 2002, the World Bank and IMF recognized the Financial Stability Forum's twelve key standards—and only those twelve key standards.[108] By April 2003, the Fund had conducted 291 separate ROSCs in seventy-four different jurisdictions.[109] The chairman of the British Financial Services Authority commented in 2003 that surveillance of national compliance with these standards and codes is, "now consuming a significant proportion of the Fund's resources."[110] The IMF Executive Board agreed, noting that, "standards assessments are being increasingly integrated into Fund operations."[111]

---

[105] Reisen, "Standards and Codes in the Global Financial Architecture," 2.

[106] IMF Policy Development and Review Department, "Quarterly Report on the Assessments of Standards and Codes," June 29, 2001, available at http://www.imf.org/external/pubs/ft/stand/q/2001/eng/062901.htm, accessed March 31, 2006.

[107] Lamonte, "Reforming the International Financial Architecture; Park and Wang, "What Kind of International Financial Architecture for an Integrated World Economy?"

[108] "List of Standards, Codes and Principles Useful for Bank and Fund Operational Work and for which Reports on the Observance of Standards and Codes Are Produced," November 2002, available at http://www.imf.org/external/standards/scnew.htm, accessed March 31, 2006.

[109] Information available at http://www.imf.org/external/np/rosc/rosc.asp.

[110] Howard Davies, "Is the Global Regulatory System Fit for Purpose in the 21st Century?" Monetary Authority of Singapore Lecture speech, May 13, 2003.

[111] "IMF Executive Board Reviews International Standards," Public Information Notice No. 03/43, Washington, DC: International Monetary Fund. Raghuram Rajan, the IMF's chief economist,

The great powers were able to maximize the legitimacy of their club-derived standards by relying on a universal IGO with treaty status to help with enforcement. As John Eatwell concludes, "the IMF is using a treaty-sanctioned surveillance function to examine adherence to codes and principles that are not themselves developed by accountable treaty bodies."[112] At the same time, because of the IMF's universal membership and consensus decision-making structure, the G-7 was thwarted from achieving all of its enforcement goals within the IFI structure.

The great powers relied on club IGOs to ensure that the most flagrant violators of the financial codes and standards—countries with offshore financial centers or significant amounts of official corruption—faced additional sanctions. The choice of club IGOs was quite conscious. One American policymaker described the problem with regard to money laundering:

> [A]ny strategy had to be global and multilateral, since unilateral actions would only drive dirty money to the world's other financial centers. Yet Washington could not afford to take a "bottom-up" approach of seeking a global consensus before taking action; if the debate were brought to the U.N. General Assembly, for example, nations with underregulated financial regimes would easily outvote those with a commitment to strong international standards.[113]

Because of this distribution of preferences, the great powers turned to club IGOs—namely, the Financial Action Task Force on Money Laundering (FATF), OECD, and the FSF. The OECD was tasked with clamping down on uncooperative tax havens. The Financial Stability Forum was tasked with developing a blacklist of unregulated OFCs. Of the three club IGOs, however, the FATF initiative to enforce anti-money-laundering standards functions as an exemplar case of club standards enforcement.

In June 1999, the G-7 heads of state pushed for FATF to take an even more aggressive posture toward nonmembers whose laws appeared to tolerate money laundering.[114] In February 2000, FATF published criteria to identify "non-cooperative countries and territories" (NCCTs), a schedule for selecting and evaluating jurisdictions for NCCT status, and a menu of "countermeasures" for those governments that refused to comply with FATF requests. The countermeasures ranged from the issuance of advisories to domestic financial institutions to the

---

recently observed in an interview that the IMF was paying more attention to the question of financial regulation. See the interview at http://www.rediff.com/money/2003/jul/04inter.htm, accessed March 31, 2006.

[112] John Eatwell, "The Challenges Facing International Financial Integration," unpublished manuscript, Queens College, Cambridge University, Cambridge, UK, 2000, 10.

[113] Wechsler, "Follow the Money," 41.

[114] See the June 18, 1999 Communiqué by G-7 Heads of State and Government at http://www.g7.utoronto.ca/g7/summit/1999koln/g7statement_june18.htm.

most serious possible sanction: "conditioning, restricting, targeting, or even prohibiting financial transactions with non-cooperative jurisdictions."[115]

FATF members reviewed the first group of possible NCCTs between February and June 2000. Twenty-nine jurisdictions were assessed, and fifteen were listed as NCCTs (see table 5.2). The jurisdictions ranged from microstates in the South Pacific to the Russian Federation. FATF demanded that these countries take the legislative and administrative steps to criminalize money laundering, establish centralized financial intelligence units, cooperate with other national authorities in money laundering investigations, and require banks to file suspicious activity reports to the government. With regard to the NCCTs, FATF warned, "should those countries or territories identified as non-cooperative maintain their detrimental rules and practices despite having been encouraged to make certain reforms, FATF members would then need to consider the adoption of countermeasures."[116] A month later, the G-7 finance ministers strongly supported FATF's NCCT initiative as well as the potential sanctions that backed up the threat. The G-7 stated: "We are prepared to act together when required and appropriate to implement coordinated countermeasures against those NCCTs that do not take steps to reform their system appropriately, including the possibility to condition or restrict financial transactions with those jurisdictions."[117]

Table 5.2 summarizes the extent of NCCT concessions, as well as the FATF response. Of the fifteen NCCTs, four of them—The Bahamas, Cayman Islands, Liechtenstein, and Panama—acquiesced completely, passing all of the necessary anti-money-laundering laws and staffing the requisite agencies to implement those laws. Another seven countries—Cook Islands, Dominica, Israel, Lebanon, Marshall Islands, St. Kitts and Nevis, and Russia—made significant concessions, enacting comprehensive legislation but not implementing it immediately. Three more jurisdictions—Niue, the Philippines, and St. Vincent and the Grenadines—passed laws that addressed enough FATF demands to temporarily avoid sanctions. Finally, Nauru made minor but insufficient concessions, leading to the FATF imposition of financial sanctions in December 2001. In total, 73 percent of the target countries made major concessions prior to the implementation of any economic sanctions. The demonstration effect of the first round of the NCCT process, combined with the enhanced salience of money laundering

---

[115] Financial Action Task Force, *Report on Non-Cooperative Countries and Territories*, Paris, February 14, 2000, 8.

[116] Financial Action Task Force, *Review to Identify Non-Cooperative Countries and Territories: Increasing the Worldwide Effectiveness of Anti-Money Laundering Measures*, Paris, June 22, 2000, 12.

[117] G-7 Finance Ministers report, "Actions against the Abuse of the Global Financial System," July 21, 2000, available at http://www.g7.utoronto.ca/summit/2000okinawa/abuse.htm, accessed 25 October 2004.

TABLE 5.2
Success of FATF Threats of Economic Coercion

Target Country	Concessions to FATF	FATF Response
The Bahamas	Complete acquiescence (Comprehensive anti-money-laundering laws enacted and implemented)	Sanctions threat lifted (Removed from NCCT list)
Cayman Islands	Complete acquiescence (Comprehensive anti-money-laundering laws enacted and fully implemented)	Sanctions threat lifted (Removed from NCCT list)
Cook Islands	Moderate concessions (Comprehensive anti-money-laundering laws enacted; implementation plan in progress)	Sanctions threat suspended indefinitely
Dominica	Moderate concessions (Comprehensive anti-money-laundering laws enacted; implementation plan in progress)	Sanctions threat suspended
Israel	Moderate concessions (Comprehensive anti-money-laundering laws enacted; implementation plan in progress)	Sanctions threat suspended indefinitely
Lebanon	Moderate concessions (Significant anti-money-laundering laws enacted; implementation plan in progress)	Sanctions threat suspended indefinitely
Liechtenstein	Complete acquiescence (Comprehensive anti-money-laundering laws enacted and implemented)	Sanctions threat lifted (Removed from NCCT list)
Marshall Islands	Moderate concessions (Comprehensive anti-money-laundering laws enacted; implementation plan in progress)	Sanctions threat suspended indefinitely
Nauru	Minor concessions (Incomplete anti-money-laundering laws enacted)	Sanctions imposed in December 2001
Niue	Minor concessions (Incomplete anti-money-laundering laws enacted)	Sanctions threat suspended
Panama	Complete acquiescence (Comprehensive anti-money-laundering laws enacted and fully implemented)	Sanctions threat lifted (Removed from NCCT list)
Philippines	Minor concessions (Incomplete anti-money-laundering laws enacted)	Sanctions threat suspended
Russia	Moderate concessions (Significant anti-money-laundering laws enacted; implementation plan in progress)	Sanctions threat suspended
St. Kitts and Nevis	Moderate concessions (Comprehensive anti-money-laundering laws enacted; implementation plan in progress)	Sanctions threat suspended indefinitely
St. Vincent and the Grenadines	Minor concessions (Incomplete anti-money-laundering laws enacted)	Sanctions threat suspended

in the wake of the 9/11 attacks, caused several other potential targets of coercion to preemptively adopt rigorous anti-money-laundering measures.[118]

There is clear evidence to support the contention that these jurisdictions altered their laws in direct response to the FATF threat of economic coercion. When Lebanon passed its anti-money-laundering legislation, its central bank governor explicitly stated that the law was designed to meet FATF's criteria.[119] Dominica's finance minister urged for the passage of an anti-money-laundering bill in order to escape the FATF "blacklist."[120] When Russia was debating its anti-money-laundering legislation, the Russian finance minister and the chairman of the Duma's banking committee explicitly urged passage in order to avoid FATF countermeasures.[121] Other targets expressed similar sentiments, either in public or in negotiations with FATF officials.[122] Although media coverage of this initiative was scant, what reporting there was confirms this assessment.[123]

The G-7 countries used persuasion and inducements as well as sanctions to ensure broad acceptance of the need to ratchet up anti-money-laundering standards. The G-7 encouraged the creation of FATF-style regional bodies in the developing world, such as the Caribbean Financial Action Task Force and the Asia-Pacific Group on Money Laundering. By 2001 five regional bodies had been created with a collective membership of 108 jurisdictions.[124] For these regional groups, the G-7 proffered technical assistance to ensure adherence and recognition of the FATF Forty Recommendations on Money Laundering. By August 2001, over 140 countries and territories had publicly acknowledged the FATF 40 as the accepted international standard for anti–money laundering. Through club IGOs like the G-7 and FATF, great powers were able to cajole, coerce, and enforce a global anti-money-laundering standard into existence.

ALTERNATIVE EXPLANATIONS AND THE INTERNATIONAL
FINANCIAL ARCHITECTURE

The FSF was not the only institutional response to the Asian financial crisis— the Group of Twenty (G-20) was also established in 1999. This forum includes

---

[118] Daniel W. Drezner, "The Hidden Hand of Economic Coercion: The Case of Money Laundering," paper presented at the 4th pan-European meeting of the European Consortium on Political Research's Standing Group on International Relations, Canterbury, UK, September 2001.

[119] "Lebanon Approves Money Laundering Law," Reuters, April 10, 2001.

[120] "Opposition in Dominica Blasts Anti-Money-Laundering Bill," Reuters, June 16, 2001.

[121] Marta Srnic, "Russians Tackle Money Laundering," Bloomberg News, June 25, 2001; Svetlana Kovalyova, "Russian Government Urges Passage of Anti-Money-Laundering Bill," Reuters, June 26, 2001.

[122] Canute James and Michael Peel, "Tax Havens Tighten Rules," *Financial Times*, June 17, 2001.

[123] See the *Economist*, "Fighting the Dirt," June 21, 2001.

[124] Membership lists can be found at http://www1.oecd.org/fatf/Members_en.htm#OBSERVERS, accessed March 31, 2006.

all G-7 members, a few other developed countries, and the significant emerging markets, including Argentina, Brazil, China, India, Indonesia, Mexico, and Russia.[125] Given the disparate preferences of these members, the G-20 cannot be categorized as a club IGO. Tony Porter argues that the G-20 was just as important as the FSF in legitimizing the regulatory response.[126] However, there are significant problems with this interpretation. First, the G-20 is institutionally thinner than either the G-7 or the FSF. In contrast to either of the latter clubs, the G-20 meets only once a year, and has no secretariat or working groups. Although the grouping was ostensibly designed to oversee the codes and standards initiative, European officials insisted at the inaugural meeting that it would have no decision-making authority over the FSF—a fact reflected in the 1999 communiqué.[127] According to interviews with U.S. Treasury officials, the G-20 was designed to act as one mechanism among many to legitimize the output of the FSF, and was never considered to be a governance substitute.[128]

In contrast to the great power concert of the FSF, efforts by other actors to generate new rules of the global financial game floundered. The creation of the FSF and the promulgation of stringent standards diverged significantly from what the epistemic community of financial experts wanted.[129] Most experts agreed that the IMF should pay greater attention to the relevant financial codes and standards in its surveillance function. However, the bulk of this discourse focused on how to reallocate the division of labor between the Bank and the Fund, how to improve IFI accountability, and whether the IMF should play a role as the lender of last resort.[130] The failure of this consensus to affect real change in G-7 policy preferences undercuts epistemic community or ideational arguments about the regulation of globalization. As Porter concludes, "The strong and overt political guidance exercised by the G-7 over the FSF was a marked change from the earlier heavily technical governance of the regime."[131]

Some scholars have asserted that the changes in financial codes and standards have been made at the behest of the big firms in the financial sectors of

---

[125] See membership list at http://www.g20.org/public/index.php?page=members&skin=1, accessed July 30, 2004.

[126] Tony Porter, "The G-7, the Financial Stability Forum, the G-20, and the Politics of International Financial Regulation," paper presented at the International Studies Association annual meeting, Los Angeles, CA, March 15, 2000.

[127] Cited in Porter, "The G-7, the Financial Stability Forum, the G-20, and the Politics of International Financial Regulation," 5. For the 1999 communiqué, see http://www.g20.org/download/public/19991216_kommuniques_berlin_minist_en.pdf, accessed July 30, 2004.

[128] Interviews with Treasury officials, August 2001.

[129] Contrary to assertions that there was no agreement among the experts, John Williamson concludes that, "the degree of consensus exhibited is quite significant." See Williamson, "The Role of the IMF."

[130] See the citations in footnote 4.

[131] Porter, "The G-7, the Financial Stability Forum, the G-20, and the Politics of International Financial Regulation," 10.

the great powers.[132] However, this does not fit with important aspects of the new codes and standards. For example, the G-7 pushed for a ratcheting up of anti-money-laundering standards in direct opposition to financial sectors in the United States and Europe. Private sector actors were more concerned about the costs of complying with new regulations. Banks, for example, were concerned about the added cost of implementing know-your-customer regulations.[133] Attempts were made by the larger financial firms to set up a private order as a means of warding off further state regulations.[134] In the United States, firms in the financial sector did relay concerns to Treasury officials about the regulatory shift.[135] Those pressures failed to dissuade Treasury officials from their course of action.

As for other states, East Asian governments made the most concerted effort to alter the international financial architecture—to little avail. Japan's efforts in September 1997 to establish an Asian Monetary Fund during the height of the crisis as a means of bypassing IMF strictures failed when U.S. officials pressured other Asian countries to reject the proposal. Eisuke Sakakibara, the Japanese vice minister of finance who floated the proposal, acknowledged afterward, "We were taught a valuable lesson on the influence the United States wields in Asia."[136] A drive by the Asian countries to apply more direct regulation of hedge funds came to naught because of disagreements between the United States and European countries over the merits of such efforts.[137]

Conclusions

The process of creating and enforcing global financial regulation clearly follows a club standards model of global governance. In designing the content of global financial regulations, the great powers largely bypassed the IFIs. Instead, the United States and European Union created club IGOs—like the Financial Stability Forum—and empowered other club IGOs—such as the Basle Committee and the Financial Action Task Force—to ensure control over the establishment and enforcement of common financial standards. The G-7 countries then pushed to have the IFIs act as enforcement regimes for these new standards, with moderate success. Developing country IGOs, in contrast, had no influ-

---

[132] Stiglitz, *Globalization and Its Discontents*; Susanne Soederberg, "The Promotion of 'Anglo-American' Corporate Governance in the South: Who Benefits from the New International Standard?" *Third World Quarterly* 24 (February 2003): 7–27.

[133] See Florini, "Does the Invisible Hand Need a Transparent Glove?"

[134] For the efforts at private order, see Mark Peith and Gemma Aiolfi, "The Private Sector Become Active: The Wolfsberg Process," *Journal of Financial Crime* 10 (April 2003): 359–65.

[135] Interviews with U.S. Treasury officials, August 2004.

[136] Quoted in Blustein, *The Chastening*, 168.

[137] Eichengreen, "Governing Global Financial Markets," 195.

ence over the setting of global financial standards, and were badly weakened from the financial crises and their aftermath.[138]

The normative and positive implications to draw from this chapter are quite significant. Normatively, the results suggest that correcting the "democratic deficit" and transparency of global economic governance will be significantly harder than is commonly understood. To NGOs, social movements, and anti-globalization protestors, the focal point for global economic governance has been the Bretton Woods institutions. Global civil society advocates particularly deride the "green room" process, in which key decisions are made by powerful states behind closed doors.[139] However, the model of global governance presented here suggests that once the great powers achieve a concert on an issue, they will design governance structures that ensure the permanence of the green room. One obvious prediction of the theory presented here is that the more successful global civil society is at democratizing the Bretton Woods institutions, the more the great powers will rely on alternative IGOs to devise and enforce the rules of globalization.

Positively, the analysis suggests that the tendency of most IPE scholars to focus on the IFIs obscures much of the politics involved in the creation of global financial regulation. Important bargaining is done in club IGOs such as the G-7, OECD, Basle Committee on Banking Supervision, and Financial Stability Forum. It also suggests, consistent with the Rational Design approach to international organizations, that even when universal-membership IGOs are designated as the "lead" international agency, their unwieldiness leads the great powers to create new clubs in order to better control policy outcomes.[140]

---

[138] Shaun Narine, "ASEAN in the Aftermath," *Global Governance* 8 (April–June 2002): 179–95.

[139] O'Brien et al., *Contesting Global Governance*; Elliott et al., "Assessing Globalization's Critics."

[140] Barbara Koremenos, Charles Lipson, and Duncan Snidal, eds., "The Rational Design of International Institutions," special issue of *International Organization* 55 (Autumn 2001): 761–1103.

CHAPTER SIX

Rival Standards and Genetically Modified Organisms

THE PREVIOUS TWO CHAPTERS demonstrated that even in issue areas where the structural forces of globalization have been thought to be at their strongest—global finance and the Internet—the great powers still dictate when and how global regulatory governance will be effective. When the United States and the European Union faced minimal adjustment costs and recognized the substantial benefits that came with coordination, the establishment of common regulatory and technical standards was swift. In the instances where the regulatory question intersected with broader societal concerns—censorship and privacy rights—the adjustment costs were much higher, and effective coordination did not take place.

This chapter looks at a regulatory issue that generates high adjustment costs—the treatment of genetically modified organisms (GMOs). This issue is an ideal one to examine the power of the revisionist framework in comparison to alternative explanations of how globalization affects regulatory coordination. Global civil society explanations, for example, emphasize the power and influence of nongovernmental organizations or epistemic communities. Because the disputes about GMOs are at their core scientific questions, this would potentially be an arena where epistemic communities would hold sway. Similarly, the genetic engineering of food is a topic that inspires environmental NGOs and consumer groups across the globe into political activism.

This case is also an excellent one to compare the revisionist approach to other state-based theories of regulatory coordination. A realist approach that assumes American hegemony would predict the global regulatory outcome to mirror American preferences on genetically modified organisms. A California effect model would assume convergence toward the upper bound of the regulatory spectrum—that is, more stringent handling of GMOs. Scholars emphasizing the importance of regulatory networks would predict European preferences to trump the American position on GMOs. Neoliberal institutionalists would predict that the rewards from regulatory coordination should lead to an accommodation between the United States and the European Union.

As this chapter will demonstrate, none of these models accurately predict the outcome of this regulatory case. Despite the visibility of nonstate actors in dealing with this issue, the GMO case also demonstrates the limits of their influence. Despite America's hegemonic position in agriculture and Europe's constant ratcheting up of its standards, neither great power has had a demonstrable effect on the other's preference ordering. The health and safety regulations governing GMOs affect groups with extremely high barriers to exit—agricultural producers, biotechnology firms, and consumer groups. The initial divergence of preferences between Americans and Europeans on this issue, combined with the high adjustment costs of regulatory harmonization, ensured the absence of a bargaining core between the two governments. The result has been a rival standards outcome between the American preference for "substantial equivalence" and the European preference for the "precautionary principle." The lack of a bargaining core has created an intense competition between the two great powers to bolster their position in friendly international fora, and to recruit as many allies from among the smaller states as possible. On the margins, nonstate actors have had an effect—particularly in hardening European public opinion—but because these actors also lack consensus, their influence on the rival standards outcome has been minimal.

The rest of this chapter is divided into seven sections. The next section looks at the state of the science on GMO and the salient regulatory questions posed by the use of genetically modified products. The third section examines actor preferences on the GMO question, which left the European Union with a preference for very stringent regulatory standards. The fourth and fifth sections examine how both great powers have exploited friendly fora to advance their regulatory preferences at the global level. The sixth section examines how well alternative theories of regulatory coordination do at explaining the GMO case. The final section summarizes and concludes.

A PRIMER ON GENETIC ENGINEERING

The genetic modification of plant and animal life has been around for as long as organized agriculture—the simple decision to cultivate crops or raise livestock with desirable traits is the earliest and crudest example of genetic manipulation. However, in popular and political parlance the terms "genetically modified" or "transgenic" refers to newer and more sophisticated forms of genetic engineering—altering organisms at the cellular level via the introduction or elimination of specific gene sequences using recombinant DNA techniques. That is how the term shall be used here as well.

This type of genetic engineering had been a subject of theoretical discussion in the scientific community since the late 1960s. In 1987, however, a practical technique was developed to insert genetic material from one plant species into another at the intracellular level. Since then, the variety and sophistication of genetic modification techniques has proliferated.[1] At present, genetic modifi-

---

[1] For an excellent historical primer, see Paul Lurquin, *The Green Phoenix: A History of Genetically Modified Plants* (New York: Columbia University Press, 2001). For descriptions of newer techniques, see National Academy of Sciences, *Safety of Genetically Engineered Foods: Approaches to Assessing Unintended Health Effects* (Washington, DC: National Academy Press, 2004), Glossary A.

cation has been commercialized for plants and agricultural crops, particularly cotton, maize, soybeans, and tobacco.[2] There are active research efforts for other transgenic crops—such as coffee—as well as trees, fish, shellfish, and pigs.[3]

GMOs raise regulatory concerns with regard to consumer health and safety and the preservation of biodiversity. The immediate concern is the effect of GMOs on humans. Because most cultivated crops can produce harmful substances—allergens, toxins, or antinutritional elements—the genetic engineering of agricultural outputs could have an adverse effect on consumers, particularly those with allergies. However, this risk is present in conventional forms of agricultural cultivation as well, so it is far from clear that GMOs pose a categorically distinct risk. The National Academy of Sciences (NAS) has concluded that GM foods did not merit any special form of health and safety regulation: "it is the final product of a given modification, *rather than the modification method or process*, that is more likely to result in an unintended adverse effect."[4] The scientific consensus on this point is relatively strong and hardly limited to the United States; over eighty scientific studies sponsored by the European Union over fifteen years found no scientific evidence of added harm to humans from the consumption of GMOs.[5] Nevertheless, the NAS report also concluded that, "our ability to interpret the consequences to human health of changes in food composition is limited."[6]

To date, there is no hard evidence that genetically modified foods have created any unique health hazards for humans.[7] The allegations that have been

---

[2] For a fuller list of approved GM products, see Jan-Peter Nap et al., "The Release of Genetically Modified Crops into the Environment: Overview of Current Status and Regulations," *The Plant Journal* 33 (January 2003): Table 2.

[3] Hillary Rosner, "Turning Genetically Engineered Trees into Toxic Avengers," *New York Times*, August 3, 2004; Dan Baum, "Feeding Our Deepest Fears," *Playboy*, June 2004, 5; Andrew Hay, "Brazil Maps Coffee Genome to Create 'Super Beans,'" Reuters, August 10, 2004; Paul Elias, "Pursuing Healthier Bacon through Biotech," Associated Press, March 26, 2006. Data on new GM crops can be found at http://www.agbios.com.

[4] National Academy of Sciences, *Safety of Genetically Engineered Foods*, 5 (emphasis in original).

[5] National Academy of Sciences, *Genetically Modified Pest-Protected Plants: Science and Regulation* (Washington, DC: National Academy Press, 2002); Charles Kessler and Ioannis Economidis, eds., *EC-Sponsored Research on Genetically Modified Organisms: A Review of Results* (Brussels: Research Directorate-General, European Commission, 2001); Robert Paarlberg, "Reinvigorating Genetically Modified Crops," *Issues in Science and Technology* 19 (Spring 2003): 86–93; Mike Mendelsohn et al., "Are Bt Crops Safe?" *Nature Biotechnology* 21 (September 2003): 1003–9; Harry Kuiper et al., "Assessment of the Food Safety Issues Related to Genetically Modified Foods," *The Plant Journal* 27 (September 2001): 503–28.

[6] National Academy of Sciences, *Safety of Genetically Engineered Foods*, 5. See also John Heritage, "The Fate of Transgenes in the Human Gut," *Nature Biotechnology* 22 (February 2004): 170–72.

[7] Beyond humans, one study found that certain strands of GM corn were harmful to monarch butterflies, because the transgene inserted into the corn was designed to repel insects in the same biological family. However, further research suggests that the real-world magnitude of this effect was small. See Mark Sears et al., "Impact of Bt Corn Pollen on Monarch Butterfly Populations: A Risk Assessment," *Agricultural Sciences* 98 (September 14, 2001): 11937–42; Pat Byrne et al.,

made have not withstood scientific scrutiny. For example, in August 1998, biochemist Arpad Pusztai claimed on British television that rats fed with genetically engineered potatoes developed cancerous tumors; he subsequently submitted his findings to *The Lancet*.[8] However, the medical journal's peer review rejected the essay because of poor methodology; a Royal Society internal review concluded that the study was, "flawed in many aspects of design, execution, and analysis" and therefore "no conclusions should be drawn from it."[9] In the end, the article was published by the medical journal—with a disclaimer from the editors and several letters critiquing the findings—in order to confront allegations that the editors had rejected the submission on political rather than scientific grounds.[10]

The most prominent health scare concerning GMOs in the United States involved accidental exposure to a GM product not intended for human consumption. The StarLink variety of corn was genetically modified for pest resistance by using a *bacillus thuringiensis* (Bt) toxin that cannot be broken down by human digestion. This variety of GM corn was intended for animal feed and ethanol production. However, tests revealed that 1 percent of StarLink corn found its way into taco shells manufactured by Kraft, at which point they were recalled. However, there were no reports of anyone becoming sick from consumption of StarLink corn.[11]

The second regulatory concern about GMOs is their potential effect on biological diversity. Because the seeds of GM crops can float with the wind, it is difficult to contain the spread of GMOs in an ecosystem.[12] The possible spread of genetically engineered DNA variants into natural habitats—via seed dispersal, cross-kingdom digestion, or pollination—triggers two biodiversity concerns. First, there is the possibility of superweeds or superinsects. If transgenic crops engineered to tolerate herbicides or to resist diseases and pests were to pass these resistant genes to naturally occurring plants, it could create

---

"Monarch Butterflies and Bt Corn," Department of Soil and Crop Sciences, Colorado State University, 2004, available at http://www.colostate.edu/programs/lifesciences/TransgenicCrops/hotmonarch.html, accessed April 2, 2006.

[8] Stanley W. B. Ewen and Arpad Pusztai, "Effect of Diets Containing Genetically Modified Potatoes Expressing *Galanthus nivalis* Lectin on Rat Small Intestine," *The Lancet* 354 (October 16, 1999): 1353–54.

[9] Richard Horton, "Genetically Modified Foods: 'Absurd' Concern or Welcome Dialogue?" *The Lancet* 354 (October 16, 1999): 1314–15. See also Harry A. Kuiper, Hub P.J.M. Noteborn, and Ad A.C.M. Peijnenburg, "Adequacy of Methods for Testing the Safety of Genetically Modified Foods," in the same issue.

[10] David Whitehouse, "The Pusztai Affair—Science Loses," *BBC News*, October 15, 1999; for a more sympathetic take on Pusztai's research, see Michael Sean Gillard, Laurie Flynn, and Andy Rowell, "Food Scandal Exposed," *The Guardian*, February 12, 1999, 1.

[11] For a summary of the StarLink episode, see National Academy of Sciences, *Biological Confinement of Genetically Engineered Organisms* (Washington, DC: National Academy Press, 2004).

[12] Andrew Pollack, "Can Biotech Crops Be Good Neighbors?" *New York Times*, September 26, 2004.

a new variant of weed immune to chemical control. A related concern is if insects ingesting GM crops were to develop resistance to pesticides. Such plants or animals would threaten to crowd out other forms of wildlife. Second, if GMOs crossbreed with their wild relatives, it could lead to the extinction of the original species. If the transgenic variant of the species was better suited for wildlife growth, it would overrun the original plant.

As with concerns for human health and safety, biodiversity concerns are hardly unique to GMOs—conventional-bred cultivars can have a similar effect. Since the Green Revolution, the Middle East has lost 85 percent of its wheat varieties and India has lost 30,000 varieties of rice.[13] Furthermore, the scientific consensus suggests that many transgenic crops are no more likely to act as "colonizers" in the wild than conventional crops.[14] There is also no evidence that pests have developed any resistance to the insecticide toxins introduced into GM crops.[15]

However, the introduction of transgenic crops unquestionably reinvigorated valid debates about crop cultivation and biodiversity.[16] The chair of a 2004 National Academy of Sciences report on biocontainment emphasized, "Deciding whether and how to confine a genetically engineered organism cannot be an afterthought. . . . Confinement won't be warranted in most cases, but when it is, worst-case scenarios and their probabilities should be considered."[17] The problem is that sophisticated forms of biocontainment—spatial segregation, temporal isolation, or engineered sterility in the affected GMO— are often expensive and/or technologically advanced, posing acute challenges for developing countries in particular. As a United Nations report concluded, "Countries where most centers of [biological] diversity are found are among those least likely to have the resources needed to protect against the risks of the technology."[18] Furthermore, even these forms of containment are not foolproof.

As with the threat to health and safety, the biggest scare to date on the biodiversity ramifications from GMOs has come from a disputed journal article. In November 2001, David Quist and Ignacio Chapela published an article

[13] Jane Rissler and Margaret Mellon, *The Ecological Risks of Engineered Crops* (Cambridge, MA: MIT Press, 1996), 112.

[14] M. J. Crawley et al., "Transgenic Crops in Natural Habitats," *Nature* 409 (February 8, 2001): 682–83; Anthony J. Conner, Travis R. Glare, and Jan-Peter Nap, "The Release of Genetically Modified Crops into the Environment: Overview of Ecological Risk Assessment," *The Plant Journal* 33 (January 2003): 19–46. See also the citations in footnote 5.

[15] Jeffrey Fox, "Resistance to Bt Toxin Surprisingly Absent from Pests," *Nature Biotechnology* 9 (September 2003): 958–59.

[16] Norman C. Ellstrand, "When Transgenes Wander, Should We Worry?" *Plant Physiology* 125 (April 2001): 1543–45.

[17] Quoted in NAS press release, "Integrated, Redundant Approach Best Way to Biologically Confine Genetically Engineered Organisms," January 20, 2004, available at http://www4 .nationalacademies.org/news.nsf/isbn/0309090857?OpenDocument, accessed May 12, 2006.

[18] Quoted in Rissler and Mellon, *The Ecological Risks of Engineered Crops*, 117.

in *Nature* asserting that transgenic DNA constructs had been found in indigenous maize species in Oaxaca, Mexico. The authors warned: "Our discovery of a high frequency of transgene insertion into a diversity of genomic contexts indicates that introgression events are relatively common."[19] However, this supposition was challenged on empirical grounds. Five months later, in response to multiple critiques of the Quist and Chapela finding, the editors of *Nature* concluded: "the evidence available is not sufficient to justify the publication of the original paper."[20] The North American Commission on Environmental Cooperation issued a report on the maize issue that urged precautions in dealing with GM products—but because of sociocultural rather than biodiversity concerns. As the report concluded, "There is no reason to expect that a transgene would have any greater or lesser effect on the genetic diversity of landraces or teosinte than other genes from similarly used modern cultivars. . . . the introgression of a few individual transgenes is unlikely to have any major biological effect on genetic diversity in maize landraces."[21]

The findings to date suggest three tentative conclusions relevant to the promulgation of regulatory standards. First, GMOs have no adverse health or safety effects on humans because of the process by which they are engineered. Second, GMOs have no adverse effects on biodiversity because of the process by which they are engineered—although scientists do acknowledge concerns about their possible impact. Third, there is no evidence to suggest that GMOs pose either an enhanced or unique public policy concern compared to conventionally bred organisms. Given the degree of consensus on these conclusions within the scientific community, as well as agreement on the methodologies to falsify these conclusions, one could posit the presence of an epistemic community on this topic.[22]

ACTOR PREFERENCES ON GMOS

Despite some initial interest from European biotech and chemical firms, the European Union was reluctant to embrace GMO technology. For the European Commission, the trouble with commercial GM crops centered on both agricul-

[19] David Quist and Ignacio Chapela, "Transgenic DNA Introgressed into Traditional Maize Landraces in Oaxaca, Mexico," *Nature* 414 (November 29, 2001): 541–43. The quotation is from page 542.

[20] "Editorial Note," *Nature* 416 (April 11, 2002): 600. For the critiques, see the correspondence (including Quist and Chapela's admission of partial error) in pages 600–602 of that issue.

[21] North American Commission on Environmental Cooperation, *Maize and Biodiversity: The Effects of Transgenic Maize in Mexico*, Quebec, Canada, November 2004, 12. See also M. R. Bellon and J. Berthaud, "Transgenic Maize and the Evolution of Landrace Diversity in Mexico: the Importance of Farmers' Behavior," *Plant Physiology* 134 (March 2004): 883–88.

[22] Peter Haas, "Introduction: Epistemic Communities and International Policy Coordination," *International Organization* 46 (Spring 1992): 1–35.

tural policy and consumer preferences. A complex web of quotas, tariffs, price controls, and subsidies protected European agriculture. The EU's Common Agricultural Policy (CAP) managed this system of protection, representing over 50 percent of the EU budget, and was designed to subsidize European farmers from foreign competition. During the 1990s, CAP subsidies largely operated by subsidizing exports to make them competitive with world market prices. A large (albeit decreasing) fraction of CAP subsidies are tied to production: farmers received a larger subsidy with increased crop yields. The relative amounts of these subsidies were considerable—in the late 1990s, approximately 44 percent of all European farm receipts came from CAP subsidies.[23] If GMOs increased European agricultural productivity, the CAP system would mandate an increased outlay of subsidies, posing a considerable strain on the EU budget. Reducing or untying the link between subsidies and production would be one way to address the issue, but this would cut against the interests of agricultural producers. EU agricultural politics over the last two decades demonstrate that these groups specialize in deploying the use of political voice to prevent CAP reform.[24]

This distribution of interests, combined with a history of strong environmental protection at the European Commission level, makes it unsurprising that the first two EU directives on GMOs in 1990 were considered particularly stringent on GMO regulatory approval.[25] The biotechnology sector in Europe was disorganized in lobbying for less stringent regulatory standards, allowing the European Commission to have its way on the issue.[26] Furthermore, the EU's initial resistance to GM technology created a resistance to the technology by European agricultural producers; farmers rendered less competitive from an absence of GMOs would have an incentive to resist any regulatory coordination allowing the importation of genetically engineered foods.[27] Biotech firms, deterred from making large investments in GM technology, were not compelled to exercise their voice option.

---

[23] Christina Davis, *Food Fights over Free Trade* (Princeton, NJ: Princeton University Press, 2003), 230. The percentage has declined since the early 1990s; see the *Economist*, "Agricultural Subsidies," June 19, 2003.

[24] Davis, *Food Fights over Free Trade*, chap. 7.

[25] Directives 90/129 (Contained Use) and 90/230 (Deliberate Release). Yves Tiberghien and Sean Starrs, "The EU as Global Trouble-Maker in Chief," paper presented at the 2004 Conference on Europeanists, Chicago, IL, March 2004, 7; Gregory Shaffer and Mark Pollack, "Reconciling (or Failing to Reconcile) Regulatory Differences: The Ongoing Dispute over the Regulation of Biotechnology," in *The Future of Transatlantic Economic Relations*, ed. David Andrews et al. (Florence: European University Institute, 2005).

[26] Claire Dunlop, "GMOs and Regulatory Styles," *Environmental Politics* 9 (Summer 2000): 152; Aseem Prakash and Kelly Kollman, "Biopolitics in the EU and the U.S.: A Race to the Bottom or Convergence to the Top?" *International Studies Quarterly* 47 (March 2004): 627.

[27] Tiberghien and Starrs point out in "The EU as Global Trouble-Maker in Chief" that the more competitive components of European agriculture did favor GM research in the early 1990s.

At the same time, European consumers also exhibited a considerable degree of hostility to the idea of GM foods—indeed, the common term for genetically engineered foods in Europe is "Frankenfoods."[28] This uneasiness only intensified in the aftermath of food safety crises that have plagued Europe.[29] The outbreaks of mad cow disease, the presence of dioxin in Belgian farm animal feed, the discovery of *salmonella* in British eggs, and the plague of hoof-and-mouth disease were all associated with the introduction of more complex agro-industrial processes and the failure of regulatory authorities to monitor these changes.[30] Previous health crises were directly cited as the cause behind the European Commission's 2000 White Paper on food safety.[31]

These repeated failures in food safety had a pronounced effect on European preferences regarding food safety. Eurobarometer polls repeatedly showed a growing skepticism toward biotechnology throughout the 1990s. Optimism about biotechnology increased between 1999 and 2002, but skepticism about GM foods and crops remains high. Even when offered positive reasons for purchasing GM foods, a majority of Europeans said they would not buy such products; 65 percent of Europeans said they would not buy GM foods even if they were less expensive. The survey concluded, "A majority of Europeans do not support GM foods. These are judged not to be useful and to be risky for society."[32] There is a clear link between GMO attitudes and a more general concern about globalization's effect on regulation. Across EU countries, there is a strong statistical correlation between opposition to GMOs and fear of "uncontrolled globalization."[33]

Given the combination of agricultural interests and strong public preferences on the issue, it is not surprising that the European Union reacted by ratcheting up regulatory preferences on the GMO issue throughout the 1990s. As early as 1990, European officials promoted the precautionary principle as the standard for regulating aspects of biotechnology. This principle states that potentially dangerous activities can be restricted or prohibited *before* they are scientifically proven to cause serious damage.[34] In 1997, this principle was ex-

---

[28] Mark Pollack and Gregory Shaffer, "The Challenge of Reconciling Regulatory Differences," in *Transatlantic Governance in a Global Economy*, ed. Pollack and Shaffer (Lanham, MD: Rowman and Littlefield, 2001).

[29] Shaffer and Pollack, "Reconciling (or Failing to Reconcile)," 179.

[30] Juan Enriquez, "Green Biotechnology and European Competitiveness," *Trends in Biotechnology* 19 (April 2001): 135.

[31] Available at http://europa.eu.int/scadplus/leg/en/lvb/l32041.htm, accessed April 2, 2006.

[32] George Gaskell, Nick Allum, and Sally Stares, *Europeans and Biotechnology in 2002: Eurobarometer 58.0* (London: London School of Economics, March 2003), 1.

[33] Tiberghien and Starrs, "The EU as Global Trouble-Maker in Chief," 23.

[34] For the official EU explanation, see "Communication from the Commission on the Precautionary Principle," February 2, 2000, at http://europa.eu.int/comm/dgs/health_consumer/library/pub/pub07_en.pdf.

plicitly codified into European law with the Treaty of Amsterdam. Even this standard was insufficient to allay public anxiety on the issue—leading the European Council to impose an unofficial moratorium on the use of GM crops and foods beginning in 1999.[35] The European Commission also favored the clear labeling of any product that contained even trace amounts of genetically engineered material. The labeling requirement covers any product with GM additives or ingredients.

In contrast to the European Union, the United States embraced GM technology more than any other country. Starting in the 1980s, the U.S. logic on GMOs was similar to the scientific consensus—the product and not the process should be regulated. Using that reasoning, the U.S. position was one of "substantial equivalence": GMOs should receive the same regulatory treatment as other agricultural products.[36] In 1992, the Food and Drug Administration conferred Generally Recognized as Safe status to GM crops, obviating the need for additional tests to satisfy FDA requirements.[37] No government agency mandated that producers label GM products when marketing them to consumers. The Congressional Research Service reported in 1999 that, "In the United States, the regulation of biotechnology food products does not differ fundamentally from regulation of conventional food products."[38]

With a more permissive regulatory environment, GMO use in the United States expanded dramatically after 1996. The Agriculture Department estimated that by 2002, GM crops represented 75 percent of soybean plantings, 34 percent of corn plantings, and 71 percent of total cotton plantings.[39] GMOs are found in most processed foods in American supermarkets. The leading multinational corporations in the development of commercial GMOs are American-based: Monsanto, DuPont, and Dow Chemicals.[40]

Public opinion in the United States was also more receptive to the idea of GM foods—despite scares such as the StarLink episode discussed above. A 2001 Food Policy Institute survey revealed strong support—more than 75 percent—for specific genetic modifications of both plants and animals.[41] A 2003

---

[35] Alasdair Young, "Political Transfer and 'Trading Up'?: Transatlantic Trade in Genetically Modified Food and US Politics," *World Politics* 55 (July 2003): 457–84.

[36] Ibid., 462–64.

[37] Felicia Wu and William Butz, *The Future of Genetically Modified Crops* (Santa Monica, CA: RAND Corporation, 2004), 56.

[38] Donna Vogt and Mickey Parish, *Food Biotechnology in the United States: Science, Regulation, and Issues* (Washington, DC: Congressional Research Service, June 2, 1999), 2.

[39] K. T. Arasu, "US Farm Group Says Europe's GMO Plan Unworkable," Reuters, July 3, 2002.

[40] Andrew Pollack, "The Green Revolution Yields to the Bottom Line," *New York Times*, May 15, 2001.

[41] William K. Hallman, Adesoji O. Adelaja, Brian J. Schilling, "Public Perceptions of Agricultural Biotechnology in the United States in 2001," Food Policy Institute, Rutgers University, 2001, 452, available at http://www.foodpolicyinstitute.org/docs/reports/horticulture.pdf, accessed August 26, 2004.

survey revealed that a plurality (49 percent to 39 percent) supported the commercial use of GM plant products. It could be argued that American acceptance of GM crops is due to lack of awareness about the prevalence of GM technology; only half of Americans knew that foods with GM ingredients were sold in supermarkets. However, the same poll demonstrated that Americans were significantly better informed than Europeans about the science of genetic modification.[42]

The benefits to the economies of the developing world from the introduction of GMOs were potentially much greater than the benefits to the developed world. The use of genetically engineered cotton provides one example of the magnitude of this benefit. In China, the use of Bt cotton reduced the costs of production by more than $750 per hectare per season.[43] In Africa, yield increases and savings from reduced chemical use associated with Bt cotton easily outweighed the higher seed costs.[44] In India, average pest-related losses in cotton cultivation ranged from 50 to 60 percent, whereas in the United States they are less than 15 percent. As a result, yields from the introduction of GM cotton in India increased on average by 60 percent. One 2003 survey concluded, "GM crops can have significant yield effects that are most likely to occur in the developing world, especially in the tropics and subtropics . . . the biggest yield gains are expected in South and Southeast Asia and Subsaharan Africa."[45] In the future, nutritionally enhanced GMOs, such as "golden rice" or "golden maize" offer the possibility of reducing malnutrition in Asia and Africa.[46] Given the utility of GMOs for developing countries, it was not surprising that the first commercial plantings of transgenic crops took place in 1992, in the People's Republic of China.

Despite the attractiveness of GM products for agricultural producers in the third world, there were and are significant barriers to entry for local producers in emerging markets. High startup costs, fragmented markets for research and development, and underinvestment in basic research made it prohibitive for most of these countries to move down the GMO learning curve.[47] As previously noted, the use of transgenic crops requires significant asset-specific invest-

[42] William K. Hallman et al., "Public Perceptions of Genetically Modified Foods," Food Policy Institute, Rutgers University, October 2003.

[43] Jikun Huang et al., "Plant Biotechnology in China," *Science* 295 (January 25, 2002): 675.

[44] Jennifer A. Thomson, "Research Needs to Improve Agricultural Productivity and Food Quality, with Emphasis on Biotechnology," *Journal of Nutrition* 132 (November 2002): 3441S. See also Mark Lacey, "Engineering Food for Africans," *New York Times*, September 8, 2002.

[45] Matin Qaim and David Solberman, "Yield Effects of Genetically Modified Crops in Developing Countries," *Science* 299 (February 7, 2003): 900–902.

[46] Peter Beyer et al., "Golden Rice," *Journal of Nutrition* 132 (November 2002): 506S–508S. See also Christopher Surridge, "The Rice Squad," *Nature* 416 (April 2002): 576–77.

[47] Matin Qaim, Anatole Krattiger, and Joachim von Braun, *Agricultural Biotechnology in Developing Countries* (Boston: Kluwer, 2000), 3; Wu and Butz, *The Future of Genetically Modified Crops*, 40.

ments, which can be daunting for risk-averse third-world farmers. The cost of obtaining patents from first-world corporations to advance GM research was also significant.[48]

Corporate and NGO actors had wildly divergent preferences on the regulation of GMOs. Transgenic products were attractive to agricultural, chemical, and biotech firms for several reasons. For farmers, GMOs offered a way to increase crop yields and simplify the chemical dimension to agriculture. For example, farmers using established herbicides like Roundup must be careful when spraying conventional crops, because the chemical kills plantings as well as weeds. However, crops can be genetically modified to survive exposure to Roundup, making weed control easier. For chemical firms like Monsanto, the ability to patent and market GM crops was a highly lucrative opportunity. The global market for transgenic seeds was roughly $3 billion in 2000, and estimated to approach $25 billion by 2010. Agricultural economists calculated in 2000 that approximately 80 percent of the welfare benefits created through the use of GM cotton and soybeans went to agricultural and biotech firms.[49] By 2003, Monsanto's seed and genomic division was profitable, earning gross profit margins 50 percent greater than their chemicals division.[50]

For corporate actors, the asset-specific investments of GMO production and use were also high.[51] For GMO producers, only 1 in 10,000 GM seeds ever makes it to the field trial stage, and the time from initial research to commercial use can be as long as a decade. The estimated costs of research and development range from the hundreds of millions into the billions.[52] As for agricultural producers, the cross-pollination of GM seeds within a confined agricultural area made it costly for farmers to segregate GM crops from non-GM crops, leading to an all-or-nothing approach to GM technology.[53] Once these actors decided to invest in GM technology, the value of those investments depended on a stable regulatory environment.

[48] Pollack, "The Green Revolution Yields to the Bottom Line."

[49] José Benjamin Falck-Zepeda, Greg Traxler, and Robert Nelson, "Surplus Distribution from the Introduction of a Biotechnology Innovation," *American Journal of Agricultural Economics* 82 (May 2000): 360–69; Falck-Zepeda, Traxler, and Nelson, "Rent Creation and Distribution from Biotechnology Innovations: The Case of Bt Cotton and Herbicide-Tolerant Soybeans in 1997," *Agribusiness* (February 2000). This does not mean that consumers have not benefited from other crops; by one estimate, the use of Bt corn led to a welfare gain of $530 million for American consumers. See Wu and Butz, *The Future of Genetically Modified Crops*, 63–64.

[50] Mark Tatge, "Piracy on the High Plain," Forbes.com, April 12, 2004, available at http://www.forbes.com/forbes/2004/0412/135_print.html, accessed August 23, 2004.

[51] Peter Newell, "Globalization and the Governance of Biotechnology," *Global Environmental Politics* 3 (May 2003): 58–59.

[52] Rick Weiss, "Seeds of Discord," *Washington Post*, Wednesday, February 3, 1999; Clive James, "Transgenic Crops Worldwide: Current Situation and Future Outlook," in *Agricultural Biotechnology in Developing Countries*, ed. Qaim, Krattiger, and von Braun, 16–18.

[53] D. S. Bullock and M. Desquilbet, "The Economics of Non-GMO Segregation and Identity Preservation," *Food Policy* 27 (February 2002): 82–100.

A broad swath of global civil society was virulently opposed to the introduction of GMOs into the food chain. Their objections centered on the perceived threat to biodiversity. In its campaign against GMOs, Greenpeace stressed the precautionary doctrine that long-term environmental risks of GMOs could not be assessed by existing scientific means.[54] There were other concerns, however. As previously noted, GM technology disproportionately benefited first-world biotech firms, and promised the global consolidation of the biotechnology and agriculture sectors.[55] These trends ran counter to GCS preferences for small businesses, small-scale agriculture, and traditional farming techniques.

Because of these nonenvironmental issues, NGOs were hostile to the idea of allowing the scientific community to assess the risks from GM crops—they suspected agricultural and plant scientists of being in league with corporate and/or government interests.[56] The fact that the first batch of commercially available GM crops dealt with first-world agricultural problems (resistance to herbicides) as opposed to developing country concerns reinforced these assumptions. As a result, even groups committed to combating world hunger—which would be expected to be more accepting of GM use—were hostile to permissive regulatory standards. Groups such as Oxfam repeatedly called for a moratorium on GM use.[57]

The preferences of the great powers diverged sharply on the question of GMO technology—as Aseem Prakash and Kelly Kollman conclude, "The two paths taken by the EU and the U.S. in the area of biotech regulation could hardly be more different."[58] In Europe, initial EU resistance, combined with massive public hostility, led to strong preferences for very strict regulatory standards on the use of GMOs. In the United States, active interest from agricultural producers and biotech firms, combined with consumer receptivity, led to regulatory standards based on scientific risk. By the late 1990s, the adjustment costs of altering regulatory standards were high for both governments. In the United States, the asset-specific investments by farmers and biotech firms in the existing set of regulations was significant; in Europe, the

---

[54] See, for example, quotations in "Lies and Hype—NGOs Denounce United Nations Report on Biotech," at http://www.organicconsumers.org/gefood/ngosUN.cfm, accessed August 25, 2004.

[55] This assumption was well founded. See Steven W. Collins, "Interfirm Alliances and Globalization in the Biotechnology Industry," paper presented at the International Studies Association annual meeting, Toronto, Canada, March 1997.

[56] Robert Tripp, "GMOs and NGOs: Biotechnology, the Policy Process, and the Presentation of Evidence," *Natural Resource Perspectives* no. 60, London, Overseas Development Institute, September 2000; Jean-Eric Aubert, "NGOs on GMOs: The Reasons for Resistance," *OECD Observer* no. 220, Paris, OECD, April 2000.

[57] OxFam press release, June 13, 2002. Available at http://www.oxfam.org/eng/pr020613_world_cup_and_food_summit.htm, accessed August 25, 2004.

[58] Prakash and Kollman, "Biopolitics in the EU and the U.S.," 626.

groups affected by a change in regulatory standards specialized in the use of political voice.[59] The differences in approval processes between the two countries were great enough to impose very high adjustment costs for policy change for the relevant political institutions.[60] In developing countries, regulatory preferences remained in flux. There was a bias toward more permissive standards among agricultural exporters and large emerging markets, and a bias toward more stringent regulation among smaller less developed countries.[61] The interest in GMO technology clashed with a lack of state resources to cope with even American safety standards on the handling of GMOs.

The Emergence of Rival Global Standards

Compared to capital markets, the market for agricultural goods is commonly perceived as heavily protected and more immune from the pressures of globalization. However, by any empirical measure—trade flows, tariff levels, subsidies as a percentage of output, strength of commodity cartels—the agricultural sector underwent considerable liberalization between 1975 and 1995.[62] The fall in border barriers to agriculture, combined with the introduction of GM technology into agricultural products, triggered demands for regulatory coordination on GMO technology. In the early 1990s, the OECD and various United Nations agencies released a plethora of documentation on possible ways to regulate biotechnology; however, none of these regimes filled the regulatory gap created by the growth in GMOs.[63] As the issue heated up, the United States and the European Union competed to develop regulatory standards consistent with their national preferences. In doing so, both of the great powers relied on friendly international fora for codification.

The United States—supported by other food exporters in the "Miami group" (Argentina, Australia, Canada, Chile, and Uruguay)—relied on the World Trade Organization's legal authority to legitimize their own regulatory preferences on GMOs. This preference was grounded in the 1994 Sanitary and Phytosanitary (SPS) agreement established during the Uruguay round of world

---

[59] Henry Miller, "The Biotechnology Industry's Frankenstein Creation," *Trends in Biotechnology* 19 (April 2001): 130–31.

[60] Young, "Political Transfer and 'Trading Up?'" 460.

[61] Sybil Rhodes, "The Politics of Frankenfood: The Role of States, Corporations, and Interest Groups in the Genetically Modified Foods Debate," paper presented at the International Studies Association annual meeting, New Orleans, LA, March 2002.

[62] Davis, *Food Fights over Free Trade*, chap. 1; Arvind Panagariya, "Liberalizing Agriculture," *Foreign Affairs* special ed. (December 2005): 56–66.

[63] Robert Falkner, "Regulating Biotech Trade: the Cartagena Protocol on Biosafety," *International Affairs* 76 (April 2000): 303.

trade talks. The SPS required WTO members and adjudicating bodies to defer to safety standards established by the Codex Alimentarius Commission to determine whether national food regulations were appropriate or merely a disguised form of protectionism.[64] Countries were allowed to promulgate standards considered more stringent than Codex-issued standards, but they would be deemed illegal if not based on "sufficient scientific evidence."[65]

Although the Codex was a universal IGO, it was well suited to advance American preferences on food safety standards. First, its focus on promoting international trade suggested that the regulatory standards agreed upon in the Codex would not be overly stringent. As one observer pointed out, "There is no codified standard requiring Codex to apply precautionary principles . . . to assess whether consumer health is protected adequately.[66] Second, the United States and other agricultural exporters were active participants in the Codex process, ensuring that anti-GMO countries could not capture the IGO. Third, the Codex had greater barriers to access for nongovernmental organizations than the other relevant international bodies.[67]

There are several reasons why the European Union agreed to the SPS agreement despite its deleterious effect on their regulatory preferences regarding GMOs. First, at the time of the negotiations, GMOs were not a significant component of trade in agricultural or food products. Second, the SPS agreement covers issues beyond GMOs to include products where the Europeans preferred more lax regulatory standards, such as unpasteurized cheeses. Third, many of the food safety scandals that triggered the use of political voice and hardened EU preferences on GMOs took place *after* the SPS agreement was completed. For all of these reasons, the SPS agreement was a low-priority issue for the European Union during the Uruguay round. EU negotiators allocated much more attention to the agricultural portion of the Uruguay round than the SPS negotiations, as the former set of negotiations had a direct impact on agricultural interests. As a result, the European Union was not a major

---

[64] GATT Article XX(b); Agreement on the Application of Sanitary and Phytosanitary Measures, Article 2.2. For a legal analysis, see David Victor, "WTO Efforts to Manage Differences in National Sanitary and Phytosanitary Measures," in *Dynamics of Regulatory Change*, ed. David Vogel and Robert Kagan (Berkeley: University of California Press, 2004).

[65] Bruce Silverglade, "The WTO Agreement on Sanitary and Phytosanitary Measures: Weakening Food Safety Regulations to Facilitate Trade?" *Food and Drug Law Journal* 55 (2000): 518.

[66] Lucinda Sikes, "FDA's Consideration of Codex Alimentarius Standards in Light of International Trade Agreements," *Food and Drug Law Journal* 53 (1998): 328.

[67] Urs Thomas, "The Codex Alimentarius and Environmental Issues," paper presented at the International Studies Association annual meeting, New Orleans, LA, March 2002; Diahanna Post, "Diffusion of International Food Safety Standards," paper presented at the 2003 American Political Science Association annual meeting, Philadelphia, PA, August 2003; Sikes, "FDA's Consideration of Codex Alimentarius Standards in Light of International Trade Agreements," 329; Victor, "WTO Efforts to Manage Differences in National Sanitary and Phytosanitary Measures."

player in the SPS negotiations.[68] In 1998, the European Commission proposed revisiting the SPS agreement because of its GM-friendly content. The United States, comfortable with the status quo, rebuffed the proposal.[69]

Given the bias against the precautionary principle in both the WTO and the Codex, the European Union switched fora to another United Nations emanation to advance its regulatory preferences. Negotiations over the biosafety protocol to implement the 1992 Rio Convention on Biological Diversity provided the ideal fora for European officials. The initial Declaration on Environment and Development already affirmed that the precautionary principle should "be widely applied."[70] From 1996 onward, European negotiators pushed to have the precautionary principle included in the protocol, and to have the agreement exempted from WTO rules.[71]

While the United States participated in the negotiations, it resisted the European push to ratchet up environmental standards. The chief U.S. negotiator articulated the American position as "no deal is better than a bad one."[72] However, U.S. officials were negotiating from a position of weakness. Because the United States never ratified the Rio Convention, they only had observer status in these negotiations. Although American officials were admitted to all informal negotiations, and their great power status could not be dismissed, their outsider position put them at a negotiating disadvantage.[73] Furthermore, most agricultural importers were sympathetic to the EU position, leaving the United States heavily outnumbered at the negotiations. Only the Miami group of agricultural exporters supported the U.S. position. One African negotiator described the distribution of interests at the negotiations as, "five nations against the world."[74]

Nevertheless, the Miami group was able to thwart the European Union at the February 1999 Cartagena conference, leading to a draft treaty that was heavily bracketed with unresolved issues. It was the first time in twenty years that a UN environmental treaty had not been concluded by a self-imposed deadline. The head of one environmental NGO blasted the setback to the negotiations, concluding: "There was no moral high ground here. . . . It was just cheap power politics."[75]

---

[68] David, *Food Fights over Free Trade*, 329.

[69] William Kerr, "International Trade in Transgenic Food Products: A New Focus for Agricultural Trade Disputes," *World Economy* 22 (March 1999): 245.

[70] Rio Declaration of Environment and Development, Principle 15, available at http://www.unep.org/Documents/Default.asp?DocumentID=78&ArticleID=1163, accessed August 18, 2004.

[71] Falkner, "Regulating Biotech Trade," 304.

[72] Ibid., 304.

[73] Vogt and Parish, *Food Biotechnology in the United States*.

[74] Quoted in Andrew Pollack, "U.S. Sidetracks Pact to Control Gene Splicing," *New York Times*, February 25, 1999.

[75] Ibid.

As the negotiations continued, the United States tried to shift the bargaining forum back to the WTO. In the run-up to the December 1999 WTO Ministerial meeting in Seattle, the United States proposed strengthening the WTO rules governing trade in GM products, and establishing a WTO working group on biotechnology. As Robert Falkner observes: "Both proposals raised the spectre of a shift in the institutional context within which biosafety issues would be debated, away from the [Rio Convention's] emphasis on biodiversity and towards the WTO's objective of trade liberalization."[76] However, the American proposal foundered in the end. Although EU trade commissioner Pascal Lamy initially agreed to the idea, the EU's General Affairs Council rejected it.

In January 2000, the Cartagena Protocol on Biosafety was finalized in Montreal.[77] The agreement reaffirmed employing the precautionary principle in the treatment of living modified organisms in the preamble. In the text, the agreement added, "Lack of scientific certainty due to insufficient relevant scientific information and knowledge . . . shall not prevent that Party from taking a decision, as appropriate, with regard to the import of the living modified organism."[78] The advance informed agreement provision required exporters to provide detailed information to importing countries about the GMO exports.

The United States did not object to the Cartagena Protocol, despite not being a signatory to the agreement, because the final language ensured that the treaty did not govern GM products (as opposed to seeds or other *living* modified organisms). However, Falkner's assessment of the treaty concluded:

> The EU's position has been strengthened by the Protocol; while the treaty does not add significantly to the EU's existing regulatory system, it does provide it with greater international legitimacy. The establishment of the precautionary principle within the Protocol's [Advanced Informed Agreement] procedure . . . serves to challenge the United States' insistence on full scientific proof as the basis for risk assessment, as is customary in WTO dispute settlement cases.[79]

The result, by 2000, was a legal stalemate, with the biosafety protocol's precautionary principle flatly contradicting the trade regime's norm of scientific proof of harm. Legal and development experts agreed that it would be difficult at best to reconcile the WTO and Cartagena regimes.[80]

---

[76] Davis, *Food Fights over Free Trade*, 305.

[77] Andrew Pollack, "130 Nations Agree on Rules for Biotech Food," *New York Times*, January 30, 2000. The Protocol went into effect in September 2003.

[78] Cartagena Protocol on Biosafety, article 10, paragraph 6, available at http://www.biodiv.org/biosafety/articles.asp?lg=0&a=bsp-10, accessed April 2, 2006.

[79] Falkner, "Regulating Biotech Trade," 313.

[80] Urs P. Thomas et al., "The Biosafety Protocol: Regulatory Innovation and Emerging Trends," *Revue Suisse de Droit International et de Droit Européen* 10 (April 2000): 513–58; Erik Millstone and Patrick van Zwanenberg, "Food and Agricultural Biotechnology Policy: How Much Autonomy Can Developing Countries Exercise?" *Development Policy Review* 21 (September 2003): 655–67.

The Post-Cartagena Rivalry for Regulatory Standards

The U.S. and EU governments remain far apart in their preferences for regulating genetically modified organisms.[81] In 2001, the European Commission imposed the most stringent set of regulations in existence on GMOs, centralizing the approval process and requiring a GM label if the food contained as little as 0.9 percent of modified DNA material.[82] According to one estimate, it would cost up to $400 million for American firms to simultaneously use GM technology and still be able to export non-GM food that would satisfy the labeling requirement to the European Union.[83] Approval is limited to ten years, after which the GMO product needs to be resubmitted. In contrast, policy change in the United States has been modest—the only change in U.S. standards was the FDA's decision to promulgate guidelines for a voluntary labeling system of GM products.[84]

Both great powers appear to be locked in to their preferred set of regulations. In 2002, an EU trade official characterized European hostility to GM food as "a political fact," elaborating that, "People don't see any value added in genetically modified foods. They don't want it." In July 2003, EU agricultural commissioner Franz Fischler told an American audience that, "there is simply no social consensus in Europe for accepting GM products."[85] In March of 2004, the European Union did end the unofficial moratorium in place on the sale of GMO crops. Even with the end of the moratorium, however, powerful member states remain committed to prohibiting all GMO imports.[86] The CEO of Monsanto admitted in 2004, "I'd love to see our seeds being planted in Europe, but that won't be happening for a long, long time."[87] Syngenta's representatives echoed these sentiments.[88]

U.S. Trade Representative Robert Zoellick blasted the EU's informal moratorium as "Luddite" in January 2003.[89] The threat of WTO action became reality

---

[81] Gilbert Winham, "Regime Conflict in Trade and Environment: The Cartagena Protocol and the WTO," paper presented at the International Studies Association annual meeting, Chicago, IL, February 2001; Jeffrey Lewis and David Nixon, "Transnational Regulatory Conflict and the Problems of Deeper Integration," paper presented at the International Studies Association annual meeting, Chicago, IL, February 2001.

[82] Michael Mann, "EU Food Move May Raise Trade Tensions," *Financial Times*, July 25, 2001.

[83] Wu and Butz, *The Future of Genetically Modified Crops*, 60.

[84] Young, "Political Transfer and 'Trading Up?'" 472.

[85] Trade official quoted in Greg Burns, "Europe Shows Little Taste for U.S. Biotech Crops," *Chicago Tribune*, October 30, 2002. Fischler quoted in "Genetically Modified Food Still Hot Topic," *Deutsche Welle*, July 30, 2003.

[86] Young, "Political Transfer and 'Trading Up?'" See also Fiona Harvey, "Five EU States Win Right to Keep Ban on Modified Crops," *Financial Times*, June 25, 2005.

[87] Quoted in Tatge, "Piracy on the High Plain."

[88] Shaffer and Pollack, "Reconciling (or Failing to Reconcile)," 204.

[89] Edward Allen, "Congress Presses Zoellick on Biotech Foods," *Financial Times*, March 5, 2003.

later in 2003 when a WTO panel was convened on the issue at the behest of the United States. In February 2006 a preliminary WTO panel ruled against the European Union.

The divergence of preferences between the United States and the European Union have stymied efforts to develop common global regulations on GMOs.[90] However, both of the great powers invested considerable resources into converting other states to adopt their position on the matter. American actors pushed for greater acceptance of the U.S. regulatory principles regarding GMOs using a mixture of carrots and sticks. Officially, the Department of Agriculture and the U.S. Trade Representative lobbied governments across the globe on the virtues of GMO crops. Beginning with the Clinton administration's Initiative on Biotechnology, the USDA openly stated as one of its goals "to facilitate the marketing of bioengineered products in both the domestic and international markets."[91] The United States Agency for International Development made a similar pledge in 2002.[92]

At the 2002 World Food Summit, the U.S. government made no secret of its powerful advocacy of biotechnology. At the summit the U.S. secretary of agriculture announced a ten-year, $100 million Collaborative Agriculture Biotechnology Initiative to "advance research on [GM] varieties better suited to growing conditions in developing countries."[93] Official American food aid is also likely to contain genetically engineered products.[94] U.S. officials have also tried to use the logic of appropriateness to advance their regulatory preferences on GMOs. The U.S. ambassador to the Holy See lobbied for the Vatican to speak out in favor of genetically modified foods as a way of addressing world hunger; Vatican officials subsequently voiced cautious optimism about the potential for GMOs.[95]

The United States has also pushed countries to accept U.S. safety certifications for GMO products or to develop their own protocols as quickly as possible. For example, Chinese officials told U.S. officials in fall 2001 that they would accept U.S. safety certifications for GMO crops. After Beijing reversed course in early 2002, the U.S. Trade Representative and agriculture secretary

[90] Associated Press, "Countries 'Polarized' on Safety of Genetically Modified Products," February 23, 2004.

[91] U.S. Department of Agriculture, "Agricultural Biotechnology—Frequently Asked Questions," available at http://www.usda.gov/agencies/biotech/faq.html, accessed August 22, 2004.

[92] Paarlberg, "Reinvigorating Genetically Modified Crops."

[93] Quotations from Hilmi Toros, "World Food Summit Endorses Biotechnology to Combat Hunger," Inter Press Service, June 12, 2002.

[94] "U.S. Food Aid Runs into Biotech Resistance," Environmental News Service, June 14, 2002.

[95] Peter Popham, "Vatican Looks to GM Food as Panacea for Hungry and Burgeoning Global Population," *The Independent*, November 11, 2003; Associated Press, "Vatican Plays Host for GMO Talks," November 10, 2003; address by Archbishop Renato R. Martino, June 23, 2003, available at http://www.vatican.va/roman_curia/secretariat_state/2003/documents/rc_seg-st_20030625_gmo-martino_en.html, accessed August 22, 2004.

issued a joint statement characterizing the situation as "unacceptable." In response, the Chinese government issued temporary safety certificates permitting GMO imports until permanent regulations were drafted in February 2004.[96] One NGO official complained in early 2004 that, "the U.S. is trying to impose its standards on the rest of the world."[97]

Implicit in U.S. diplomacy over the GMO issue has been the specter of WTO arbitration rulings in their favor. The SPS agreement gave the United States a mechanism through which it could promulgate its preferred set of standards on GMO regulation—the WTO dispute resolution mechanism. Beginning with the EU beef hormone case, WTO panels have consistently sided with the American position that attempts to restrict agricultural products without credible scientific evidence of possible harm violate international trade law.[98] In 1998, the U.S. Trade Representative used the specter of the WTO to attack the European Union's labeling requirements for foods containing transgenic material, arguing that "such labeling is unnecessary, in the absence of an identified and documented risk to safety or health." That language was consciously phrased to invoke the SPS agreement.[99] The secretary of agriculture made similar remarks in 1999.[100] Four years later, the United States carried out its threat and brought the case to the WTO. Beyond the European Commission, other governments are aware that the United States can use the WTO to legitimize and authorize economic sanctions for failing to permit GM imports.

The revisionist model predicts that economic coercion among the great powers does not lead to regulatory coordination. Consistent with the EU's economic size, it has been unmoved by WTO-supported American sanctions on the beef case.[101] However, the uses of economic statecraft should have a powerful effect on countries asymmetrically dependent on access to U.S. markets. Significant developing countries have taken steps toward producing and/ or consuming GM products. In 2002, the Indian government approved the

[96] Evelyn Iritani, "U.S., China at Impasse over Genetically Modified Crops," *Los Angeles Times*, February 9, 2002; *Dow Jones Newswires*, "China Says No GMO Permits Needed from Health Ministry for Now," July 1, 2002; *People's Daily Online*, "Gene-Altered Crops are Safe: Officials," February 26, 2004.

[97] Sean Young, "Countries 'Polarized' on Safety of Genetically Modified Products," Associated Press, February 23, 2004.

[98] Silverglade, "The WTO Agreement on Sanitary and Phytosanitary Measures," 518–19; Davis, *Food Fights over Free Trade*, chap. 9; Victor, "WTO Efforts to Manage Differences in National Sanitary and Phytosanitary Measures." See also Georgetown University's Institute of International Economic Law, "GMOs in the WTO," available at http://www.law.georgetown.edu/iiel/current/gmos/gmos_wto.html.

[99] Allen, "Congress Presses Zoellick on Biotech Foods."

[100] Dan Glickman, "New Crops, New Century, New Challenges," speech delivered to the National Press Club, Washington, DC, July 13, 1999, available at http://www.usda.gov/news/releases/1999/07/0285, accessed August 25, 2004.

[101] Davis, *Food Fights over Free Trade*, chap. 9.

commercial cultivation of Bt cotton.[102] The Brazilian government permitted the commercial cultivation of soybeans. South Korea, Egypt, Kenya, South Africa, and Thailand have pilot programs for GM crops. The first two countries to agree with American standards for GMO labeling were Mexico and Canada.[103] As large developing markets accept GM seeds, the competitive incentive for other countries to coordinate standards at a level that permits GM cultivation increases.[104] The number of approved field trials for transgenic crops in the developing world has increased since 2000. Industry analysts forecast annual increases of 12 percent in market demand for transgenic seeds. One assessment concluded, "The global adoption rate of GM crops is among the highest for any new technology in agriculture."[105]

Using similar tools of statecraft, European actors have pushed equally hard to promote the precautionary principle and resist the diffusion of GMO-friendly regulations. The European campaign against GMO proliferation, combined with the six-year EU moratorium on GMO imports, encouraged trade-dependent countries to adopt the EU position on genetically modified crops. As the EU expanded into Central and Eastern Europe, those countries agreed to pass laws on GMOs consistent with the EU position. Most potential entrants have taken steps to conform to EU regulations with regard to GMOs.[106]

The European Union has lobbied African governments to ratify the Cartagena Protocol, and offered technical assistance to set up regulatory systems that embrace the precautionary principle.[107] In August 2002, European Commission officials rebuffed a U.S. request to reassure famine-stricken African countries about the safety of American-supplied GM food aid.[108] The European Union has also advanced its agenda through its support of European environmental NGOs. The European Commissioner for Consumer Protection and Health acknowledged that the European Union funds nongovernmental orga-

---

[102] Edward Luce, "India Allows Farms to Grow Genetically Modified Cotton," *Financial Times*, March 27, 2002; Associated Press, "Monsanto's Gene-Altered Crops in India," February 10, 2003.

[103] Mark Stevenson, "Mexico Becomes First Importer Nation to Adopt U.S.-Backed Standards on Labeling for Genetically Modified Grains," Associated Press, February 12, 2004.

[104] Lacey, "Engineering Food for Africans"; John Mason, "Gaining Ground," *Financial Times*, March 27, 2002; "Government Working on GMO Development," *Korea Herald*, September 12, 2002.

[105] Nap et al., "The Release of Genetically Modified Crops into the Environment: Overview of Current Status and Regulations," 6. On market projections, see Freedonia Group, "World Agricultural Biotechnology: Transgenic Seeds to 2006," Cleveland, OH, March 2002.

[106] Nap et al., "The Release of Genetically Modified Crops into the Environment: Overview of Current Status and Regulations," 12–13.

[107] Paarlberg, "Reinvigorating Genetically Modified Crops."

[108] U.S. State Department, "Biotechnology and U.S. Food Assistance to Southern Africa," August 21, 2002; "EU Disapproves of US GM Food Aid to Africa," EurActiv.com, August 23, 2002, available at http://www.euractiv.com/cgi-bin/cgint.exe/2571909-112?204&OIDN=1503811&-home=search, accessed August 22, 2004.

nizations that oppose GMO products.[109] The head of Greenpeace's Genetic Engineering Campaign noted in early 2004: "Europe has been very vocal in its skepticism about GMOs and of course that travels everywhere."[110]

The EU's lobbying yielded results in sub-Saharan Africa. Zambia's president said in early 2003 that his nation would "rather starve" than accept U.S. food aid with GM corn. The country's agriculture minister expressed concern that if the GM corn seed were to pollute the country's seed stock, Zambian agricultural exports would be blocked from the European Union. Other African nations followed suit; governments across the drought-ridden region feared being shut out of European markets if they invest in GMO technology.[111] Beyond the African continent, other emerging markets such as Thailand have resisted using GM seeds because of fears that European agricultural exports would be adversely affected.[112] In May 2003, President Bush went so far as to accuse the European Union of undermining efforts to eradicate hunger in Africa because of their GMO position.[113]

The result of the combined U.S. and EU pressure has been a single global cleavage on the GMO issue.[114] In one camp are countries that specialize in agricultural exports, have internal markets of sufficient size to exploit the possibilities of GMOs, or are vulnerable to U.S. coercive pressure. In the other category are countries that either rely on subsistence agriculture or are trade dependent on the European Union. Efforts to develop policy on GMOs in international governmental organizations like the World Bank and the Food and Agricultural Organization have foundered over the EU-U.S. split.[115] A RAND study concluded: "The regulations in these two parts of the world, and the battle between these two factions over the place of GM crops in global food production, are shaping the regulations in other nations worldwide."[116]

---

[109] Lizette Alvarez, "Europe Shows a Growing Distaste for Genetic Foods," *New York Times*, February 10, 2003.

[110] Quoted in Jeremy Smith, "World Awaits More GM Crops as Safety Debate Rages," Reuters, February 27, 2004.

[111] George B. Pyle, "Food That Starving People Won't Eat," *Chicago Tribune*, September 2, 2002; Wu and Butz, *The Future of Genetically Modified Crops*, 61. Consistent with the revisionist model, the one country not to object to GM food aid was Swaziland, a country that became increasingly reliant upon U.S. export markets following the passage of the Africa Growth and Opportunity Act. See Noah Zerbe, "Feeding the Famine? American Food Aid and the GMO Debate in Southern Africa," *Food Policy* 29 (December 2004): 593–608.

[112] Mason, "Gaining Ground"; "U.S. Food Aid Runs into Biotech Resistance," Environmental News Service, June 14, 2002.

[113] David E. Sanger, "Bush Links Europe's Ban on Bio-Crops with Hunger," *New York Times*, May 22, 2003.

[114] Millstone and van Zwanenberg, "Food and Agricultural Biotechnology Policy," 656; Nap et al., "The Release of Genetically Modified Crops into the Environment: Overview of Current Status and Regulations."

[115] Paarlberg, "Reinvigorating Genetically Modified Crops."

[116] Wu and Butz, *The Future of Genetically Modified Crops*, 54.

Despite the incentives for private and public actors in developed and developing countries, the distribution of investment in GMOs across the globe has been uneven. More than half of the world's soybeans are now genetically engineered, and the percentages have been steadily rising for cotton, maize, and canola. Eighteen countries planted GM crops in 2003. However, 99 percent of the world's GM crops are grown in only five countries: Argentina, Brazil, Canada, China, and the United States.[117] The number of countries that use EU standards for labeling has also increased to more than thirty.

EVALUATING OTHER EXPLANATIONS

Explanations that stress the role of nonstate actors are of limited utility in explaining the GMO case. The causal impact of these actors ranges from marginal to insignificant. The epistemic community argument provides little explanatory power. Despite the overwhelming degree of scientific consensus on the relative safety of using GMOs, that consensus has not been widely accepted by major portions of the globe. In 2003, one group of exasperated plant scientists observed: "The problem is partly that the relevant questions have been repeatedly asked for over 15 years, and keep being asked, despite the fact that all the supposedly relevant research has been performed. The answers given are apparently not satisfactory."[118]

Rather than the epistemic community acting as the key independent variable, in this case the scientific community has become the dependent variable. In the case of the Pusztai paper in *The Lancet*, the GM controversy has caused scientists to violate their own validity norms and publish work in order to quell a public controversy. As the BBC's science editor concluded, "It is there not because it is good science. It is there because it has caused a fuss. A fuss brought about by single-interest pressure groups. . . . But what is worse is that its publication is essentially an admission that science has failed to get its arguments across to the people."[119]

An editorial in *Nature* also deplored the deterioration of scientific standards as a result of the GMO dispute among others. The editorial was even more scathing of the epistemic community approach:

> Some scientists believe that "science" alone provides a sufficient basis for decision-making, in that a problem is identified, various hypotheses are tested, remedial poli-

---

[117] Clive James, "Global Status of Commercialized Transgenic Crops: 2003," ISAAA Briefs No. 30, International Service for the Acquisition of Agri-Biotech Applications, Ithaca, NY, November 2003.

[118] Nap et al., "The Release of Genetically Modified Crops into the Environment: Overview of Ecological Risk Assessment," 20.

[119] Whitehouse, "The Pusztai Affair—Science Loses."

cies suggested and implemented—then the situation improves. But putting the onus of problem resolution on science brings all the messy realities of politics into the practice of science. Rather than making politics more scientific, this approach, in fact, makes science more political. *Indeed, I have never come across any real-world policy issue involving science and decision-making that has resolved itself in this logical but oversimplistic manner.*[120]

Multinational corporations would appear to have had more influence, given the prominence of Monsanto in the spread of GM technology. This confuses prominence with influence, however. Because of their high adjustment costs, American biotech firms undoubtedly exercised voice to influence the American government.[121] However, the effect of multinational corporations waned outside North America. A PR effort by Monsanto to improve the public image of GM products in the European Union backfired; in the three years after the Cartagena Protocol was signed, Monsanto's stock valuation fell by 25 percent. Other multinational firms spun off their agri-biotech divisions in order to shelter their profitable brands from association with the GMO controversy.[122] By 1999, Deutsche Bank was recommending to its clients to sell their agricultural biotechnology stocks, concluding that, "GMOs are good science but bad politics."[123] The Transatlantic Business Dialogue persistently advocated for American-style regulatory standards on GMOs since the Cartagena Protocol. European-based multinationals lobbied furiously for the European Commission to relax its regulatory standards on GMOs.[124] However, beyond the United States, multinational corporations have had limited influence.

The influence of global civil society on the GMO outcome suffers from the same problem as discussing the role of multinational corporations—explaining one set of great power preferences but nothing else. Many scholars contend that environmental groups were able to mobilize European public

[120] Roger A Pielke Jr., "Policy, Politics, and Perspective," *Nature* 416 (March 28, 2002): 367–68. The quote is from p. 367 (emphasis added).

[121] For the case of Monsanto, see Kurt Eichenwald, Gina Kolata, and Melody Peterson, "Biotechnology Food: From the Lab to a Debacle," *New York Times*, January 25, 2001.

[122] Shaffer and Pollack, "Reconciling (or Failing to Reconcile)," 181; Prakash and Kollman, "Biopolitics in the E.U. and the U.S.," 632; Oliver Cadot, Akiko Suwa-Eisenmann, and Daniel Traça, "Trade-Related Issues in the Regulation of Genetically Modified Organisms," paper prepared for the workshop on European and American Perspectives on Regulating Genetically Engineered Food, INSEAD, Cedex, France, June 7, 2001; Rachel Schurman, "Fighting 'Frankenfoods': Industry Opportunity Structures and the Efficacy of the Anti-Biotech Movement in Western Europe," *Social Problems* 51 (May 2004): 243–68.

[123] Quoted in William Leiss, "The Trouble with Science: Public Controversy over Genetically Modified Foods," *Environmental Health Review* 44 (Summer 2000): 42–53.

[124] Transatlantic Business Dialogue, Cincinnati Recommendations, November 2000, 10–11, available at http://128.121.145.19/tabd/media/2000CincinnatiCEOReport.pdf, accessed August 25, 2004; "EU Biotech Industry Blasts Genetic Crop Labeling Law," Dow Jones, July 9, 2002; Shaffer and Pollack, "Reconciling (or Failing to Reconcile)," 184–85.

opinion against GM use. Without question, these NGOs consciously and explicitly linked the GMO issue to the food safety catastrophes that took place during the mid-1990s.[125] European-based NGOs influenced the behavior of smaller states as well. African scientists have argued that European-based NGOs—including Oxfam and Save the Children—frightened African governments into rejecting food aid that contained GM technology.[126]

There are a few flaws in this narrative, however. Global civil society failed to mobilize a similar shift in consumer preferences in the United States. This has not been due to a lack of effort. By 1999, the Transatlantic Consumer Dialogue, Greenpeace USA, Sierra Club, and Friends of the Earth had launched active campaigns against GMOs. Furthermore, after 2000 there were at least two significant food safety scares in the United States—the StarLink episode and the limited outbreak of mad cow disease. These crises gave GCS elements a policy window through which they could ratchet up regulatory stringency.[127] However, there was no significant change in the American regulatory system with regard to GM use, and only a modest shift in public opinion.[128]

Even in countries where NGOs supposedly had a pronounced effect, the duration of their influence has been limited. In the case of the European Union, the regulatory environment was already relatively strict prior to the mid-1990s activism on the GMO issue. EU scholars argue that the success in the GMO case had as much to do with citizen frustration at the opacity of EU decision-making as the substantive issues of the GM dispute.[129] Since the European Union ratcheted up its regulatory standards in 2001, these groups have had limited influence. Despite a fierce lobbying effort, they were unable to prevent the European Commission from lifting the unofficial moratorium on approving new GM products. The European Union also rejected the labeling of eggs and poultry fed with GM feed, against the wishes of environmental groups. The *Economist* observed in mid-2004, "the environmentalist lobby has been suffering as many setbacks as victories in its drive to rid the world of 'frankenfoods.' "[130]

As for the developing world, the NGO policy advice proffered to African governments was less persuasive than the reluctance of the European Union itself to endorse GM food aid.[131] The environmental groups themselves ac-

---

[125] Schurman, "Fighting 'Frankenfoods,' " 254–62.

[126] Tamar Kahn, "Modified Food-Aid Fears Slammed," *Business Day*, March 6, 2003.

[127] Leiss, "The Trouble with Science," 45; Shaffer and Pollack, "Reconciling (or Failing to Reconcile)," 207–8.

[128] Young, "Political Transfer and 'Trading Up?' " 475–78.

[129] Tiberghien and Starrs, "The EU as Global Trouble-Maker in Chief"; Grace Skogstad, "Legitimacy and/or Policy Effectiveness?: Network Governance in the European Union," *Journal of European Public Policy* 10 (June 2003): 321–38.

[130] "Another Genie Out of the Bottle," *Economist*, May 19, 2004.

[131] Paarlberg, "Reinvigorating Genetically Modified Crops."

knowledge that they have been unable to dissuade farmers in these countries from embracing GM technology. A Greenpeace spokesman stated in 2002 that, "Whenever you see these crops come to market you see significant take-up because farmers see it as their salvation."[132]

In the end, the best one can say about the different nonstate actors is that their advocacy resonated in places that were predisposed to hearing such arguments—and as a result, these messages cancelled each other out at the global level. Environmental NGOs and less competitive farmers preferred the most stringent set of regulatory standards for the handling of GMOs, while scientists and biotech corporations preferred a science-based approach. As noted in chapter 3, without a universal consensus among these actors, it is impossible for nonstate actors to change a rival standards outcome. Biotech firms have had limited success with the regulatory approval of GM crop plantings, and global civil society has had some success with the extent of GM food labeling. However, neither global regulatory coordination nor effective global governance has been established for either question.

Other state-based models of regulation do poorly in explaining the GMO case as well. David Vogel's "California effect" model would predict that the United States should adopt EU-style regulations for GMOs.[133] Aseem Prakash and Kelly Kollman argue that this has taken place: "starting in 1999, there has been a subtle but noticeable change in the policy agenda surrounding biotechnology issues in the U.S., signifying movement (though not a drastic change) towards some sort of convergence with EU standards."[134] As evidence, they point to the proliferation of proposed legislation at the federal and state level installing more stringent regulatory standards and labeling requirements for GM products, the passage of referenda at the state and county level banning some types of GM products, and the FDA's promulgation of voluntary standards on the labeling of GM food. Furthermore, in February 2004, Monsanto had to retreat from its efforts to market a genetically engineered wheat plant in the United States. Farmers were concerned that their exports would not be accepted by GM-unfriendly importers.[135]

It would be an exaggeration to claim any real shift in the U.S. position since 1999. Prakash and Kollman acknowledge that, "new laws and regulations have yet to be enacted at the federal level and the U.S. Trade Representative (USTR) continues to threaten the EU with WTO action."[136] Indeed, the USTR decision to launch a WTO dispute underscores this point. As the previous section demonstrated, the U.S. government has not substantially altered its position on

---

[132] Quoted in Mason, "Gaining Ground."

[133] David Vogel, *Trading Up: Consumer and Environmental Regulation in a Global Economy* (Cambridge, MA: Harvard University Press, 1995).

[134] Prakash and Kollman, "Biopolitics in the EU and the U.S.," 629.

[135] Andrew Martin, "Monsanto Retreats on Biotech Wheat," *Chicago Tribune*, May 11, 2004.

[136] Prakash and Kollman, "Biopolitics in the EU and the U.S.," 621.

GM regulation since the Cartagena Protocol. Reviewing the recent history of the GMO dispute, Alasdair Young concluded that "de facto trading up has been modest," and that while public wariness of GM products increased, "the changes in U.S. *policy* are modest."[137] David Vogel, in reviewing the increasing acceptance of GMO crops within the United States, concludes: "in this area of regulatory policy, not only is there no move toward regulatory convergence but American and European regulatory policies have become *more* divergent."[138]

The outcome—a stalemate with neither camp gaining a decisive edge—also contradicts predictions grounded in the assumption of American economic hegemony. In terms of agricultural production, food trade, and biotechnology, American primacy is unquestioned. However, consistent with the model developed here, the source of state power in a globalized economy is not share of production but share of consumption. On this dimension, the European Union is a coequal of the United States. As Robert Paarlberg concludes:

> Many observers originally assumed that once the United States began growing GM food and feed products, the technology would quickly become pervasive. The United States is the world's biggest exporter of agricultural goods, so these products would have to be accepted worldwide. That was the wrong way to look at the matter. *In international commodity markets, the big importers, not the big exporters, usually set standards*—and the biggest importers are Europe and Japan, which together import $90 billion in agricultural products annually. Europe imports 75 percent more food and farm products from developing countries every year than the United States does. Accordingly, developing countries that aspire to export farm products must pay close attention to European consumer preferences and import regulations.[139]

CONCLUSION

The case of genetically modified organisms provides an exemplary case of rival standards. The United States and the European Union promulgated different regulatory standards to govern the production and consumption of GMOs. The initial divergence of standards created domestic groups with large asset-specific investments in these sets of standards, increasing the adjustment costs for both governments to switch standards later. The absence of a bargaining core between the great powers, combined with the absence of strong preferences from other countries, led to a rival standards outcome. Both the United States and the European Union pushed to legitimize their preferred standards

---

[137] Young, "Political Transfer and 'Trading Up?'" 469, 474.

[138] David Vogel, "The Dynamics of Regulatory Convergence," paper presented at a conference on "Regulation in Europe," November 1999, 26 (emphasis in original). See also Shaffer and Pollack, "Reconciling (or Failing to Reconcile)."

[139] Paarlberg, "Reinvigorating Genetically Modified Crops," 90 (emphasis is added).

in friendly fora, and competed to recruit as many allies as possible among the other countries of the world. Because of the large market size of both of these countries, the result has been an uneasy stalemate.

In the case of GMOs, the outcome suggests an intriguing paradox—in a bipolar economic order, great power rivalries can be an efficacious source of policy *convergence*, if not policy *coordination*. Divergent preferences among large states, combined with the increasing returns to scale of regulatory harmonization, lead these actors to attract as many allies as possible. In a bipolar distribution of power, the result is a bifurcation of policies, but strong policy convergence at two different nodes. Without this great power rivalry, it is highly unlikely that any degree of policy convergence would have taken place. The case of GMOs strongly underscores this type of convergence process.

CHAPTER SEVEN

The "Semi-Deviant" Case: TRIPS and Public Health

WHEN the 1994 Agreement on Trade-Related Intellectual Property Rights (TRIPS) came into force, NGOs, public health advocates, and transnational activists asserted that the agreement imposed excessive restrictions on access to life-saving drugs in the developing world. The TRIPS accord was thought to be particularly damaging in the treatment of HIV/AIDS, because of the high cost of patented antiretroviral drugs (ARVs). In the late 1990s, these elements of global civil society banded together to push for less stringent IPR enforcement for most countries in the world.

Soon afterward, both the United States and European Union began softening their stance on the strict enforcement of TRIPS. In November 2001, at the Doha Ministerial meeting of the World Trade Organization (WTO), member governments addressed this concern by signing off on the "Declaration on the TRIPS Agreement and Public Health" or Doha Declaration. This Declaration stated that:

> [T]he TRIPS Agreement does not and should not prevent members from taking measures to protect public health. Accordingly, while reiterating our commitment to the TRIPS Agreement, we affirm that the Agreement can and should be interpreted and implemented in a manner supportive of WTO members' right to protect public health and, in particular, to promote access to medicines for all.[1]

The Declaration went on to delineate the various conditions under which countries could use the "flexibilities" of TRIPS to address public health problems. In August 2003, an additional WTO agreement was reached to clarify remaining ambiguities from the Doha Declaration.[2] In December 2005, these agreements were codified through a permanent amendment to the TRIPS accord.[3] These events were the culmination of a sustained campaign by global civil society designed to scale back intellectual property restrictions on the production and distribution of generic drugs to the developing world. A devel-

---

[1] "Declaration on the TRIPS Agreement and Public Health," http://www.wto.org/english/thewto_e/minist_e/min01_e/mindecl_trips_e.htm, accessed April 4, 2006.

[2] "Implementation of paragraph 6 of the Doha Declaration on the TRIPS Agreement and public health," August 30, 2003, available at http://www.wto.org/english/tratop_e/trips_e/implem_para6_e.htm, accessed April 4, 2006.

[3] "Amendment of the TRIPS Agreement," December 6, 2005, available at http://www.wto.org/english/news_e/news05_e/trips_decision_e.doc, accessed April 4, 2006.

oping country delegate told one researcher, "what negotiators like me failed to accomplish Oxfam and MSF [Médecins Sans Frontières] have accomplished."[4]

The revisionist approach developed here would appear to have a tough time accounting for the shift in global governance emanating from the Doha Declaration. The two largest trading powers (the United States and European Union) and powerful economic sectors embedded in those economies (pharmaceutical companies) had heartily embraced the status quo of stringent IPR regulations, despite opposition from much of the developing world. According to the revisionist model, global civil society should not be able to alter the outcome in a club standards situation. And yet, according to GCS scholarship, this appears to be exactly what happened.[5] The Doha Declaration appears to be a deviant case for the revisionist model.

A deviant case presents an opportunity for theory testing and theory development.[6] Closer examination of the event can reveal limitations of the proposed theory, highlight unforeseen causal mechanisms or newly relevant variables, or lead to a reevaluation of how the case is coded. This chapter takes a closer look at the TRIPS case to examine why the revisionist argument failed to hold up, and to see if GCS arguments hold up to empirical scrutiny. The data suggest that global civil society did have some causal effect on great power foreign policies and the changes to the TRIPS regime with regard to public health. This influence, however, has been overstated in several ways. As with other prominent cases, the GCS narrative omits alternative explanatory variables and exaggerates the extent of the policy shift.

Examination of this case also reveals three useful concepts for further theory development. First, national preferences on regulatory standards can be affected by the *securitization* of the relevant issue.[7] The key to the U.S. policy shift was less the GCS campaign than the viewing of HIV/AIDS through a national security lens. Second, this is a deviant case for the revisionist model because of the unusually high costs of forum-shopping that were unique to the timing and circumstances surrounding the Doha Ministerial. The great powers conceded more than they would have preferred at Doha, but this was due to transient factors unrelated to the GCS campaign. Third, even if extreme

---

[4] Quoted in Peter Drahos, "Developing Countries and International Intellectual Property Standard-Setting," *Journal of World Intellectual Property* 5 (May 2002): 765.

[5] Aseem Prakash and Susan Sell, "Using Ideas Strategically: The Contest between Business and NGO Networks in Intellectual Property Rights," *International Studies Quarterly* 48 (Spring 2004): 143–75; Drahos, "Developing Countries and International Intellectual Property Standard-Setting."

[6] Arend Lijphart, "Comparative Politics and the Comparative Method," *American Political Science Review* 65 (September 1971): 692.

[7] The concept of securitization that is developed here is distinct from its treatment by the "Copenhagen School" of international relations theory. For an introduction to their approach, see Michael Williams, "Words, Images, Enemies: Securitization and International Politics," *International Studies Quarterly* 47 (December 2003): 511–31.

values of a variable can lead to an anomalous short-run outcome, the revisionist model holds up better over the long haul. After the Doha Declaration, the United States and European Union acted to ensure that the carve-out for public health fit with their preferences rather than those of global civil society. As time has passed great power governments have appropriated the normative frame of improving public health to advance their own policy aims. In the end, the preferences of the great powers strongly conditioned the final extent of the shift.

This chapter is divided into six parts. The next section recounts the GCS narrative of how a public health exception to TRIPS was negotiated. The third section critically examines whether global civil society was solely responsible for the change in great power preferences, and concludes that national security concerns played a more prominent role than is commonly understood. The fourth section looks at the negotiations surrounding the Doha Ministerial conference to see why the United States and European Union agreed to such a sweeping declaration. This section exposes one temporary weakness of the typology of global governance processes developed here; it assumes there are minimal costs to forum-shopping. The fifth section examines developments on this issue since the 2001 Doha Declaration, and finds that the revisionist model outperforms GCS narratives in explaining the retrenchment of intellectual property rights. The final section summarizes and concludes.

GETTING TO THE DOHA DECLARATION: THE GCS NARRATIVE

The TRIPS regime was designed to deal with the protection of all forms of intellectual property—patents, trademarks, and copyrights. As the prime mover behind the creation of TRIPS, it was not surprising that the United States immediately began to make aggressive use of the TRIPS provision to crack down on IPR violations in the developing world.[8] In the first five years of the WTO's existence, the United States filed more TRIPS cases than any other country.[9]

A majority of these filings were triggered at the behest of the Pharmaceuticals Research and Manufacturers of America (PhRMA), the principal lobbying organization for the pharmaceuticals sector. The motivations behind these TRIPS cases were varied; however, one obvious driver was the issue of antiretroviral drugs that combat the HIV virus. By the 1990s, the AIDS crisis in Africa

---

[8] Susan Sell, *Power and Ideas: North-South Politics of Intellectual Property and Antitrust* (Albany: State University of New York Press, 1998); Sell, *Private Power, Public Law: The Globalization of Intellectual Property Rights* (Cambridge: Cambridge University Press, 2003).

[9] Sell, *Private Power, Public Law*, 129.

had become particularly acute. Of the 40 million persons with the HIV virus, 25 million lived in Africa. In 1998, 200,000 Africans lost their lives because of war; more than 2 million died from AIDS. By 2010, the economies in the region are estimated to be roughly 20 percent lower than they would have been without AIDS. Because of AIDS, life expectancy in sub-Saharan Africa has fallen by twenty to thirty years, while infant mortality has increased from 50 to 300 percent. By the late 1990s, approximately 8,000 people per day died of AIDS in the developing world.[10]

The spread and cost of the disease prompted some developing-country governments to search for ways to widen citizen access to life-saving drugs. One attractive policy option was compulsory licensing—allowing local pharmaceutical firms to manufacture low-cost generic versions of ARVs without the permission of the patent holder. For countries lacking domestic production facilities, another option was parallel importation—allowing the product made by the patent owner to be imported into the country without the patent owner's permission. This creates differential prices for the same drug in the same market.

PhRMA, representing the patent holders for ARVs, had a vested interest in the status quo of strict enforcement of the TRIPS accord. The economics of pharmaceutical production consist of massive fixed costs and very small marginal costs once a drug has been developed. Patents permit the inventor to hold an artificial monopoly on the product, allowing the firm to recoup its fixed costs. Without a strong IPR regime, the pharmaceutical sector feared it would begin to see its profits diminish. Even though developing countries were not a significant market, PhRMA worried that any exception made to TRIPS would trigger a general erosion of intellectual property rights. For example, if the practice of parallel importation spread to the developed countries, the monetary losses stemming from an inflow of generic ARVs would be considerable. Drug company representatives told South African president Thabo Mbeki that their problem with his government's moves toward the compulsory licensing of AIDS drugs was that, "what South Africa does is a precedent for other developing countries."[11] Thailand's government received a similar mes-

---

[10] Data in this paragraph comes from Council on Foreign Relations, *More Than Humanitarian: A Strategic U.S. Approach toward Africa* (New York: Council on Foreign Relations, 2005), 63; UNAIDS, *Report on the Global HIV/AIDS Epidemic* (Geneva: UNAIDS, 2000); United Nations Development Program, *Human Development Report 2004*, 143–46; National Intelligence Council, "The Global Infectious Disease Threat and Its Implications for the United States," January 2000, available at http://www.cia.gov/cia/reports/nie/report/nie99-17d.html, accessed September 13, 2005; Channing Ardt and Jeffrey D. Lewis, "The Macro Implications of HIV/AIDS in South Africa," World Bank Africa Region Working Paper Series No. 9, Washington, DC, December 2000; Ellen 't Hoen, "TRIPS, Pharmaceutical Patents, and Access to Essential Medicines," *Chicago Journal of International Law* 3 (Spring 2002): 27.

[11] Quoted in Barton Gellman, "A Conflict of Health and Profit," *Washington Post*, May 21, 2000.

sage from the United States government when that country contemplated compulsory licensing.[12]

To change the status quo, a group of AIDS activists and public health advocates formed the Access Campaign to lobby the governments and IGOs that the TRIPS accord should not interfere with the production and exchange of generic ARVs. Leading NGOs involved in the effort included ACT UP, Médecins Sans Frontières (MSF), Health Action International, Oxfam, CARE, and the Consumer Project on Technology. When MSF won the Nobel Peace Prize in 1999, it donated all of its award money to the Access Campaign.

A typical GCS effort was the November 1999 Amsterdam Statement signed by more than 350 participants, which averred the following:

> In the developing world, a lucrative or "viable" market for lifesaving drugs simply does not exist. But clearly what does exist is need. The market has failed both to provide equitably priced medicines and to ensure research and development for infectious disease. This lack of affordable medicines and research and development for neglected diseases is causing avoidable human suffering. Market forces alone will not address this need: political action is demanded.[13]

According to the coordinator for MSF's globalization project, the Amsterdam Statement served as a guide for the work of global civil society on TRIPS and public health.[14]

Transnational activist networks influenced the TRIPS regime through three mechanisms. First, NGOs played a crucial role in raising the issue to governments of all stripes. According to Susan Sell and Aseem Prakash, the NGO network supported and encouraged developing-country governments to issue compulsory licenses for life-saving drugs. NGOs were particularly crucial in providing legal expertise to developing countries, permitting them to take an active role in TRIPS negotiations. Peter Drahos documents the extent to which the African countries' increased influence within the TRIPS Council was enabled by partnerships with NGOs.[15]

The same GCS coalition also lobbied American and European trade officials by providing information on the connection between TRIPS and the public health crises in the developing world. In 2000, United States trade representative Charlene Barshefsky told the *Washington Post*: "Largely it was the activities of ACT-UP and the AIDS activists that galvanized our attention [to the fact] that there was an absolute crisis. . . . [In the past] I was certainly not aware

---

[12] Nathan Ford et al., "The Role of Civil Society in Protecting Public Health over Commercial Interests: The Case of Thailand," *The Lancet* 363 (February 14, 2004): 560.

[13] Available at http://www.accessmed-msf.org/upload/ReportsandPublications/17122001173935/ Amsterdam%20statemt.pdf, accessed August 5, 2005.

[14] 't Hoen, "TRIPS, Pharmaceutical Patents, and Access to Essential Medicines," 34.

[15] Drahos, "Developing Countries and International Intellectual Property Standard-Setting."

of this at all."[16] Other USTR and European Commission officials have also acknowledged their ignorance of the public health dimensions of their work prior to the Access Campaign.[17]

Second, GCS activists tried to raise public awareness of the issue in the developed world as a means of pressuring political leaders in these countries. Again, there is preliminary evidence of success on this front. ACT UP disrupted the official start to Al Gore's 2000 presidential campaign to protest Gore's alleged involvement in pressuring South Africa to strictly enforce the TRIPS accord. The NGO gained additional publicity by disrupting later campaign events.[18] Sell and Prakash observe that by 2001, news stories containing the terms "patents" and "public health" in the same article had increased seven-fold from three years prior.[19] To push the "public health" frame of thinking about IPR and TRIPS, GCS efforts also focused on encouraging nontrade international governmental organizations, such as the World Health Organization, the Joint United Nations Programme on HIV/AIDS (UNAIDS), and the European Parliament to get involved on the issue.[20]

Third, public health advocates worked to combat the messages and memes of PhRMA and governments that opposed weakening the enforcement of TRIPS. GCS activists engaged in research designed to counter the claim that patent protection was necessary to fund research and development for new drugs. In the run-up to the Doha Ministerial, both USTR and PhRMA put out repeated statements minimizing the role that patent protections played in hindering the treatment of AIDS in the developing world; GCS activists responded by pointing out the internal contradictions of such a claim. As one activist put it: "If patents in developing countries are not important to Pharma, why so much concern about obtaining and enforcing them?"[21]

According to the GCS narrative, this activist campaign led to two tangible and significant policy shifts in the global governance of public health and intellectual property. First, prior to Doha, both the United States and the European Union scaled back efforts to enforce the TRIPS accord against countries affected by the AIDS crisis. Initially, the Clinton administration applied limited economic sanctions and threatened more against South Africa unless that

---

[16] Gellman, "A Conflict of Health and Profit."

[17] Anna Lanoszka, "The Global Politics of Intellectual Property Rights and Pharmaceutical Drug Policies in Developing Countries," *International Political Science Review* 24 (May 2003): 192.

[18] For a chronology of these events from ACT-UP's perspective, see Mark Milano, Alan Berkman, and David Hoos, "Breaking the Silence: Activist Efforts to Improve Global Access to AIDS Medications," paper presented at the 13th International AIDS Conference, Durban, South Africa, July 2000.

[19] Prakash and Sell, "Using Ideas Strategically," 166.

[20] 't Hoen, "TRIPS, Pharmaceutical Patents, and Access to Essential Medicines," 35–38.

[21] Frederick Abbott, "The Doha Declaration on the TRIPS Agreement and Public Health," *Journal of International Economic Law* 5 (Spring 2002): 485.

country repealed its Medicines and Related Substances Control Amendment Act of 1997. The law allowed for the compulsory licensing of generic ARVs. The European Commission applied similar pressure. In 2001, the Bush administration filed a complaint with the WTO over Brazil's AIDS program, which relies heavily on competition from generic drug producers.

In both cases, the threats of coercion prompted widespread protests from GCS activists. In the case of South Africa, the Office of the Vice President interceded with the USTR to change American policy. In both cases, the great powers—and PhRMA—retreated from their initial positions and chose not to challenge these domestic laws. In the United States, these changes were codified into a more general policy. In December 1999, at the Seattle WTO Ministerial, President Clinton declared that, "the United States will henceforward implement its health care and trade policies in a manner that ensures that people in the poorest countries won't have to go without medicine they so desperately need."[22] In May 2000, this policy was codified into an executive order dictating that the United States "shall not seek, through negotiation or otherwise, the revocation or revision of any intellectual property law or policy" for countries in sub-Saharan Africa. The Bush administration reaffirmed this principle in February 2001, and later in the year agreed to negotiate with Brazil rather than pursue WTO enforcement.

The second major achievement was the Doha Declaration itself. Various articles of the original TRIPS accord allowed for "limited exceptions" to stringent IPR enforcement, but they were vaguely worded.[23] The legal uncertainty associated with that issue had deterred many developing countries from even skirting the boundaries of TRIPS due to their fear of running afoul of either the United States or the European Union in a WTO dispute panel. The Doha Declaration greatly reduced that uncertainty.[24] In addition, the agreement also gave least developed WTO members an additional ten-year exemption to the implementation of patent protections of pharmaceutical products.[25]

Experts and media reports interpreted the Doha Declaration as a clear victory for developing countries as opposed to the developed world or PhRMA. The "blowback" of negative publicity for the pharmaceutical sector—caused almost entirely by global civil society—made this outcome inevitable. One reporter concluded: "Going into Doha, U.S. drug companies had become a

---

[22] Remarks by President Clinton, December 1, 1999, available at http://usembassy-australia.state .gov/hyper/WF991202/epf402.htm, accessed April 4, 2006.

[23] For example, Article 30 reads in full: "Members may provide limited exceptions to the exclusive rights conferred by a patent, provided that such exceptions do not unreasonably conflict with a normal exploitation of the patent and do not unreasonably prejudice the legitimate interests of the patent owner, taking account of the legitimate interests of third parties." Available at http:// www.wto.org/english/tratop_e/trips_e/t_agm3_e.htm, accessed August 1, 2005.

[24] As will be shown later in this chapter, however, this uncertainty was not eliminated.

[25] "Declaration on the TRIPS Agreement and Public Health," paragraph 7.

public relations liability for the cause of preserving patent protection for corporations. Headlines at home and abroad depicted them as heartless profiteers that charged dying, impoverished Africans exorbitant prices for AIDS medicines."[26] Indeed, by 2001, the pharmaceutical industry had become sufficiently stigmatized to become villains in popular culture.[27]

Analysts also credited transnational activist networks as the pivotal actors responsible for the Doha Declaration.[28] Economist Arvind Panagariya concluded, "The credit for pushing through the Declaration on the TRIPS Agreement and Public Health must go largely to civil society groups from both North and South, which spoke with one voice and rallied behind an undeniably worthy cause."[29] An EU trade expert confirmed that "it is beyond doubt that [the Doha Declaration] has legal value."[30] Reflecting on the policy changes between the Uruguay round and the Doha round, Prakash and Sell conclude:

> The NGO network presented a normative frame and proposed policy solutions that the business network opposed. In the end, with its successful strategies of mobilizing a transnational coalition, framing policy problems, disseminating information, grafting its agenda as a solution to policy problems, and exploiting political opportunities . . . the NGO network has clearly won some substantive victories and brought about normative change in the IPR debate.[31]

Since the Doha Declaration, the United States has publicly proclaimed its restraint in pushing patent protection for pharmaceuticals in its bilateral and regional free trade agreements (FTA). On its Web site, the USTR stresses that, "The FTAs we have negotiated similarly contain the flexibility needed in order to address public health crises."[32] FTAs with Chile, Morocco, and Bahrain do not contain any restrictions on compulsory licensing. Typical of these arrangements is the Central American Free Trade Agreement (CAFTA), which comes with a side letter specifying that CAFTA's intellectual property provisions "do not affect a Party's ability to take necessary measures to protect public health by promoting access to medicines for all, in particular concern-

---

[26] Jeff Faux, "A Trade Deal Built on Sand," *The American Prospect* Online, December 4, 2001, available at http://www.prospect.org/webfeatures/2001/12/faux-j-12-04.html, accessed August 8, 2005. See also Abbott, "The Doha Declaration on the TRIPS Agreement and Public Health," 473.

[27] John le Carré, *The Constant Gardener* (New York: Scribner, 2000).

[28] Helen Epstein and Lincoln Chen, "Can AIDS Be Stopped?" *New York Review of Books* 49 (March 14, 2002).

[29] Arvind Panagariya, "Developing Countries at Doha: A Political Economy Analysis," *The World Economy* 25 (September 2002): 1226.

[30] Jean Charles Van Eeckhaute, "The Debate on the TRIPs Agreement and Access to Medicines in the WTO: Doha and Beyond," *Pharmaceuticals Policy and Law* 5 (2002): 14.

[31] Prakash and Sell, "Using Ideas Strategically," 167.

[32] Office of the USTR, "Fact Sheet on Access to Medicines," July 9, 2004, available at http://www.ustr.gov/Document_Library/Fact_Sheets/2004/Fact_Sheet_on_Access_to_Medicines.html, accessed April 6, 2006.

ing cases such as HIV/AIDS."[33] The Doha Declaration is also explicitly mentioned in the understanding.

The effect of these shifts in policy on the cost of AIDS drugs was significant. According to Médecins Sans Frontières, the price of most first-line ARVs per patient-year in the developing world fell from $10,000 in 2000 to $150 in 2005.[34] As a matter of course, pharmaceutical companies began to allow generic drug manufacturers to license newer drugs for use in poorer countries.[35] From the GCS perspective, this is a case where actors that possess little in the way of conventional material capabilities were able to alter the preferences of great power actors. GCS activists accomplished this task despite the implacable opposition of multinational corporations with enormous specific assets invested in the status quo ante.

THE SHIFT IN GREAT POWER PREFERENCES: A REVISIONIST INTERPRETATION

The narrative and evidence put forward to support the GCS paradigm on this issue cannot be summarily dismissed. Interviews with USTR officials confirm that U.S.-based NGOs acted as an effective "fire alarm" in alerting trade officials to the AIDS crisis in Africa.[36] However, in other issue areas—such as land mines, investment, and the environment—prior claims of GCS effects have suffered from one of two flaws.[37] First, GCS accounts have tended to neglect alternative explanations and causal pathways for the outcome.[38] The connection between GCS activity and the desired outcome has often been made without an examination of alternative explanations. Second, GCS accounts have overestimated the magnitude of any perceived policy shift. While there may be a change in policy, the change is neither significant nor permanent. This section considers whether there are factors beyond GCS activity that can explain the shift in great power behavior.

In the case of the United States, one alternative explanation can account for the shift in preferences—the decision to securitize infectious diseases in gen-

---

[33] Office of the USTR, "Understanding Regarding Certain Public Health Measures," August 5, 2004, available at http://www.ustr.gov/assets/Trade_Agreements/Bilateral/CAFTA/CAFTA-DR_Final_Texts/asset_upload_file697_3975.pdf, accessed August 9, 2005.

[34] Available at http://www.accessmed-msf.org/prod/publications.asp?scntid=28620052030274&contenttype=PARA&, accessed August 9, 2005.

[35] Donald McNeil, "Bristol-Myers Allows Powerful AIDS Drug to Be Sold Cheaply," *New York Times*, February 15, 2006.

[36] On the role that interest groups and NGOs can play as "fire alarms" in international negotiations, see Helen V. Milner, *Interests, Institutions, and Information: Domestic Politics and International Relations* (Princeton, NJ: Princeton University Press, 1997).

[37] See the discussion in chapters 1 and 8 for more on these cases.

[38] Michelle Betsill and Elisabeth Corell, "NGO Influence in International Environmental Negotiations: A Framework for Analysis," *Global Environmental Politics* 1 (November 2001): 65–85.

eral, and HIV/AIDS in particular, as a serious transnational threat to American interests.[39] With the end of the cold war, and the decline of traditional security threats, there was a serious scholarly and policy debate over what constituted a security threat.[40] Over the course of Bill Clinton's second term, the national security bureaucracies in general, and the National Security Council in particular, devoted an increasing amount of attention to the problem of transnational threats.[41] Threats ranging from terrorism to financial contagion to infectious diseases had the potential to breach U.S. borders. Securitizing these issues had the advantage of mobilizing the state and reallocating resources toward that policy concern.[42]

While conventional security analysts dismissed most of these new threats as overblown, the idea of disease as a transnational threat found wider acceptance among policymakers and the mass public alike.[43] Historically, disease has been an important factor in determining the balance of power in world politics.[44] Although the direct threat to American security might not have been large, the indirect threat was a source of concern. There was a growing consensus among U.S. security experts that HIV/AIDS had the capacity to trigger regional instability, war, or massive refugee flows in areas with weak or failing states.[45]

[39] This explanation is not limited to the United States; there is evidence that Japan and other developed countries evinced a similar concern. See Roland Paris, "Human Security: Paradigm Shift or Hot Air?" *International Security* 26 (Fall 2001): 90.

[40] See, in particular, the debate surrounding the concept of "human security." On the scholarly debate over whether to focus on "nontraditional" threats, see Stephen Walt, "The Renaissance of Security Studies," *International Studies Quarterly* 35 (June 1991): 211–39; Edward Kolodziej, "Renaissance of Security Studies? Caveat Lector!" *International Studies Quarterly* 36 (December 1992): 421–38; United Nations Development Programme, *Human Development Report 1994: New Dimensions of Human Security* (New York: Oxford University Press, 1994); Sean M. Lynn-Jones and Steven E. Miller, eds., *Global Dangers: Changing Dimensions of International Security* (Cambridge, MA: MIT Press, 1995); Keith Krause and Michael C. Williams, "Broadening the Agenda of Security Studies: Politics and Methods," *Mershon International Studies Review* 40 (October 1996): 229–54; Paris, "Human Security."

[41] David Rothkopf, *Running the World* (New York: Public Affairs, 2005), 364 and 382. See, more generally, Richard Clarke, *Against All Enemies* (New York: Free Press, 2004).

[42] David E. Sanger, "Sometimes, National Security Says It All," *New York Times*, May 7, 2000.

[43] At the policymaker level, see PDD NTSC-7, "Addressing the Threat of Infectious Diseases," June 12, 1996, available at http://www.fas.org/irp/offdocs/pdd_ntsc7.htm, accessed September 13, 2005. At the mass public level, see John E. Rielly, ed., *American Public Opinion and U.S. Foreign Policy 1999* (Chicago: Chicago Council on Foreign Relations, 1999), 15.

[44] William McNeill, *Plagues and Peoples* (New York: Doubleday, 1976); Jared Diamond, *Guns, Germs, and Steel: The Fates of Human Societies* (New York: W. W. Norton, 1999); Andrew T. Price-Smith, *The Health of Nations: Infectious Disease, Environmental Change, and Their Effects on National Security and Development* (Cambridge, MA: MIT Press, 2002).

[45] International Crisis Group, *HIV/AIDS as a Security Threat*, Issues Report No. 1, Washington, DC, June 2001, available at http://www.crisisgroup.org/home/index.cfm?id=1831&l=1, accessed January 2006; United States Institute for Peace, "AIDS and Violent Conflict in Africa," USIP Special Report No. 75, October 2001; P. W. Singer, "AIDS and International Security," *Survival* 44 (Spring 2002): 145–58; Susan Peterson, "Epidemic Disease and International Security," *Security*

Among infectious diseases, HIV/AIDS is unique in that it targets the most productive and pivotal members of society—adults between 18 and 45. Infection rates among peacekeeping forces, policy officers, government bureaucrats, and skilled professionals are higher than the general population. In some sub-Saharan countries, the practice of concurrent sexual partners further facilitates the spread of the disease.[46] This disease vector has a disastrous effect on economic growth, social stability, and the likelihood of war. AIDS increases infant mortality rates, which has been found to be one of the important triggers for state failure.[47] It would not be surprising, therefore, to see the United States prioritize public health concerns over intellectual property rights as the decade of the 1990s progressed.

In weighing the relative explanatory effects of the national security explanation and the GCS hypothesis, there are several factors that suggest privileging the securitization hypothesis as the primary cause for the shift in U.S. preferences. First, official directives and unofficial statements demonstrate that before and after the GCS campaign, high-ranking executive branch officials framed HIV/AIDS increasingly as a transnational threat to security rather than as a humanitarian or public health problem. In June 1996, President Clinton issued a Presidential Decision Directive addressing the threat of infectious diseases, stating, "Emerging infectious diseases such as Ebola, drug-resistant tuberculosis, and HIV/AIDS present one of the most significant health and security challenges facing the global community."[48] Announcing the directive, Gore said, "Today, guaranteeing national security means more than just defending our borders. . . . Now it also means defending our nation's health against all enemies, foreign and domestic."[49] Madeleine Albright wrote in her memoirs that, "At the start of my term I expected AIDS to be a significant threat to democracy, prosperity, and security in Africa. I soon realized it was the dominant one."[50] HIV/AIDS was raised as a national security matter at both the CIA and the NSC prior to the protest actions by GCS activists in 1999.

Studies 12 (Winter 2002/3): 43–81; Stefan Elbe, "HIV/AIDS and the Changing Landscape of War in Africa," *International Security* 27 (Fall 2002): 159–77; Jeremy Youde, "Enter the Fourth Horseman: Health Security and International Relations Theory," paper presented at the 2004 International Studies Association annual meeting, Montreal, Canada, March 2004; Laurie Garrett, *HIV and National Security: Where Are the Links?* (New York: Council on Foreign Relations, 2005).

[46] Daniel T. Halperin and Helen Epstein, "Concurrent Sexual Partnerships Help to Explain Africa's High HIV Prevalence," *The Lancet* 364 (July 3, 2004): 4–6.

[47] Daniel Esty et al., *The State Failure Task Force Report: Phase II Findings* (McLean, VA: Science Applications International Corporation, 1998).

[48] PDD NTSC-7, "Addressing the Threat of Infectious Diseases."

[49] Quoted in Peterson, "Epidemic Disease and International Security."

[50] Madeleine Albright, *Madame Secretary: A Memoir* (New York: Miramax Books, 2003), 452. See also Bill Clinton, *My Life: The Presidential Years* (New York: Vintage Press, 2004), 379 and 418, and Hillary Clinton, *Living History* (New York: Scribner, 2003), 404.

The concern about the transnational threat from disease also appeared in U.S. national security strategies. The 1999 U.S. National Security Strategy (NSS) stated:

> Environmental and health problems can undermine the welfare of U.S. citizens, and compromise our national security, economic and humanitarian interests abroad for generations. These threats respect no national boundary. History has shown that international epidemics, such as polio, tuberculosis and AIDS, can destroy human life on a scale as great as any war or terrorist act we have seen.[51]

A January 2000 National Intelligence Estimate concurred:

> New and reemerging infectious diseases will pose a rising global health threat and will complicate US and global security over the next 20 years. These diseases will endanger US citizens at home and abroad, threaten US armed forces deployed overseas, and exacerbate social and political instability in key countries and regions in which the United States has significant interests.[52]

By the late 1990s, stopping the global spread of HIV/AIDS was not merely a priority of global civil society—it was a priority for national security specialists as well. Vice President Gore's national security advisor, Leon Fuerth, stated that "HIV by definition was undercutting our state interests." He phrased the administration's evolving position as "a sense of national interest informed by ethics," concluding: "We approached the HIV problem from a sense what was right to do and what was in our interest to do, and we had no problem with seeing these as congruent."[53] In December 1999, UN ambassador Richard Holbrooke independently decided to put HIV/AIDS on the UN Security Council Agenda after his first trip to sub-Saharan Africa.[54]

A crude measure of this shift in national security focus can be seen in the attention devoted to public health vs. intellectual property in the series of National Security Strategies promulgated by the Clinton and Bush administrations. A new NSS was introduced every year except one. Because the NSS is designed for a national security audience, and not distributed to nongovernmental actors prior to publication, one would expect GCS influence over the drafting process to be minimal. As table 7.1 demonstrates, there was a noticeable shift over time emphasizing public health in general—and AIDS in partic-

---

[51] White House, "A National Security Strategy for a New Century," Washington, DC, December 1999, 3, available at http://www.fas.org/man/docs/nssr-1299.pdf, accessed August 15, 2005.

[52] National Intelligence Council, "The Global Infectious Disease Threat and Its Implications for the United States."

[53] Interview with Leon Fuerth, September 15, 2005.

[54] Steve Sternberg, "Former Diplomat Holbrooke Takes on Global AIDS," *USA Today,* June 10, 2002; Gwyn Prins, "AIDS and Global Security," *International Affairs* 80 (October 2004): 941–45.

TABLE 7.1
Alternative Frames in the National Security Strategy

Year	Mentions of "AIDS" or "public health"	Mentions of "transnational threat"	Mentions of "intellectual property" or "patents"
1996	3	1	3
1997	1	6	2
1998	5	7	9
1999	13	6	4
2000	18	6	5
2002	11	3	1

Note: Searchable documents retrieved from http://www.fas.org/man/doctrine.htm#nation (1996–1999); http://www.au.af.mil/au/awc/awcgate/nss/nss_dec2000_contents.htm (2000), and http://www.whitehouse.gov/nsc/nssall.html (2002).

ular—as a national security issue. In contrast, concerns about intellectual property rights enforcement waned as the years passed.

As the 2002 numbers show, this concern was not strictly a partisan one—HIV/AIDS remained a priority concern of the Bush administration as well, despite the Bush team's frostier relations with global civil society.[55] At his confirmation hearings for secretary of state, Colin Powell said AIDS was a "national security problem." His undersecretary of state, Paula Dobriansky, also said that "HIV/AIDS is a threat to security and global stability, plain and simple." P. W. Singer observes that, "a significant continuity between Clinton and Bush administration worldviews is the perception of a link between AIDS and increased instability and war."[56]

The second factor favoring a security explanation for the switch in policy is that global civil society was neither directly nor indirectly responsible for the emergence of this "transnational threat" frame—if anything, they shunned the language of national interest.[57] There is no mention of the national security implications of infectious diseases in the Amsterdam Statement, or in similar NGO documents. A search of online press release archives of the significant

[55] The decline of mentions in the 2002 document can be traced to the decline in length of the overall document. The Council on Foreign Relations concluded, "The rethinking of the U.S. approach to global security, post-9/11 . . . placed heavy emphasis on global health and the imperative to check the destructive power of runaway global infectious diseases, especially HIV/AIDS," Council on Foreign Relations, *More Than Humanitarianism*, 63.

[56] All quotes from Singer, "AIDS and International Security," 145.

[57] Stefan Elbe, "Should HIV/AIDS Be Securitized? The Ethical Dilemmas of Linking HIV/AIDS and Security," *International Studies Quarterly* 50 (March 2006): 121.

NGOs involved in the Access Campaign also failed to turn up any positive use of the transnational threat argument.

This may have been because such arguments were seen as insufficiently altruistic. From a GCS perspective, the drawback to securitizing the issue was that it permitted states to think about the problem through the narrow lens of interest rather than the expansive lens of social justice.[58] Indeed, the president of MSF's International Council, in a June 2000 speech, deplored the use of any national security logic to promote TRIPS flexibility—while still acknowledging the role that security interests played in the policy shift:

> *Now that the sufferings and diseases of the poor are a "threat" to national security and to expanding global markets, there is political interest.* Well this is not good enough. We must take this new-found political interest, and not allow a fiscal and state-security agenda to drive our agenda, which is one that is irreducibly committed to social justice.[59]

Third, the national security explanation is more consistent with the bureaucratic origins for the shift in the Clinton administration's position on AIDS and TRIPS. When South Africa passed its generic ARV measure, the USTR advocated moving South Africa to a "priority watch list" under section 301 of U.S. trade law. However, both Gore's national security advisor *and* the National Security Council staff opposed the move on national security grounds—prior to the launch of the GCS protests that hounded Gore's campaign.[60] Contrary to claims made by AIDS activists and GCS scholars that Gore needed to be persuaded to support their cause, both press reports at the time and interviews conducted with former trade officials confirm that Gore "led the way" in opposing any move toward economic coercion against South Africa.[61] When asked about the role that activists and protestors on the presidential campaign trail played in the resolution of that case, Fuerth replied: "You could draw the conclusion that it was the demonstrations that brought us to closure, and I'm not sure I can disprove that, *but it is simply not true.*"[62] Both Gore and Fuerth

[58] Ibid., 119–44; Marcella David, "Rubber Helmets: The Certain Pitfalls of Marshalling Security Council Resources to Combat AIDS in Africa," *Human Rights Quarterly* 23 (August 2001): 560–82.

[59] Dr. James Orbinski, speech to the Health Forum, June 14, 2000, available at http://www.msf.org/msfinternational/invoke.cfm?component=article&objectid=B6533B59-3EBB-4416-81F1367425329FE3&method=full_html, accessed April 4, 2006 (emphasis added). Ironically, this concern about securitizing AIDS has also been voiced by traditional security scholars—in part because of fears of conceptual overstretch by linking traditional security with "human security," and in part because such a move would relieve states from any moral obligation to assist. See Peterson, "Epidemic Disease and National Security," and Paris, "Human Security."

[60] Gellman, "A Conflict of Health and Profit"; interviews with NSC and USTR officials.

[61] Interviews with NSC and USTR officials; see also Jonathan Weisman, "Gore's Campaign Disrupted over South African AIDS Drugs," *Baltimore Sun*, June 22, 1999.

[62] Emphasis added. Quoted in Gellman, "A Conflict of Health and Profit."

cited the transnational threat posed by AIDS as a recurrent foreign policy theme throughout the 2000 campaign.[63] Holbrooke's UN initiative was also independent of the GCS campaign.

Finally, the anthrax scare in the fall of 2001 also reinforced the transnational threat frame.[64] The spread of anthrax through the mail to multiple American cities—including Washington, DC—stirred calls to license the generic manufacture of Cipro, an antibiotic patented by Bayer. Health officials in both Canada and the United States threatened to bypass Bayer's patent to ensure sufficient quantities of the antibiotic could be procured affordably.[65] Both governments eventually backed down from that threat after negotiations with Bayer. In the run-up to Doha, however, the incident caused negotiating difficulties for the United States, as developing countries argued that the HIV/AIDS epidemic was on par with the anthrax scare.[66] This situation forced the USTR's office to explicitly address what the Doha Declaration would later reiterate:

> Given the discovery of anthrax in New York, Florida, and the Washington, DC metropolitan area, and the risk of individuals being infected with a potentially deadly virus, the United States would be permitted under TRIPs to exercise its rights to go outside the patent process. . . . *These flexibilities are not limited to the United States. They are available to every other member of the WTO.*[67]

Global civil society was not superfluous in affecting great power preferences on this issue—the GCS campaign likely accelerated the change in TRIPS policy. Any counterfactual analysis, however, would have to conclude that because of the securitization phenomenon, the shift in U.S. preference over the issue was merely a matter of time. As Gwyn Prins points out, "If an issue can be 'securitized,' it is the equivalent of playing a trump at cards, for at once it leapfrogs other issues in priority."[68] The continuity between the Clinton and Bush administrations on this issue also supports the argument that security concerns were the main driver behind the switch in preferences. The United States scaled back its eagerness to unilaterally enforce the strictest interpretation of the TRIPS accord against countries suffering from epidemic levels of AIDS in order to prevent state failure and protect U.S. security interests.

[63] See, for example, "Vice President Gore's Remarks on AIDS to UN Security Council," January 10, 2000, at http://www.aegis.com/news/usis/2000/US000102.html, accessed August 9, 2005.

[64] Lanoszka, "The Global Politics of Intellectual Property Rights," 1823.

[65] Kristin Johnson, "Thompson May Seek to Void Cipro Patent If Talks Fail," Bloomberg News, October 23, 2001.

[66] Interview with former USTR official. See also Paul Blustein, "Drug Patent Poses Trade Threat," *Washington Post*, October 26, 2001; Sabin Russell, "U.S. Push for Cheap Cipro Haunts AIDS Drug Dispute," *San Francisco Chronicle*, November 8, 2001.

[67] Office of the USTR, "TRIPs and Health Emergencies," November 10, 2001, available at http://www.ustr.gov/Document_Library/Press_Releases/2001/November/.TRIPs_Health_Emergencies.html, accessed August 10, 2005. [emphasis added]

[68] Prins, "AIDS and Global Security," 940.

What Happened at Doha?

The November 2001 USTR statement reveals that the United States did not think the Doha Declaration was necessary. Indeed, the shift in the U.S. position prior to Doha is more consistent with the national security explanation than the GCS narrative. The American negotiating position was that the original TRIPS accord *already* contained public health exceptions for epidemics and the like.[69] Consistent with the national security frame, the U.S. position was that exceptions to TRIPS should apply only to poor countries with weak state institutions that suffer from epidemics—but that the carve-out should not go any further. Whereas the final Declaration actually said that the TRIPS accord, "does not and should not prevent members from taking measures to protect public health," the United States preferred narrower language, asserting a right "to take measures necessary to address these public health crises, in particular to secure affordable access to medicines."[70] The European Commission's position on the TRIPS accord was similar.[71] GCS advocates, in contrast, wanted as broad a "public health" exception to TRIPS as possible, covering any and all forms of illness—and got what they wanted in the Doha Declaration.

While securitization can explain the shift in great power preferences, it cannot explain what happened at Doha. The great powers acceded to a Declaration at Doha that contained very broad language on public health—an outcome more consistent with the GCS narrative. The problem is that GCS activity had no direct effect on the United States; in interviews, multiple USTR officials have refuted the notion that they felt pressure to cut a deal at Doha because of NGO pressure or activities.[72] GCS scholars counter that civil society influence in this event was indirect; transnational activists influenced the position of developing country members. The sheer number of supporting countries—and the improved coordination among the developing bloc—isolated the great powers and forced the United States and European Union to shift their positions.

Again, this is factually plausible,[73] but conceptually incomplete. The distribution of preferences on this issue is a classic example of club standards; under

[69] See, in particular, articles 7, 8, 30, and 31 of the original TRIPS agreement.

[70] Elizabeth Olson, "Drug Issue Casts a Shadow on Trade Talks," *New York Times*, November 2, 2001.

[71] European Commission, "Agreement on Intellectual Property Rights Relating to Trade and Pharmaceutical Patents," available at http://europa.eu.int/scadplus/leg/en/lvb/l21168.htm, accessed August 11, 2005.

[72] Interviews and e-mail exchanges with current and former USTR officials, June–August 2005.

[73] Although it should be noted that at the time of the negotiations, the coherence of the developing country bloc was open to question. The *Financial Times* reported during the Doha conference that, "Western negotiators say satisfying developing countries' grievances is made more difficult because they are so diverse and often poorly defined. 'They do not have a very clear position. Trying to make progress is very frustrating,' one European official said" (Guy de Jonquières and Frances Williams, "Poor Countries Raise Hurdle at WTO," *Financial Times*, November 9, 2001).

this scenario, the revisionist model would predict the great powers to create institutions guaranteeing that their regulatory preferences were locked in. In the past and present both the United States and the European Union have run into roadblocks at universal-membership IGOs. At these junctures in the past, great powers have evinced the willingness and the ability to either act unilaterally or shift fora to friendlier IGOs.[74] This would have been especially true of the Bush administration in late 2001, given their position toward the utility of multilateral diplomacy.[75] The important counterfactual question worth asking is why the great powers agreed to the Doha Declaration when there were alternative strategies outside the WTO process.

The answer, in part, appears to rest with the costs that come with forum-shopping. Although there are always some costs to switching fora, those costs were uniquely prohibitive for the great powers at the time of the Doha Ministerial—for reasons that had little to do with the Access Campaign. In the aftermath of the September 11 attacks, the United States was determined to launch a trade round at Doha for two reasons. First, the United States wanted to counter impressions that the terrorist attacks would weaken the process of economic globalization and/or undercut U.S. leadership.[76] Second, the great powers wanted a successful trade round in order to reinvigorate a global economy slumping from the aftereffects of the terrorist attacks and the concomitant slowdown in global trade.[77]

U.S. and European leaders were quite conscious of the link between a successful round and the terrorist attacks. Nine days after the attacks, Federal Reserve chairman Alan Greenspan testified before the Senate that, "A successful [trade] round would not only significantly enhance world economic growth but also answer terrorism with a firm reaffirmation of our commitment to open and free societies."[78] U.S. trade representative Robert Zoellick echoed these remarks in a *Washington Post* op-ed the very same day, stating, "We need to infuse our global leadership with a new sense of purpose and lasting resolve . . . the Bush administration has an opportunity to shape history by raising the flag of American economic leadership. The terrorists deliberately chose the World Trade towers as their target. While their blow toppled the towers, it

---

[74] Stephen D. Krasner, *Structural Conflict* (Berkeley: University of California Press, 1985); Krasner, "Global Communications and National Power: Life on the Pareto Frontier," *World Politics* 43 (April 1991): 336–66.

[75] Daniel W. Drezner, "Lost in Translation: The Transatlantic Divide over Diplomacy," in *Growing Apart: America in a Globalizing World*, ed. Jeffrey Kopstein and Sven Steinmo (Cambridge: Cambridge University Press, 2002).

[76] Panagariya, "Developing Countries at Doha," 1205.

[77] Sandra Cordon, "Slowdown Adds Pressure at WTO," *Ottawa Citizen*, November 1, 2001; Frances Williams, "Growth in Trade Unlikely to Top 2%," *Financial Times*, October 26, 2001.

[78] Alan Greenspan, "The condition of the financial markets," testimony before the Senate Committee on Banking, Housing, and Urban Affairs, September 20, 2001, available at http://www.federalreserve.gov/boarddocs/testimony/2001/20010920/default.htm, accessed January 2006.

cannot and will not shake the foundation of world trade and freedom."[79] As the Ministerial started in Doha, the British trade and industry secretary warned that the "war on terrorism could be lost here."[80] Media coverage of the run-up to Doha also stressed the importance of a successful Ministerial meeting to buttress perceptions of U.S. leadership.[81]

The failure to launch a trade round at Seattle three years earlier also increased the stakes at Doha for the ability of the WTO regime to advance trade liberalization. As Zoellick pointed out in October 2001, "the WTO stumbled badly in its first effort, in Seattle in 1999, to launch a round of global trade liberalization. It has not been keeping up with the challenges of a changing world economy. The meeting in Doha needs to get the WTO back on track."[82] Even prior to the September 11 attacks, WTO director-general Mike Moore stressed the importance of a successful Ministerial meeting at Doha given what transpired at Seattle: "failure to reach consensus on a forward work programme that would advance the objectives of the multilateral trading system, particularly in the light of the earlier failure at Seattle, would lead many to question the value of the WTO as a forum for negotiation. It would certainly condemn us to a long period of irrelevance."[83] Following the Doha meeting, Zoellick declared, "We have removed the stain of Seattle."[84] Contemporaneous media accounts confirm the shadow that Seattle cast over American and European trade negotiators in the run-up to Doha.[85]

[79] Robert Zoellick, "Countering Terror with Trade," *Washington Post*, September 20, 2001. In November 2001, Zoellick reiterated this point: "Just as the Cold War reflected a contest of values, so will this campaign against terrorism. Just as America's Cold War strategy recognized the interconnection of security and economics, so must its strategy against terrorism." Quoted in Denis Staunton, "Terrorist Threat Overshadows Key Trade Meeting," *Irish Times*, November 9, 2001. See also "American Trade Leadership: What Is at Stake," speech at the Institute for International Economics, Washington, DC, September 24, 2001, available at http://www.ustr.gov/assets/Document_Library/USTR_Speeches/2001/asset_upload_file522_4267.pdf, accessed January 2006.

[80] Quoted in Oliver Morgan and Gaby Hinsliff, "War on Terrorism Could be Lost Here," *The Observer*, November 4, 2001. See also Guy de Jonquières, "Dealing in Doha," *Financial Times*, November 6, 2001.

[81] Joseph Kahn, "A Trade Agenda Tempts Murphy's Law," *New York Times*, November 9, 2001; Siti Hajiar Sulaiman, "Call for Full Turnout at WTO Meeting," *Business Times Malaysia*, September 25, 2001; Staunton, "Terrorist Threat Overshadows Key Trade Meeting."

[82] Zoellick, "The WTO and New Global Trade Negotiations: What's at Stake," speech at the Council on Foreign Relations, Washington, DC, October 30, 2001, availalbe at http://www.ustr.gov/assets/Document_Library/USTR_Speeches/2001/asset_upload_file821_4260.pdf, accessed January 2006.

[83] Statement by the Director-General to the Informal General Council, July 30, 2001, available at http://www.wto.org/english/thewto_e/minist_e/min01_e/min01_dg_statement_gcmeeting30july01_e.htm, accessed January 2006.

[84] Quote to Agence-France Presse found at http://www.wto.org/trade_resources/quotes/new_round/new_round.htm, accessed January 2006.

[85] See references in footnote 74.

Finally, the ability of the great powers to shift fora on intellectual property from WIPO to the WTO in the Uruguay round made it that much more difficult to try and shift governance structures less than a decade later. Ironically, the efforts to create enforceable "hard law" on IPR in the first place also raised the costs on future forum-shifting.[86] Because the Americans and Europeans had invested so much in the WTO, any legal weakening of the TRIPS regime would be costly to them for other aspects of WTO enforcement, such as the dispute settlement mechanism. One European Commission trade negotiator observed after Doha that, "in the absence of any Declaration on public health, *de facto* non-compliance by several developing countries was a real risk."[87]

The uniquely binding venue and timing of Doha prevented the United States from substituting across governance structures. The multiplicity of linked trade issues also benefited the developing-country position. Because so many issues were being negotiated for inclusion in the Doha development agenda at the same time—textiles, agricultural subsidies, investment, procurement, the environment, and such—the developing countries were able to link issues to ensure concessions on TRIPS. Because the United States was committed to securing an agreement at Doha to launch a new trade round, USTR officials decided that making concessions on IPR early on would increase the odds of success.[88] As Haochen Sun observes, "[WTO] members came to understand that no broad negotiating mandates such as investment and competition would emerge from the conference in the absence of a meaningful result on medicines."[89]

GCS actors and developing-country governments were astute to exploit the unique opportunity presented by Doha. The uniqueness, however, should be stressed. In the fall of 2001, great powers faced extreme values of two control variables: (a) higher costs for forum-shopping than normal, and (b) an urgent need for forward momentum on WTO trade negotiations in order to cement the WTO's legitimacy. This suggests that, like domestic analyses of "policy windows," there are moments when GCS actors can seize the stage at the global level.[90]

---

[86] On this point, see Kenneth Abbott and Duncan Snidal, "Hard and Soft Law in International Governance," *International Organization* 54 (Summer 2000): 421–56.

[87] Eeckhaute, "The Debate on the TRIPs Agreement and Access to Medicines in the WTO," 22.

[88] According to one interview with a former USTR official, Zoellick explicitly made this calculation in signing off on the Doha Declaration. This has also been the post-Doha pattern on TRIPs and public health. Breakthroughs in negotiations over TRIPS preceded both the Cancun and Hong Kong Ministerials in 2003 and 2005 respectively.

[89] Haochen Sun, "The Road to Doha and Beyond: Some Reflections on the TRIPS Agreement and Public Health," *European Journal of International Law* 15 (February 2004): 136. See also Guy de Jonquières, "All Night Haggling in Doha Leads to Agreement," *Financial Times*, November 15, 2001.

[90] John W. Kingdon: *Agendas, Alternatives, and Public Policies*, 2nd ed. (New York: Longman, 1995). See also John Braithwaite and Peter Drahos, *Global Business Regulation* (Cambridge: Cambridge University Press, 1999), 33.

Post-Doha Developments

Process-tracing the post-Doha developments presents an ideal testing venue to compare the GCS approach with the revisionist model developed here. If the hypothesis about global civil society narrative holds, then one would expect to see continued adherence to the norm developed at Doha. Over time, a norm cascade should take effect. The result would be the continued diffusion and internalization of the public health meme in the global governance of intellectual property rights. If the revisionist approach is correct, we should see the great powers acting to restrict and constrain the public health exception to their preferred level—flexibility on IPR in the case of epidemics affecting the poorest countries. One would also expect to see a reversion by the great powers back to forum-shifting following the aberration at Doha.

The evidence strongly suggests that as the unusual constraints faced by the great powers at Doha have lessened, the regulation of IPR has shifted back toward the great powers' preferred set of outcomes. One policy response was to push for stronger IPR protections than TRIPS—referred colloquially as "TRIPS-plus"—outside of the WTO framework.[91] The proliferation of bilateral free trade agreements (FTAs) in recent years has given the great powers an opportunity to use their market power to ratchet up IPR standards in the developing world. The European Commission and the European Free Trade Area have both inserted TRIPS-plus IPR provisions into their free trade agreements with developing countries.[92] EU agreements with Tunisia and Morocco, for example, include provisions requiring IPR protection and enforcement "in line with the highest international standards." The United States has been equally persistent in this practice. Table 7.2 demonstrates the TRIPS-plus IPR provisions in U.S. trade agreements that have been ratified since 2000. The United States has also used the carrot of bilateral investment treaties in order to secure bilateral intellectual property agreements that can include TRIPS-plus agreements.[93]

How do these TRIPS-plus provisions in FTAs jibe with the USTR trumpeting "Doha-friendly" understandings and side agreements associated with these FTAs? Oxfam argues that these understandings have "interpretive value only and will not change the binding TRIPS-plus provisions" in the FTAs

---

[91] Peter Drahos, "Bilateralism in Intellectual Property," Oxfam Research Paper, 2001, at http://www.oxfam.org.uk/what_we_do/issues/trade/bilateralism_ip.htm, accessed April 4, 2006.

[92] Ibid., 13; see also European Commission, "EU Strategy to Enforce Intellectual Property Rights in Third Countries," MEMO/04/255, November 10, 2004. For information on EFTA trade pacts, see Julien Bernhard, "Deprive Doha of All Substance," August 2004, at http://www.evb.ch/cm_data/Deprive_Doha.pdf, accessed August 12, 2005.

[93] Drahos, "Bilateralism in Intellectual Property," 6.

Table 7.2
IPR Provisions in American FTAs, 2000–2005

FTA	Mandatory Patent Extensions	Protection of Test Data	Marketing Restrictions	Limits on Parallel Imports or Compulsory Licensing
Jordan		X		X
Singapore	X	X	X	X
Chile	X	X	X	
Australia		X	X	X
Morocco	X	X	X	X
CAFTA	X	X	X	

Sources: Committee on Government Reform minority staff, U.S. House of Representatives, *Trade Agreements and Access to Medications under the Bush Administration,* Washington, DC, June 2005; Consumer Project on Technology, "Health Care, Regional Trade Agreements, and Intellectual Property," available at http://www.cptech.org/ip/health/trade/, accessed August 11 2005.

themselves.[94] Frederick Abbott argues that these side agreements "are drafted in a substantially more restrictive way" than the Doha Declaration itself.[95] At a minimum, the combination of legal texts introduces legal uncertainty, constraining the flexibility of the TRIPS accord desired by global civil society. In effect, the legal arrangements shift the status quo to the U.S.-preferred outcome; one in which flexibility is only invoked in times of crisis epidemics.

As table 7.2 demonstrates, the most prominent of the TRIPS-plus provisions is the protection of test data.[96] To satisfy government regulations, drug manufacturers are required to undergo significant amounts of testing to demonstrate safety and effectiveness, imposing additional costs on first-mover manufacturers. Data protection prevents other drug manufacturers from relying on that data to obtain approval for drugs that are chemically identical to the original patent-holder. The United States ensures data protection for five years; EU member states offer from six to ten years. In 2005, the USTR stated in its Special 301 Report to Congress that data protection would be "one of the key

[94] Oxfam, "Undermining Access to Medicines: Comparison of Five US FTAs," *Oxfam Briefing Note,* July 2004.

[95] Frederick Abbott, "The WTO Medicines Decision: World Pharmaceutical Trade and the Protection of Public Health," *American Journal of International Law* 99 (2005): 352.

[96] Carlos Correa, "Protecting Test Data for Pharmaceutical and Agrochemical Products under Free Trade Agreements," in *Negotiating Health: Intellectual Property and Access to Medicines,* ed. Pedro Roffe, Geoff Tansey, and David Vivas-Eugui (London: Earthscan, 2006).

implementation priorities" for the executive branch. The report went on to identify deficiencies in data protection for pharmaceuticals testing in more than twenty countries, including China, India, Russia, Mexico, and Thailand.[97] The continued use of Special 301 to threaten trade sanctions against countries perceived as having violated intellectual property rights is a powerful lever through which the United States has tried to advance its preferences. In the past, even an implicit threat of economic coercion has been sufficient to force dependent allies into altering their regulations on these issues.[98]

Both proponents and opponents of patent protections on pharmaceuticals agree on the post-Doha constraints placed on the "public health" frame in U.S. trade policy. One former USTR negotiator commented, "I think that individual NGO efforts got spectacular media coverage, but I'd question their real impact against the bulk of U.S. achievements since the Uruguay round."[99] Many of the same GCS analysts who claimed a victory at Doha acknowledge that the proliferation of "TRIPS-plus" provisions in free trade agreements undercuts the public health norm established at Doha.[100] Frederick Abbott, who under the auspices of the Quaker United Nations Office provided legal assistance to developing countries in TRIPS negotiations, concludes that the developing world and NGOs have, "substantially increased their negotiating effectiveness in Geneva but have yet to come to grips with the U.S. forum-shifting strategy."[101] In a May 2004 letter to U.S. trade representative Robert Zoellick, approximately ninety NGOs protested the inclusion of these TRIPS-plus provisions in FTAs, stating, "Intellectual property provisions in US free trade agreements already completed or currently being negotiated will severely delay and restrict generic competition . . . through complex provisions related to market authorization and registration of medicines."[102]

A final move by the great powers has been to try and narrow the scope of the Doha Declaration's applicability. What Doha left unresolved was how the provision on compulsory licensing would apply to countries that lacked domestic pharmaceutical industries. The Declaration promised, in paragraph six, "to find an expeditious solution to this problem" over the next twelve months.[103] NGOs and developing countries wanted the widest possible leeway granted to developing countries. The United States and European Union

---

[97] Office of the USTR, "Special 301 Report," April 2005. Quotation from page 6.

[98] Daniel W. Drezner, "The Hidden Hand of Economic Coercion," *International Organization* 57 (Summer 2003): 643–59; Drezner, "Outside the Box: Explaining Sanctions in Pursuit of Foreign Economic Goals," *International Interactions* 26 (Summer 2001): 379–410.

[99] E-mail communication from former USTR official, August 5, 2005.

[100] Sell, *Private Power, Public Law*, chap. 6; Abbott, "The WTO Medicines Decision."

[101] Abbott, "The WTO Medicines Decision," 317.

[102] "Letter from 90 NGOs to U.S. trade representative Robert Zoellick," May 27, 2004, available at http://www.cptech.org/ip/health/trade/ngos05272004.html, accessed August 11, 2005.

[103] "Declaration on the TRIPS Agreement and Public Health," paragraph 6.

sought to limit the extent of the concessions made on TRIPS in the Doha Declaration to the least developed countries and low-income developing countries.[104] The United States went so far as to push for limiting TRIPS flexibility to HIV/AIDS, tuberculosis, and malaria, excluding the "other epidemics" language from the Doha Declaration.[105]

Like Doha, and in contrast to the original TRIPS accord, NGOs were heavily involved in these negotiations between November 2001 and December 2005.[106] Unlike at Doha, however, the United States did not feel compelled to secure an agreement at a particular time. As a result, the USTR blocked an agreement from being reached by the desired deadline because of concerns over the draft language. The end result was in rough accord with great power preferences. The scope of importation primarily benefited the least developed countries, with strict limits put on parallel importation in developing countries. Procedural barriers, along with an interpretation of the chairman's statement that came with the agreed-upon amendment, limit but do not exclude the use of TRIPS flexibilities by other developing countries.[107]

This outcome conformed to American and European preferences more than global civil society, who complained that the deal was "a gift bound in red tape."[108] Reviewing the negotiation history, Duncan Matthews concluded: "ultimately the outcome, characterized by the dominance of the US and the EU as key international actors, coupled with the reluctance of developing country governments to ultimately oppose the US approach in the face of negotiating fatigue and the threat of bilateral trade sanctions, is remarkably familiar and repeats the pattern of earlier negotiations."[109] Indeed, three years after its creation, no country has availed itself of the parallel importation mechanism. Pedro Roffe writes, "Politically, it may need substantial courage for a small country to issue a compulsory license on a drug patented in the US or in a

---

[104] Duncan Matthews, "WTO Decision on Implementation of Paragraph 6 of the Doha Declaration on the TRIPS Agreement and Public Health," *Journal of International Economic Law* 7 (Winter 2004): 73–107.

[105] The USTR was concerned that the "other epidemics" language would be broadly construed to include "lifestyle" diseases such as obesity. Ibid., 86.

[106] Matthews, "WTO Decision on Implementation of Paragraph 6," 84; Abbott, "The WTO Medicines Decision," 328.

[107] Matthews, "WTO Decision on Implementation of Paragraph 6," 84; Abbott, "The WTO Medicines Decision," 328. See also M. Rafiquil Islam, "The Generic Drug Deal of the WTO from Doha to Cancun," *Journal of World Intellectual Property* 7 (September 2004): 675–92, and Roffe et al., *Negotiating Health.*

[108] Pedro Roffe, "From Paris to Doha: The WTO Doha Declaration on the TRIPS Agreement and Public Health," in *Negotiating Health*, ed. Roffe et al., 23. See also Peter Drahos, "Winning Battles, Losing the War," paper presented at the Workshop in Trade Negotiation and Developing Countries, Griffith University, Brisbane, Australia, August 2005.

[109] Matthews, "WTO Decision on Implementation of Paragraph 6," 105; for a more GCS-friendly interpretation, see Abbott, "The WTO Medicines Decision."

European Union Member State. A good political relationship may be necessary for guaranteeing access to the markets of the two global economic players."[110]

Great power behavior before and after Doha would suggest very little internalization of global civil society's preferred "public health" frame in thinking about TRIPS. One possibility is that, over time, the U.S. government has appropriated a different variation of the same frame. For example, in discussing the enforcement of intellectual property rights, the Office of the USTR repeatedly stresses the public health benefits that accrue from intellectual property protections. A July 2004 USTR fact sheet points out that because of the TRIPS-plus protections in the Jordan FTA, drug innovation in that country dramatically increased.[111] Economists and lawyers have argued that more vigorous IPR enforcement in the developing world would spur medical advances to treat diseases in those countries.[112] In the 2005 Special 301 report, there is similar language about medical innovations with regard to the marketing of pharmaceuticals.

Not surprisingly, the key players in the GCS campaign behind the Doha Declaration vigorously dispute these assertions.[113] It is beyond the scope of this book to determine which frame has greater merit. However, what matters is the emergence of an alternative frame to view IPR policy with regard to health. Some scholars argue that this leads to a battle between business and NGO networks on the issue.[114] While true, this observation omits an important implication. By playing one network off of the other, the state can actually increase its policymaking autonomy. As a result, the post-Doha regime on IPR closely conforms to great power preferences.

There is one final contributing factor to the ability of great powers to limit the scope of the public health carve-out. Five years after the Doha Declaration, the role that patents played in aggravating the HIV/AIDS pandemic appeared much smaller than it did in the late 1990s. The dramatic lowering of drug prices and increased availability of ARVs have not had a dramatic effect on the spread of the pandemic—particularly in the countries where state failure has been a concern.[115] In 2005, UNAIDS officials estimated that reduced

---

[110] Roffe, "From Paris to Doha," 15.

[111] Office of the USTR, "Fact Sheet on Access to Medicines," July 2004, available at http://www.ustr.gov/Document_Library/Fact_Sheets/2004/Fact_Sheet_on_Access_to_Medicines.html, accessed August 9, 2005.

[112] Alan Sykes, "TRIPs, Pharmaceuticals, Developing Countries, and the Doha 'Solution,'" *Chicago Journal of International Law* 3 (Spring 2002). For a contrary view, see Colleen Chien, "Cheap Drugs at What Price to Innovation: Does the Compulsory Licensing of Pharmaceuticals Hurt Innovation?" *Berkeley Technology Law Journal* 18 (Summer 2003): 853–93.

[113] Oxfam, "Undermining Access to Medicines"; Hamed El-Said and Mohammed El-Said, "TRIPS, Bilateralism, Multilateralism and Implications for Developing Countries: Jordan's Drug Sector," *Manchester Journal of International Economic Law* 2 (April 2005).

[114] Prakash and Sell, "Using Ideas Strategically."

[115] Andrew Jack, "HIV Therapy Failing to Meet Demand," *Financial Times*, March 28, 2006.

ARV prices prevented 250,000 to 300,000 deaths per year. This number is significant—but it seems small in a world with 40 million infected persons and growing.[116]

In sub-Saharan Africa, significant barriers remain to successful ARV treatment. Because the primary means of spreading the HIV virus is through sexual contact, governments in culturally conservative societies will be reluctant to publicly address the problem—thereby making it difficult to expand treatment programs within these countries.[117] Public corruption, logistical bottlenecks, and poor health infrastructures have also hampered access to drugs—even when pharmaceutical companies have donated ARV medications.[118] Despite an offer from the German firm Boehringer Ingelheim to make one ARV available for free, only two sub-Saharan governments accepted the medication in its first few years. The CEO of Abbott Laboratories was quoted in November 2005, observing, "People who simplify this into just drop-shipping gobs of drugs into remote areas of Africa, they're nuts. It's a lot more complicated than that."[119] As one economist sympathetic to the MSF campaign put it, "the root of the shortcomings in the global pharmaceutical market is not companies' policies but countries' poverty."[120] Multiple health and economic analyses concluded that the opportunity costs of focusing on treatment rather than prevention in sub-Saharan Africa are significant.[121]

While the GCS campaign to tackle the AIDS pandemic has had an effect, by 2006 the growing perception was that the IPR issue was no longer central

[116] Data from UNAIDS press release, November 21, 2005, available at http://www.unaids.org/NetTools/Misc/DocInfo.aspx?LANG=en&href=http://gva-doc-owl/WEBcontent/Documents/pub/Media/Press-Releases03/PR_EpiUpdate_Nov05_en.pdf, accessed January 2006. Some researchers disputed the 40 million figure, arguing that UNAIDS overestimated the rate of infection beyond southern Africa. See Craig Timberg, "How AIDS in Africa Was Overstated," *Washington Post*, April 6, 2006.

[117] This problem was not limited to national governments. IGOs such as UNICEF and the World Bank were also reluctant to get involved in the AIDS crisis because of the subject matter. See Sebastian Mallaby, *The World's Banker: A Story of Failed States, Financial Crises, and the Wealth and Poverty of Nations* (New York: Penguin Press, 2004), 313–19; William Easterly, *The White Man's Burden* (New York: Penguin Press, 2006), 244–46.

[118] Liz Tayler and Claire Dickenson, "The Link between Corruption and HIV/AIDS," in *Global Corruption Report 2006* (Washington, DC: Transparency International, 2006); Easterly, *The White Man's Burden*, 261.

[119] Matthews, "WTO Decision on Implementation of Paragraph 6," 98. CEO quoted in David Greising, "Africa's Tenuous AIDS Lifeline," *Chicago Tribune*, November 22, 2005.

[120] John McMillan, *Reinventing the Bazaar* (New York: W. W. Norton, 2002), 30.

[121] Andrew Creese et al., "Cost Effectiveness of HIV/AIDS Interventions in Africa: A Systematic Review of the Evidence," *The Lancet* 359 (September 14, 2002): 1365–42; Michael Kremer, "Pharmaceuticals and the Developing World," *Journal of Economic Perspectives* 16 (Fall 2002): 67–90; Warren Stevens, Steve Kaye, and Tumani Corrah, "Antiretroviral Therapy in Africa," *British Medical Journal* 328 (January 31, 2004): 66–68; Merle Sande and Allan Ronald, "Treatment of HIV/AIDS: Do the Dilemmas Only Increase?" *Journal of the American Medical Association* 292 (July 14, 2004): 267; Easterly, *The White Man's Burden*, chap. 7.

to policy in this area. In response to the worsening pandemic, the United States and the European Union have increased resources for the UN Global Fund to Fight AIDS, Tuberculosis, and Malaria. The United States also created the President's Emergency Plan for AIDS Relief (PEPFAR), a five-year, $15 billion initiative.[122] These initiatives have increased great power funding by several orders of magnitude. The United States tripled its real spending on foreign aid to combat infectious disease, to the point where in 2006 expenditures approximated budgetary allocations for military grant aid.[123] This is consistent with both the securitization and GCS hypotheses. Contradicting the latter, however, is the U.S. insistence that any country accepting PEPFAR funding comply with the TRIPS accord when purchasing drugs.[124]

Conclusions

This chapter has explored a case that at first glance seems to falsify the revisionist model and buttress the GCS narrative about global economic governance. The evidence suggests that although this is a deviant case for the revisionist model, it is not as deviant as initially thought. Global civil society did play a role in shifting policy on intellectual property rights—but the role has been exaggerated both before and after the Doha Declaration. GCS scholars argue that the United States shifted its policy because transnational activists created a new normative frame of public health to view the problem. While there is little doubt that GCS activists did push a public health frame, this version of events is incomplete—it assumes a world in which only that frame existed. The securitization hypothesis reveals that high-ranking U.S. officials increasingly deployed a transnational threat frame to analyze HIV/AIDS over the same period. Securitization allowed them to intervene on the TRIPS issue in the late 1990s and in the run-up to the Doha Declaration. Transnational activists were pushing governments toward recognizing the public health crises in the developing world, but they were pushing key governments in a direction that they already wanted to go.

After Doha, both the United States and the European Union acted within and without the World Trade Organization to place clear boundaries on IPR

---

[122] Available at http://www.usaid.gov/our_work/global_health/aids/pepfarfact.html, accessed April 4, 2006.

[123] Also consistent with the securitization hypothesis is that politicians continued to talk about disease using the language of security. For example, Senate Majority Leader Bill Frist said, "Medicine can be a currency for peace. . . . An unstable Africa, because of decimation from HIV-AIDS, does become a breeding ground for terrorism." See David Rogers, "Congress Unites to Fight against Global Pandemics," *Wall Street Journal*, January 30, 2006.

[124] Princeton Lyman, *Addressing the HIV/AIDS Pandemic* (New York: Council on Foreign Relations, 2004), 8.

flexibilities. Both economic great powers enshrined "TRIPS-plus" elements into bilateral investment treaties and free trade agreements. The United States in particular evinced a willingness to use unilateral threats of economic coercion to enforce intellectual property on pharmaceuticals as well. Two years after the Doha Declaration, a subsequent agreement on the importation of generic drugs applied some limitations on the scope of the Declaration. Consistent with the securitization hypothesis, the U.S. government was willing to carve out a public health exception to TRIPS, but believed GCS-preferred policies wanted this exception limited to the least developed countries and/or acute epidemics such as HIV/AIDS. The United States also used the "public health" frame to argue in favor of more stringent IPR protections after Doha.

A critical analysis of this case reveals a trope common to other episodes of supposed GCS influence: alternative causes are neglected and the magnitude of the policy outcome is exaggerated. Post-Doha events do not mean that GCS activity had no effect on this policy shift, but they do suggest sharp constraints on the ability of global civil society to inject new norms into global public policy. Governments can clearly adapt to the introduction of new ideas, but also assist in the "mutation" of such ideas to suit preexisting purposes.[125] Transnational activists did well to take advantage of the policy window at Doha to secure a Declaration with broad public health language. However, such policy windows are not usually a function of nonstate actors—and, over time, these windows inevitably close.

The obvious conclusion to draw from this case is that GCS influence has been overrated. And yet, going forward there are two final caveats to consider. First, it is possible that elements of global civil society have redirected their focus on this issue away from states and more toward pressuring the pharmaceutical firms into donating life-saving drugs. This would be an example of "world civic politics" at work. The second caveat is the possibility that nonstate actors have a longer-run plan of action than is commonly thought. GCS efforts have a dynamic component to them. One stated goal of global civil society is to convince governments to accept certain sets of norms, but the spread of norms is a lengthy process. It is possible that GCS activity on pharmaceutical patents is still in the initial stages of socialization, and will achieve more substantive policy shifts over time. The problem with this theory of norm change, of course, is that it is impossible to falsify.[126]

Deviant cases should yield unforeseen causal mechanisms and variables in order to better refine the falsified theory. This case has yielded both. In ascer-

---

[125] Daniel W. Drezner, "Ideas, Bureaucratic Politics, and the Crafting of Foreign Policy," *American Journal of Political Science* 44 (October 2000): 733–49.

[126] While nonfalsifiable, however, this argument is not necessarily wrong. This leads to an intriguing possibility about the future of intellectual property rights and public health: it is possible that great powers will continue to win most of the major policy skirmishes in the fight, while still losing the war.

taining great power preferences over regulation, the prospect of securitization must be considered as a means of overriding the status quo. If a regulatory issue becomes a matter of national security, the great powers might order their preferences differently than previously thought. Furthermore, the revisionist model of global governance processes assumed zero costs to forum-shifting. The situation at Doha demonstrates that this is not always the case. If there are significant transaction costs to switching fora, then the revisionist model would be a poor short-run predictor of regulatory coordination.

How much do these new factors challenge the revisionist model? They seem much more like unforeseen exceptions than rules. Policy entrepreneurs have failed to securitize most regulatory issues. There has been significant pushback from national security agencies and security scholars in areas such as environmental policy.[127] Similarly, the constraints that were in place on forum-shopping at Doha were highly unusual. While global civil society can exploit such moments, they are ephemeral. Indeed, the previous section reveals that global civil society is not a fatal roadblock to the functioning of the model developed here. Even in a deviant case like this one, global civil society can function, at best, as a temporary detour from the revisionist model's regulatory processes.

---

[127] Daniel Deudney, "The Case against Linking Environmental Degradation and National Security," *Millennium* 19, no. 3 (1990): 463–64, and Marc A. Levy, "Is the Environment a National Security Issue?" *International Security* 20 (Fall 1995): 35–62.

CHAPTER EIGHT

Conclusions and Speculations

IF THERE IS a recurring theme that runs through the literature on globalization and global governance, it is that economic globalization attenuates state power. The globalization of production has allegedly splintered the ability of governments to regulate their own economies. Whether the cause is global capital markets, international organizations, or global civil society, new actors are emerging at the expense of states, playing an ever-growing role in determining the pattern of global regulation.

This book concludes otherwise. The globalization of consumption matters more than the globalization of production; it means that all producers have a vested interest in accessing sizeable markets. Because of this, the governments that write the rules for large internal markets retain significant influence in determining the course of global regulatory and technical standards. Large markets have a gravitational effect on smaller actors. The market power, and implicit coercive power, of great power governments shapes expectations about regulatory coordination in ways that favor their preferred standards.

Economic globalization increases the rewards for international regulatory coordination. However, globalization has little effect on the adjustment costs that governments face if they need to alter their domestic regulatory frameworks. For issue areas where states face sizeable adjustment costs to changes in the rules of the economic game, there will be little in the way of effective regulatory coordination.

Most theories of globalization and global governance—including some state-centric approaches—assume that mobile sectors and factors of production gain increased leverage over domestic regulatory preferences because of their threat to exit. The argument developed here postulates that the use of political voice is the more important tool of influence. The greater the use of political voice, the higher the government's economic *and* political adjustment costs to regulatory coordination. Adjustment costs will be high when the regulatory issue in question affects relatively immobile sectors or markets—the regulation of land, labor, or consumer products.

A great power concert is a necessary and sufficient condition for effective global governance. While other actors—including NGOs, IGOs, and weaker states—can affect the process of bargaining, these actors do not affect the final outcome. Because the great powers can substitute among different governance processes, they can shift to friendly fora, such as a club IGO, if a cluster of weaker states opposes the proposed regulatory changes in a universal IGO. When the great powers cannot agree to common regulatory standards, other actors may try to fill the gap to promote and enforce global standards—but such efforts will prove to be largely ineffective.

To test these arguments, I examined four issue areas in depth—Internet governance, financial codes and standards, the treatment of genetically modified organisms, and the regulation of life-saving pharmaceuticals. The first two cases were chosen as arenas where the forces of globalization were assumed to be at their strongest; in the latter two cases, global civil society has claimed notable victories. However, contrary to assumptions that these forces weaken state power, the pattern of global regulatory coordination was consistent with the revisionist model presented here. In the case of the Internet, when the United States and the European Union saw significant benefits and low adjustment costs from coordination, the effective global governance of Internet-related issues was achieved—even if the great powers voluntarily delegated the management of these regulatory regimes to private actors. When Internet issues intersected with larger public policy questions—such as privacy or speech rights—the adjustment costs for governments dramatically increased. In the absence of a great power concert, governments used the tools of statecraft at their disposal to protect their preferred set of regulatory standards—even if such a decision heavily restricted Internet use.

The case of financial codes and standards strongly supports the revisionist model. In the aftermath of the financial crises of the 1990s, both the United States and European Union preferred to see a ratcheting up of financial regulation. The great powers, as developed economies, anticipated significant public goods benefits from coordination at a stringent level of regulation. In contrast, the domestic financial sectors in developing countries faced high adjustment costs at the prospect of stringent standards. Because of this distribution of interests, great powers chose to use club IGOs like the Financial Stability Forum as the primary fora to establish global financial regulations. Even with their weighted voting schemes, the United States and European Union encountered difficulties managing the international financial institutions, because of their strong norms of consensus decision-making. These standards were created despite the fact that financial sectors in the developed world were hardly overjoyed at the prospect of more government regulation.

The regulation of genetically modified organisms demonstrates the limits of other state-based theories of global regulation compared with the revisionist approach. The United States and the European Union promulgated different regulatory standards to govern the production and consumption of GMOs. These regulations governing GMOs affect groups with extremely high barriers to exit—agricultural producers, biotechnology firms, and consumer groups. The initial divergence of preferences between Americans and Europeans on this issue, combined with the high adjustment costs of regulatory harmonization, ensured the absence of a bargaining core between the two governments and led to a rival standards outcome. Both great powers pushed to legitimize their preferred standards in friendly international fora. Because of the large market size of both of these countries, the result has been an uneasy stalemate. Despite America's hegemonic position in the production of GM products, and despite Europe's constant ratcheting up of its standards, neither great power has had a demonstrable effect on the other government's preference ordering. The rest of the world split between the American and European set of rules regarding GM products. Consistent with the model developed here, great power divergence prevented coordination at a global level—the only equilibrium outcome for the great powers.

The emergence of a public health exemption to the regime governing intellectual property rights represents a deviant case for the revisionist model. Global civil society, health-related IGOs, and significant developing countries waged a sustained campaign to force the great powers to allow public health "flexibilities" in the enforcement of the TRIPS regime for intellectual property—and appeared to succeed with the 2001 Doha Declaration. Over time, however, this case suggests that the GCS narrative omits alternative explanatory variables and exaggerates the extent of the policy shift. Securitization also helps to explain the shift in great power preferences toward a more flexible view of TRIPS. The great powers conceded more than they would have preferred at Doha, but this was due to the unique circumstances of that Ministerial conference. The September 11 terrorist attacks and the Battle of Seattle made forum-shifting unusually costly at that particular time and place. After the Doha Declaration, the United States and European Union acted to ensure that the carve-out for public health fit with their securitized preferences rather than with what global civil society wanted. As time passed, great power governments appropriated the normative frame of improving public health to advance their own policy aims. This case pointed out that when forum-shopping is costly, the revisionist model might fail in the short run. Over the long run, however, the model holds up.

These cases were selected to maximize contrasting predictions between the revisionist model presented here and existing arguments in the literature. Global civil society scholars, for example, would posit that because nonstate actors were more prominent in the Internet, GMO, and TRIPS cases, there should be stronger global regime in those areas than in the other issue areas. Race-to-the-bottom proponents would argue that issue areas weakly related to mobile capital, such as the regulation of genetically modified organisms, are more likely to have stringent standards, while capital market regulation would have weaker standards. State-centric approaches based on hegemonic power would have predicted all of the outcomes to conform around American preferences. Approaches stressing regulatory networks would postulate outcomes reflecting European Union preferences. The revisionist approach developed

TABLE 8.1
Comparing Theoretical Predictions

Case	Race to the Bottom	Global Civil Society	U.S. as Hegemonic Producer	Strength of Regulatory Network	California Effect	Revisionist Model
TCP/IP	NP	P	P	NP	P	P
ICANN	P	NP	P	NP	P	P
Copyright protection	P	NP	P	P	P	P
Data privacy	NP	NP	NP	NP	NP	P
Content regulation	NP	NP	NP	P	NP	P
Financial codes	NP	NP	P	P	P	P
GM crops	P	NP	NP	P	NP	P
Doha Declaration	NP	P	NP	NP	NP	NP
Post-Doha TRIPS	P	NP	P	P	NP	P
Labor standards	P	NP	NP	P	NP	P
Commercial arbitration	P	P	P	P	P	P
Whaling	NP	P	NP	NP	NP	P
Anti-corruption	NP	P	P	NP	P	P
Predictive accuracy	6/13	5/13	7/13	7/13	6/13	12/13

P → theory correctly predicted outcome in that case
NP → theory did not yield a correct prediction

here argues that global regulatory standards should be strongest in the arenas where great powers have the fewest distributional conflicts—global finance, commercial arbitration, intellectual property rights, and Internet protocols.

As table 8.1 demonstrates, the approach developed here represents a significant improvement over existing explanations.

THE LIMITATIONS

This book is far from the last word on the subject of globalization and global governance. There are significant theoretical and empirical limitations to the analysis presented here; it would be disingenuous to omit any discussion of them. It is useful to highlight these limitations, as they can provide a guide for future research in this area.

Theoretically, the revisionist model omits some important questions. In the standards game used in chapter 2, the exposition emphasized the distinction between the presence and absence of a bargaining core among the great powers. The presence of a bargaining core does not guarantee that a bargain will be struck, however—it merely indicates that a bargain is *possible*. There is no guarantee that coordination will actually take place in a game where coordination is possible. While my model takes into account the role that market power plays in affecting expectations, it omits the dynamic dimensions of the bargaining process that are present in the theoretical literature.[1]

The other fact that must be acknowledged is that the process portion of the model is not an exemplar of parsimony. The predictions made in the process chapter render large-N testing next to impossible. A number of heterogeneous actors are introduced—and even then, simplifications have been made. The typology of nonstate actors is rather crude. Multinational corporations have not been designated as an independent actor—although the case studies suggest that their ability to influence regulatory preferences beyond their home country is limited at best.

The empirical limitations of the study are also formidable. Four in-depth case studies and a few pages about other issue areas are a small evidentiary base from which to draw conclusive findings. In part, this is due to the limited time period during which the questions raised in the introductory chapter have been applicable. To discuss global regulatory standards as a meaningful problem, one has to first assume that border level controls have been eliminated as a major impediment to transnational exchange. One must then assume that governments are interested in regulating the economy to some extent. The combination of these conditions has only taken place in the past twenty or thirty years.

The model and evidence presented here are incomplete. The formal model's simplicity prevents a discussion of every facet of the bargaining process. The process dimension has a fair number of working parts, with hypotheses that are difficult to test at the large-N level. The temporal domain is limited, at best, to the past two or three decades. The arguments and evidence presented here nevertheless represent a significant step forward in explaining the regulation of globalization. The revisionist model presents a unified theory that explains both the processes through which regulatory matters are negotiated at the global level, and the outcomes that are likely to take place. Heterogeneous actors are incorporated into the theory. Empirical evidence from a diverse set of cases strongly supports the model's hypotheses.

---

[1] Ariel Rubinstein, "Perfect Equilibrium in a Bargaining Model," *Econometrica* 50 (January 1982): 97–110; James A. Fearon, "Bargaining, Enforcement, and International Cooperation," *International Organization* 52 (Spring 1998): 269–306.

Theoretical Implications

The globalization phenomenon has generated considerable debate among international relations theorists. How does the revisionist model impact the major international relations paradigms? The revisionist model shares some of the precepts of these models, but also exposes some of the flaws in their explanations of the global political economy.

The argument presented here provides some support for the realist theory of international relations.[2] In many ways, it echoes Stephen D. Krasner's message in his seminal 1976 essay, "State Power and the Structure of Foreign Trade": current debates about the global political economy focus too much on transnational forces and ignore the preeminent role of the great powers.[3] However, there are three important distinctions between the revisionist model and the realist paradigm.

First, the model developed here accepts that globalization is a real and important phenomenon. Structural realists like Kenneth Waltz have tended to ignore or trivialize globalization's salience. To date, this is how they have explained away the accelerating integration of the global economy. "Globalization is the fad of the 1990s," says Waltz, adding, "What I found to be true in 1970 remains true today: the world is less interdependent than is usually supposed."[4] By any metric, however, the globalization process has intensified in the past thirty-five years. Furthermore, as previously noted, the mere existence of previous eras of globalization does not eliminate questions about global regulatory governance. Simply put, most of the demands placed on national governments today did not exist a century ago.

An approach that concedes the significance of globalization but asks how states try to maximize their relative advantage in such a world is more fruitful than the realist step of assuming the phenomenon away. Globalization does have an effect on regulatory coordination—it increases the payoff from cooperation, making global regulatory governance a more likely outcome. The approach developed here concurs with realists that globalization does not eliminate the role of states—but it does agree with liberals that, *ceteris paribus*, globalization makes policy coordination a likelier outcome.

Second, the theory presented here does not assume that state preferences are derived from the structure of the international system. A structural realist

---

[2] Kenneth Waltz, *Theory of International Politics* (New York: McGraw Hill, 1979); John J. Mearsheimer, *The Tragedy of Great Power Politics* (New York: W. W. Norton, 2001).

[3] Stephen D. Krasner, "State Power and the Structure of Foreign Trade," *World Politics* 28 (April 1976): 317–47.

[4] Kenneth Waltz, "Globalization and Governance," *PS: Political Science and Politics* 32 (December 1999): 694, 696; see also Stephen D. Krasner, *Sovereignty: Organized Hypocrisy* (Princeton, NJ: Princeton University Press, 1999), 220–23.

approach derives state preferences on any international issue from their position in the international distribution of power.[5] Instead, I have argued that state preferences on regulatory issues have their origins in the domestic political economy. Power matters in an era of globalization, in that it shapes the preferences of weaker actors in the system. However, relative differences in power among the major states are of trivial importance to questions of regulatory coordination.

The third difference is that my approach acknowledges the European Union as a great power in the global political economy. Because realists first look at the security realm, they tend to dismiss the European Union as a nonfactor in most aspects of world politics. Certainly, the idea of treating the European Union as a single actor for foreign or security policy would be a significant stretch. However, for the global political economy in general, and regulatory policies in particular, the European Union is sufficiently organized and institutionalized to treat as a single actor. As Anne-Marie Slaughter points out, "In many regulatory areas, such as competition policy, environmental policy, and corporate governance, the European Union attracts as many imitators as the United States."[6] The European Union's power in regulatory matters can neither be dismissed nor ignored.

The revisionist model shares some similarities with neoliberal institutionalism. One key result common to both arguments is that an increase in economic globalization triggers a concomitant increase in multinational cooperation. For liberals, increasing interdependence raises the costs of disagreement; for the revisionist model, globalization increases the rewards for coordination. Another commonality between the two approaches is the observation that only gross differences in power are relevant in world politics.

As noted in chapter 3, however, institutionalists universally assume that the fundamental dilemma of the global political economy is the inability of states to cooperate when cooperation is a Pareto-improving step. Institutionalist game-theoretic models also play down or ignore the significance of market power in the global political economy. The simple game structures used in this book demonstrate the flaws with these aspects of the liberal paradigm. Even in a world of globalization, there are instances where the adjustment costs of states are so high that noncooperation is the preferred outcome for all.[7]

---

[5] Even some realists have difficulties with this assumption. Randall Schweller points out that, "Leaders are rarely, if ever, compelled by structural imperatives to adopt certain policies rather than others; they are not sleepwalkers buffeted about by inexorable forces beyond their control. Rather, states respond (or not) to threats and opportunities in various ways that are determined by both internal and external consideration of policy elites" (Schweller, "Unanswered Threats: A Neoclassical Realist Theory of Underbalancing," *International Security* 29 (Fall 2004): 162.

[6] Anne-Marie Slaughter, *A New World Order* (Princeton, NJ: Princeton University Press, 2004), 5; see also Andrew Moravcsik, "Dream On, America," *Newsweek International*, January 31, 2005.

[7] This critique is hardly original to this project. More than six decades ago, E. H. Carr pointed out: "To make the harmonisation of interests the goal of political action is not the same thing as to postulate that a natural harmony of interests exists; and it is the latter postulate that has caused

Another difference comes in the role that international governmental organizations play in world politics. The neoliberal institutionalist paradigm argues that cooperation is strengthened when IGOs are endowed with strong enforcement and monitoring capabilities. This focus on enforcement capabilities obscures the functional relationship between IGOs and member states. The great powers are the actors who design the IGOs in the first place. Because of the substitutability of global governance structures, IGOs with strong monitoring and enforcement capabilities are used for regulatory matters only when a great power consensus exists on the content of the regulations to be enforced. Therefore, IGOs considered to be "strong" in the neoliberal sense matter for some distribution of interests, but not others. There are some issue areas in which the distribution of interests causes great powers to prefer IGOs with weak enforcement capabilities.

The revisionist model poses more substantive challenges to the diffuse literature on global governance and global civil society. Only by understanding the substitutability of governance structures can one acquire a greater understanding of the regulation of globalization. As Benjamin Most and Harvey Starr point out, "If scholars are genuinely interested in understanding why states do what they do, they need to move beyond efforts to focus separately on particular concrete behaviors. Rather than asking middle-range questions about specific empirical phenomena, they should begin with the initial 'grand' question with which they were allegedly concerned in the first place."[8] By failing to recognize that states can substitute unilateral measures, intergovernmental accords, and delegation to nonstate actors, scholars of global governance have unnecessarily restricted their analyses to simple comparisons of direct state involvement versus the role of nonstate actors. Ironically, globalization scholars have not erred in thinking too grandly about global governance, but in not thinking grandly enough.

Although the cases demonstrate the substitutability of governance structures, the cases also reveal instances—most obviously in the run-up to the Doha Declaration—when great powers were constrained in their ability to switch fora. Under what conditions will great power governments be constrained from forum-shopping? When are the costs associated with complexifying a regime too prohibitive?[9] Perhaps "viscosity" is a variable that should be incorporated into discussions of global governance. Some IR scholars believe that globalization has facilitated "the 'fluidization' of regulatory

---

so much confusion in international thinking" (Carr, *The Twenty Years' Crisis* [New York: Harper and Row, 1964], 51).

[8] Benjamin Most and Harvey Starr, "International Relations Theory, Foreign Policy Substitutability, and 'Nice' Laws," *World Politics* 36 (April 1984): 392.

[9] See, on this topic, Joseph Jupille and Duncan Snidal, "The Choice of International Institutions: Cooperation, Alternatives and Strategies," paper presented at the American Political Science Association annual meeting, Washington, DC, September 2005.

space."[10] In fluid mechanics, viscosity is the resistance a material has to change in form—i.e., its internal friction. It is worth contemplating whether some regime complexes suffer from higher rates of viscosity than others, and also whether some regime complexes grow more or less viscous over time.

The book also suggests that the advocacy function of global civil society is more tightly constrained than GCS scholars would like to believe. For each of the cases discussed here, transnational activists only had limited success in altering government preferences. What explains the limitations of transnational advocacy? The usual suspects of geography and history should not be discounted. Although globalization reduces the transaction costs of transnational exchanges, the dynamic density of information exchange decreases with distance and cultural dissimilarity. For example, following the collapse of communism, a panoply of transnational networks was established to encourage learning about free-market democracies in the post-Soviet space. Despite these networks, geography explains much of the variation in the creation of market economies and democratic polities. The closer a postcommunist state was to the noncommunist world, the more successful its transition. The diffusion of norms and rules may be spatially dependent.[11] Others have similarly noted the role of geographic proximity as a necessary condition for the successful transmission of ideas.[12]

One possible explanation for why "geographical determinism" would persist in an era of globalization is the distinction between the transmission of information and the transmission of knowledge.[13] Certain forms of knowledge are tacit—they cannot be codified, only experienced.[14] These forms of knowledge greatly facilitate intersubjective understanding, a precondition for advocacy groups to achieve genuine learning.[15] While the technological dynamism of globalization greatly facilitates information transmission, its effect on the transmission of knowledge is more muted. Even when the dynamic density of transnational networks is strong, history can either blunt or redirect learning effects.[16] Another possible explanation is even simpler: even in a world with

---

[10] Ronnie D. Lipschultz and Cathleen Fogel, "Regulation for the Rest of Us?" in *The Emergence of Private Authority in Global Governance*, ed. Rodney Bruce Hall and Thomas J. Biersteker (Cambridge: Cambridge University Press, 2002), 122.

[11] Jeffrey Kopstein and David Reilly, "Geographic Diffusion and the Transformation of the Postcommunist World," *World Politics* 53 (October 2000): 1–2.

[12] David Lazer, "The Free Trade Epidemic of the 1860s and Other Outbreaks of Economic Discrimination," *World Politics* 51 (Summer 1999): 447–83.

[13] I use the terms "knowledge" and "information" as they are used in economics; information is knowledge that can be codified and transmitted across space and time.

[14] Michael Polanyi, *The Tacit Dimension* (New York: Anchor, 1967).

[15] Joseph Nye, "Nuclear Learning and U.S.-Soviet Security Regimes," *International Organization* 41 (Summer 1987): 371–402; Alexander Wendt, *Social Theory of International Politics* (Cambridge: Cambridge University Press, 1999).

[16] Sarah Henderson, "Selling Civil Society: Western Aid and the Nongovernmental Organizational Sector in Russia," *Comparative Political Studies* 35 (March 2002): 139–58.

minimal barriers to cross-border exchange, the overwhelming majority of transactions will remain local and national rather than global.[17]

The results presented in this book pose a significant challenge for the globalization literature. Scholars emphasizing the singular importance of economic globalization emphasize the material and ideational strictures that are placed on all actors in the international system. However, these arguments also treat all actors in world politics as atomistic in the face of global structures. This is a grossly inaccurate description of the global political economy. Even in a world of unfettered globalization, size matters—and the great powers in the system remain large enough to advance and export their regulatory preferences. The ability of great powers to agree on norms of governance, determines the extent of policy convergence. These factors are at the core of the mainstream discourse of international political economy.[18] Globalization has led to the emergence of new issues to be analyzed by international relations scholars; it does not imply that new paradigms are needed to explain these issues.

REAL WORLD IMPLICATIONS

In *The Twenty Years' Crisis*, E. H. Carr divided international relations theory into utopian and realist categories.[19] For Carr, the former school of thought neglected the role that power and interest played in world politics, while the latter ignored the innate desire within man to seek a higher social purpose. Surveying the scholarly and activist debates about globalization and global governance, the same typology could be drawn. While activists seek to change global governance in ways that reduce the negative externalities of globalization, their failure to acknowledge how globalization and global governance actually works impedes their progress. The bulk of the analysis presented here falls under Carr's "realist" methodology. This section, however, offers some utopian asides in the form of constructive criticism.

The results presented here call into doubt several of the tenets held dear by the antiglobalization movement. First and foremost, globalization has yet to trigger a race-to-the-bottom in the issue areas that most activists care about the most.[20] While there has been little regulatory coordination in the arena of

[17] John Helliwell, *How Much Do National Borders Matter?* (Washington, DC: Brookings Institution, 1998); Jonathan Eaton and Samuel Kortum, "Technology, Geography, and Trade," *Econometrica* 70 (September 2002): 1741–79.

[18] Peter Katzenstein, Robert Keohane, and Stephen D. Krasner, eds., "Exploration and Contestation in the Study of World Politics," *International Organization* 52 (August 1998): 645–86.

[19] Carr, *The Twenty Years' Crisis*.

[20] For much fuller analyses along these lines, see Martin Wolf, *Why Globalization Works* (New Haven, CT: Yale University Press, 2004), and Jagdish Bhagwati, *In Defense of Globalization* (New York: Oxford University Press, 2004).

labor and environmental standards, the trend over time is a ratcheting up of standards among the OECD countries, and a slow and erratic upswing toward stricter regulation in the developing world. Contrary to the fears of activists and the hopes of libertarians,[21] globalization has not unleashed a Pandora's box of deregulation.

This outcome, seen in light of the revisionist model, is hardly surprising. On the one hand, the failure to witness stronger global governance for labor regulation and most forms of environmental regulation suggests that these are areas where governments face considerable adjustment costs from private actors. This leads to predictions of sham standards and rival standards outcomes. On the other hand, because of their high per capita incomes, the two great powers in the system have strict standards in these issue areas. They have further demonstrated a willingness to coerce dependent allies into adopting their preferred standards.[22] Rapid economic growth in parts of the developing world has increased domestic demands for more stringent labor safeguards. Although a global regime for these issues may not exist, globalization has not reduced national standards in these areas—if anything, economic globalization has increased the number of governments willing to ratchet up standards in the face of great power pressure.

The model developed here further suggests that global civil society's current strategy of campaigning to correct the "democratic deficit" and improve the transparency of global economic governance will either prove fruitless or counterproductive.[23] To NGOs, social movements, and antiglobalization protestors, the focal point for global economic governance has been the Bretton Woods institutions—the IMF, WTO, and World Bank.[24] Global civil society advocates particularly deride the "green room" process, in which key decisions are made by powerful states behind closed doors. Surveying the landscape of

---

[21] Libertarians and public choice theorists argue that "jurisdictional competition" has welfare-enhancing and democracy-enhancing effects. See Viktor Vanberg, "Globalization, Democracy, and Citizens' Sovereignty: Can Competition among Governments Enhance Democracy?" *Constitutional Political Economy* 11 (Winter 2000): 87–112.

[22] Daniel W. Drezner, "The Hidden Hand of Economic Coercion," *International Organization* 57 (Summer 2003): 643–59.

[23] On the ways in which global governance structures can be used to curtail democracy at home, see Klaus Dieter Wolf, "The New *Raison D'Etat* as a Problem for Democracy in World Society," *European Journal of International Relations* 5 (Fall 1999): 333–63; Daniel W. Drezner, ed., *Locating the Proper Authorities* (Ann Arbor: University of Michigan Press, 2003). On the normative implications, see Drezner, "On the Balance between International Law and Democratic Sovereignty," *Chicago Journal of International Law* 2 (Fall 2001): 321–36.

[24] Robert O'Brien, Anne Marie Goetz, Jan Aart Scholte, and Marc Williams, *Contesting Global Governance* (Cambridge: Cambridge University Press, 2000); Kimberly Ann Elliott, Debayani Kar, and J. David Richardson, "Assessing Globalization's Critics: 'Talkers Are No Good Doers?'" in *Challenges to Globalization*, ed. Robert E. Baldwin and L. Alan Winters, 17–62 (Chicago: University of Chicago Press, 2004).

globalization, ethicist Peter Singer declares that, "as more and more issues increasingly demand global solutions, the extent to which any state can independently determine its future diminishes. We therefore need to strengthen institutions for global decision-making and make them more responsible to the people they affect."[25]

The model of global governance presented here, however, suggests that once the great powers achieve a concert on an issue, they will design governance structures that ensure the permanence of the green room. Even if global civil society succeeds in democratizing the Bretton Woods institutions, the great powers will simply rely on alternative IGOs to devise and enforce the rules of globalization. As was shown in the TRIPS case, thwarting great power preferences in the WTO merely encouraged both the United States and European Union to export their regulatory preferences through bilateral and regional free trade agreements. The democratization of global governance does not retard the exercise of power—it merely diverts it through other channels. To assume otherwise is to ignore Carr's prescient warning: "Failure to recognise that power is an essential element of politics has hitherto vitiated all attempts to establish international forms of government, and confused nearly every attempt to discuss the subject. Power is an indispensable instrument of government. To internationalise government in any real sense means to internationalise power."[26]

Seen in light of the revisionist model, the push by global civil society to regulate the core security functions of the state at the global level will also be counterproductive. For both activists and policymakers, there is a near-subconscious acceptance of the old functionalist logic that once supranational coordination takes place in areas of low politics, the growth in trust and shared understandings will lead to an inexorable shift toward greater cooperation for matters of high politics.[27] The push within the European Union toward a common foreign and security policy is a regional example. The creation of the International Criminal Court, and the efforts toward stronger global regulation of land mines, weapons of mass destruction, and small arms and light weapons (SALW) are all manifestations of this impulse.[28]

[25] Peter Singer, *One World: The Ethics of Globalization* (New Haven, CT: Yale University Press, 2002), 199. See also Ethan Kapstein, *Economic Justice in an Unfair World* (Princeton: Princeton University Press, 2006).

[26] Carr, *The Twenty Years' Crisis*, 106–7.

[27] David Mitrany, *A Working Peace System* (Oxford: Oxford University Press; 1943); Ernst B. Haas, *Beyond the Nation State: Functionalism and International Organizations* (Palo Alto, CA: Stanford University Press, 1964). Ironically, this embrace by practitioners has come long after international relations scholars rejected this approach.

[28] Richard Price, "Reversing the Gun Sights: Transnational Civil Society Targets Landmines," *International Organization* 52 (Summer 1998): 639; Kenneth R. Rutherford, "The Evolving Arms Control Agenda: Implications of the Role of NGOs in Banning Antipersonnel Landmines," *World Politics* 53 (October 2000): 76.

The theoretical problem with this sort of regulatory coordination is that it impacts domestic actors who face the greatest barriers to exit of all—national military and security forces. For these actors the adjustment costs of shifting standard operating procedures to accommodate new regulations at the global level are astronomical. If a security threat emerges that poses a threat to *all* states—such as terrorism or pandemics—one would expect to see successful coordination. Otherwise, the most likely prediction for security coordination is a flurry of sham or rival standards with little practical enforcement.

Empirically, this is what one observes with regard to land mines and SALW. The overwhelming majority of the signatories to the land mine convention neither used nor produced land mines in the past; their decision to embrace the treaty is an example of coincidence of interests rather than genuine policy coordination.[29] One powerful piece of evidence that supports this argument is the virtual absence of monitoring, inspection, and enforcement provisions within the treaty itself.[30] Indeed, GCS activists *supported* the absence of enforcement mechanisms—because more stringent measures would have reduced the number of signatories.[31] The presence of China, India, Iran, Israel, Pakistan, Russia, the United States, and both Koreas on the nonsignatory list raises serious doubts about its utility.[32] Similarly, efforts to create an effective global SALW regime have foundered in the wake of great power disagreement—even as neighborhood IGOs have made limited progress on the issue.[33] On matters of security, transnational activist networks have only been successful in reinforcing coalitions of the willing. Beyond that coalition, variations in defense regulation rest on the distribution of power in the international system.

The realities of global governance pose significant problems for ethicists on the global stage. This does not mean that transnational movements cannot change the world, however; it just requires a different conceptual tool kit. One way for activists to shape the globalization process in ways they prefer is to focus less on the systemic level and more on the national level of governance. Because states remain the primary actors in the regulation of globalization, the best way to influence change at the global level is to change the rules at

---

[29] On this distinction, see Robert Keohane, *After Hegemony* (Princeton, NJ: Princeton University Press, 1984), and Jack Goldsmith and Eric Posner, *The Limits of International Law* (New York: Oxford University Press, 2005).

[30] 1997 Ottawa Convention, Articles 7–9, available at http://www.un.org/Depts/mine/UNDocs/ban_trty.htm, accessed August 1, 2005.

[31] Rutherford, "The Evolving Arms Control Process," 109–10.

[32] The International Campaign to Ban Landmines provides a complete list of nonsignatories at http://www.icbl.org/treaty/snp, accessed January 2006.

[33] Emily Meierding, "Transnational Advocates and the International Regulatory Process," presented at the University of Chicago's Program on International Political Economy and Security, Chicago, IL, May 2005.

the domestic level. The history of environmental regulation, as well as the anticorruption campaign, suggest that when great powers are forced by domestic politics to alter their national rules, they automatically switch their regulatory preferences at the global level—even when the great power government opposed the original change in domestic laws.[34]

Compared with the creation of sham standards at the global level, changing the domestic rules of great powers is a more formidable task—but one with a potentially large payoff for those who desire change at the international level. The problem with global governance is not a lack of accountability—if anything, IGOs function as perfect agents to the principal great powers.[35] GCS activists need to rethink how global governance structures can be held accountable for their actions. Combined with domestic pressure within the great powers, a delegation model of accountability—as opposed to the participation model that most GCS activists unconsciously adopt—could prove fruitful.[36]

THE FUTURE OF GLOBAL REGULATION

At first blush, there are good reasons to believe that the future of global regulation will see a great deal of successful coordination. As of this writing, there is little reason to believe that either the political or the technological imperatives behind economic globalization will be slowing down anytime soon. The reduction of communication costs, standardization of information technology software, and segmentation of business processes has facilitated the global outsourcing of an increasing range of services and goods. As the globalization process intensifies, the rewards for coordination would seem to increase. As innovation creates entirely new product sectors and production processes, the absence of asset-specific investments would suggest minimal adjustment costs for these areas. More globalization could potentially mean more coordination.

However, there are two reasons to believe that the political economy of regulatory coordination will grow more contentious over time. In the first place, the expansion of tradable activities has begun to impinge on long-standing service sectors, such as accounting, medicine, education, and the law. Many of the services that are rapidly becoming tradable—airlines, education, telecommunications, utilities—have been traditionally run by state-owned en-

[34] Elisabeth DeSombre, *Domestic Sources of International Environmental Policy* (Cambridge, MA: MIT Press, 2000).

[35] Daniel Nielson and Michael Tierney, "Delegation to International Organizations: Agency Theory and World Bank Environmental Reform," *International Organization* 57 (Spring 2003): 241–76; Darren Hawkins et al., eds., *Delegation and Agency in International Organizations* (Cambridge: Cambridge University Press, 2006).

[36] Ruth Grant and Robert Keohane, "Accountability and Abuses of Power in World Politics," *American Political Science Review* 99 (February 2005): 29–43.

terprises. This means that the forces behind globalization will affect professions, workers, and state-run institutions that have been set in their ways of doing business for centuries.[37] Because globalization will affect more nontradable sectors with high degrees of asset specificity, the adjustment costs of regulatory coordination in these areas will be extraordinarily high. Although the growth of tradable sectors may increase the long-run harmonization of regulatory policies, the use of political voice in the medium run will guarantee some large bumps in the road ahead.

Finally, if the theory presented here holds, there are reasons to believe that regulatory harmonization will be an increasingly difficult task over time. Because the period under study never saw a shift in the number of major economic powers in the system, an unstated but important hypothesis should be stressed: the scope of regulatory coordination is negatively correlated with the number of economic great powers in the system. In an economically bipolar world—as currently exists—the key question is whether a bargaining core exists between the two great powers. Furthermore, even if a core does not exist, a modest amount of regulatory convergence can still take place through competition. In a rival standards outcome, both poles try to create as large a regulatory bloc as possible.[38]

As the distribution of economic power shifts to a more multipolar world, the dynamics of regulatory coordination change. More competition among the great powers would be expected—but the increasing number of poles also increases the number of nodes at which convergence would take place. The increased number of great powers also implies reduced market and coercive power for each core state vis-à-vis the rest of the world. Therefore, as the distribution of economic power increases, so should regulatory divergence.

The shift from a bipolar distribution of market power to a more multipolar distribution is already under way. In 2003, China supplanted the United States as the largest recipient of foreign direct investment. Studies by Goldman Sachs and Deutsche Bank on growth trends for big developing economies contain some startling predictions. By 2010, the annual growth in aggregate demand from Brazil, Russia, India, and China will be greater than the combined growth of the United States, Japan, Germany, Italy, and Great Britain. By 2020, China and India are projected to have the second and third largest economies. By 2025, the annual growth in aggregate demand from the four leading devel-

---

[37] Raghuram G. Rajan and Luigi Zingales, *Saving Capitalism from the Capitalists* (Princeton, NJ: Princeton University Press, 2004), 282; Alan Blinder, "Offshoring: The Next Industrial Revolution?" *Foreign Affairs* 85 (March/April 2006): 113–28; Catherine Mann, *Accelerating the Globalization of America: The Next Wave of Information Technology* (Washington, DC: Institute for International Economics, 2006).

[38] For more discussion on this point, see Daniel W. Drezner, "Globalization, Coercion, and Competition: the Different Pathways to Policy Convergence," *Journal of European Public Policy* 12 (October 2005): 841–59.

oping economies will be *twice* that of the G-7.[39] By 2030, the combined purchasing power of China's and India's consumers is projected to be five times that of today's United States.[40] While simple extrapolations from the recent past can be misleading, economic and demographic trends suggest that the growth of India and China will shift what is currently a bipolar economic distribution of power into a more multipolar world.[41]

As the number of actors increases, the likelihood of creating a concert of common preferences among them necessarily declines.[42] This holds with particular force if these countries achieve great power market size while still having low per capita incomes. According to current projections, when China's economy will approach great power status in terms of overall size, its per capita GDP will only be a third of the developed world.[43] In addition to the current tension between the American and European varieties of capitalism, another source of preference divergence could emerge among the great powers: the tension between rich countries willing to trade off economic growth for quality of life issues, and still-developing countries that are more reluctant to sacrifice growth.[44]

China in particular has already begun to throw its weight around on technical and regulatory standards. In early 2004, the Chinese government promulgated new rules mandating that all wireless products contain data-encryption technology manufactured by Chinese companies. In response to U.S. protests, the Chinese reversed course in March 2004. China has a clear incentive to develop new technology standards, however; the United States and European Union will be anticipating future attempts at standards creation.[45] As for regulatory concerns, China has resisted efforts to ratchet up its own labor standards. Beijing has also accelerated its overseas investment in countries with no standards, such as Myanmar and Sudan.[46]

---

[39] Dominic Wilson and Roopa Purushothaman, "Dreaming with BRICs: The Path to 2050," Goldman Sachs Global Economics Paper No. 99, New York, October 2003; Stefan Bergheim, "Global Growth Centres 2020," Deutsche Bank Research Current Issues, March 2005. See also National Intelligence Council, *Mapping the Global Future* (Washington, DC: Government Printing Office, 2004), and L. Alan Winters and Shahid Yusuf, eds., *Dancing with Giants: China, India, and the World Economy* (Washington: The World Bank, 2007).

[40] UBS press release of "China and India: The Steady Progression towards Two Consumer Markets," August 23, 2004, available at http://www.ubs.com/1/e/media_overview/media_switzerland/mediareleases?newsId=65683, accessed November 11, 2004.

[41] On the demographics, see Nicholas Eberstadt, "Power and Population in Asia," *Policy Review* 123 (February 2004): 1–22.

[42] Robert Axelrod and Robert Keohane, "Achieving Cooperation under Anarchy: Strategies and Institutions," *World Politics* 38 (October 1985): 226–54.

[43] *Economist*, "The New Titans," September 16, 2006, 12.

[44] Ronald Inglehart, "Globalization and Postmodern Values," *Washington Quarterly* 23 (Winter 2000), 219. See also Inglehart, *Culture Shift in Advanced Industrial Society* (Princeton, NJ: Princeton University Press, 1990); Carr, *The Twenty Years' Crisis*, 120.

[45] Adam Segal, "Is America Losing Its Edge?" *Foreign Affairs* 83 (November/December 2004): 8.

[46] Stéphanie Giry, "Out of Beijing," *The New Republic*, November 15, 2004.

These cautionary notes suggest that globalization will *not* be generating a harmony of national interests anytime soon. This supposition would be consistent with the general take on how economic globalization affects the study of global political economy. The elimination of capital controls and the reduction of tariffs and quotas do not vitiate existing theories of international political economy, but rather point the way to new issue areas for their application. The title of this book was chosen because globalization has altered world politics through the generation of a new set of contentious global issues that were, heretofore, purely national. However, when Tip O'Neill said that all politics is local, he meant that politicians needed to heed the voices of their constituents.[47] Even if more issues are negotiated on the global stage, the sources of government power and preferences remain local. Globalization has led to new arenas of scholarly study—not a new world order.

[47] Tip O'Neill with Gary Hymel, *All Politics Is Local and Other Rules of the Game* (New York: Times Books, 1994), xvi.

Index